I0621676

Then Came Tibet

Three Years on the Roof of the World

Meredith McLeod Dunton

Edited by Jerry Payne

CH
Clarion House Publishing

Then Came Tibet

Three Years on the Roof of the World

Meredith McLeod Dunton

FIRST EDITION

Manufactured in the United States of America

Paperback ISBN: 979-8-9909488-0-8
eBook ISBN: 979-8-9909488-1-5

Library of Congress Control Number: 2024912133

Copyright © 2024, Meredith McLeod Dunton

All Rights Reserved

No part of this book may be reproduced or transmitted in any form or by any means without the written permission of the publisher.

CH
Clarion House

CONTENTS

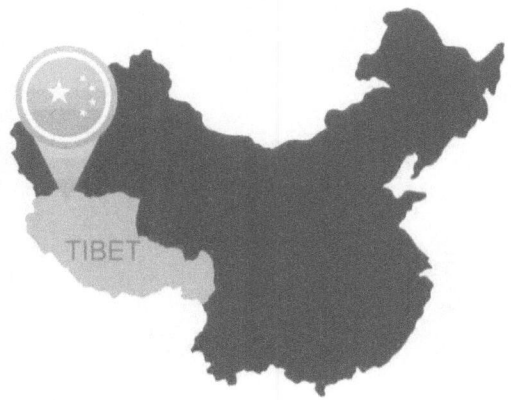

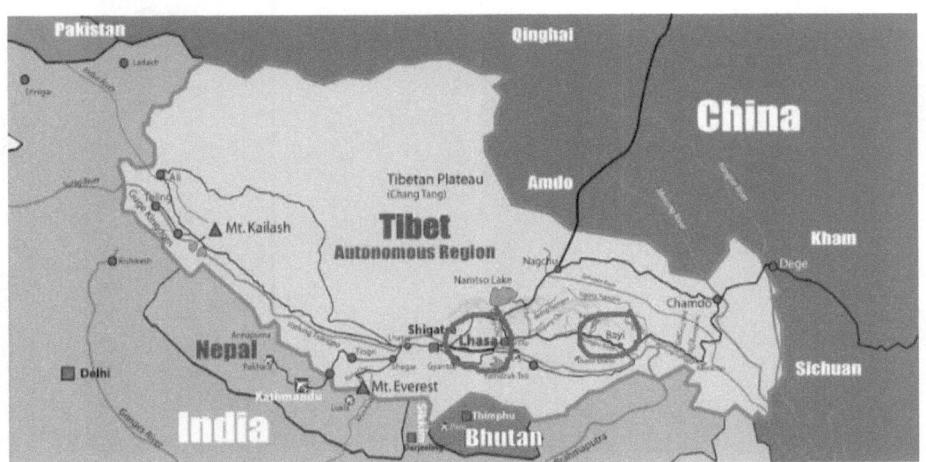

For my children and grandchildren.
One day you'll be just a memory for some people.
Do your best to be a good one.

"Travel isn't always pretty. It isn't always comfortable. Sometimes it hurts, it even breaks your heart. But that's okay. The journey changes you; it should change you. It leaves marks on your memory, on your consciousness, on your heart, and on your body. You take something with you. Hopefully, you leave something behind."

— Anthony Bourdain

INTRODUCTION

Why do people travel? More to the point, why do they travel to faraway places? For fun? For adventure? To learn about other peoples and cultures? All good answers, none of them describing my reasoning. As a child living on a farm, I'd see a plane flying overhead and wonder where it was going, who the passengers were, and could they see me waving to them from 30,000 feet below? I dreamed of flying with them for a possible adventure I knew not where. At the age of forty-eight, I finally took such an adventure, and to a faraway place, but my reason was this: to honor my teenage commitment to God, to follow Him wherever He would lead me.

Call me naïve, but I assumed, as that teenager, that the road of my life would be straightforward. Boy, was I on the wrong road! Ill-conceived decisions would derail my commitment for years. Finally, however, there I was, single again, with kids grown, and that long-ago teenage promise fresh in my thoughts. No more holding back now. As C.S. Lewis wrote, "There are far better things ahead than any we leave behind."

But where was God to lead me? Wherever the destination, I knew only that it was away from where I was. I had no reason to stay, and I toyed with the idea of going somewhere to teach English as a second language, perhaps do the Lord's work in another land. When I mentioned this to the assistant librarian—at the school I'd returned to in hopes of finishing my secondary education degree, twice as old as the other students—she said, "What about China?"

What *about* China? All I knew about China was what I'd learned as a child playing in the yard of our small-town Texas home: if I dug a hole deep enough, I'd arrive there. Now, as an adult, it seemed to me as if I'd certainly dug a deep enough hole. Now it was time to come up for air.

As it turned out, there was this magical place called Tibet that wasn't deep at all. In fact, it was remarkably high. The "Rooftop of the World," they called it. And I went there. And I found fun. And adventure. And I learned about other peoples and cultures. Most importantly, I left my past life behind me and found a new one. Or maybe it was just a new me—a me that wasn't afraid to be herself any longer, a me that felt liberated by the comfort of being a stranger in a strange place.

I didn't remain a stranger, of course. I met a lot of people and forged lifelong friendships. Yes, I taught. But I learned—more than I could have imagined. The people of Tibet were kind and curious. They were poor by American standards, but one thing I learned early was to stop looking at things by American standards. Even though I'd had to live frugally back home, I felt a kind of shame when I saw how the vast majority of Tibetans lived. On the other hand, though they had little in the way of material possessions, they were rich in other ways. I stopped thinking so much about material possessions after three years in Tibet.

Not that it was easy to assimilate. Besides traveling to Canada, I'd never been out of the country before, let alone thrown into such a unique and contrasting culture. This was not Europe, or even Eastern Europe. This was the Far East, and they don't call it "Far" for nothing. Tibet—China for that matter—is distant both geographically and culturally. It was, in short, a different world. But there were similarities too. The human condition is universal. Our beliefs, our standards, our ways of dealing with life, might all be diverse, but our joys and sorrows are the same. We laugh and we cry in the same language.

What it all meant to me was a period of three years that can never be forgotten, with stories of my times in Tibet that needed, I knew, to be written down. After all, I couldn't very well expect friends and relatives to continue to sit still every time I cornered them with tales of my journey. So here the stories are, in print, and they can now be read at leisure.

The stories are related the best that my memory will allow. I was younger then, of course. But I was younger even than my age at the time, for I was with people typically twenty-some years my junior, willing to do anything they might do (even climb mountains!), making me feel their age. And I was younger in another way. I carried the provincial naiveté of a small-town woman who thought she knew about the world. And yet on some level, I knew there had to be more. But I was penned in. By life, by the expectations of others, and by my own fears of being something more than I was.

And then...well, then came Tibet.

CHAPTER 1

DON'T LET ME DIE IN TIBET!

*"Seeing death as the end of life is like seeing the horizon
as the end of the ocean."*
—David Searls

Did I want to see a sky burial? Is that what the instructor asked me? Of course I did. A big reason I was in Tibet in the first place was to experience the ways of other cultures, to learn something about the differences from my own. There wasn't much I could think of that was as different as a sky burial. We sure didn't have those in northeast Texas.

There are other types of burials that Tibetans practice, including our more mundane earth burial, but that's probably their least preferred burial. Besides, Tibetan soil is rocky and often frozen. There is the fire burial, what we would call cremation. This was traditionally used for those who died from something contagious, but it's also used for high lamas where their ashes are preserved in religious monuments called stupas.

There is also the water burial. I had come across one of these accidentally one day while riding my bike along the river. Two young Tibetan men were stooping over the water's edge several feet below the river path. I didn't notice, but one of the other American teachers I was with told me later that she saw that they had what appeared to be a deceased newborn. In fine Tibetan tradition, they were bequeathing the body to the water, to be used as food for the fish, an act of generosity from a lifeless body to living organisms. An act, that is to say, of compassion for other living beings, compassion being a divine Buddhist virtue.

And so it was that I found myself one afternoon trudging along a path that wound higher and higher up the small mountain behind Sera Monastery, an institution founded in 1419 and one of the largest monasteries in Lhasa. Long ago, before the Chinese took control, it housed more than 5,000 monks. Now, only a few hundred lived there, but it still remained an important place.

Even though our path was a circular route up the mountain and not a direct course straight up, I still found myself breathing hard from the effects of the ever-thinning air. The group I was with was a tour guide class, all Han Chinese students of Tibet University, and we were all instructed not to make noise. Disturbing the mountain deities can bring bad luck.

Eventually, I saw a small, white temple above us which gleamed brightly in the hot, mid-afternoon sun. Down the mountain, below the temple, was where the burial site was. As if anticipating my thoughts, the instructor cautioned me to keep my camera hidden. The proceedings we were going to witness below us were sacred. No photos allowed. In fact, an attempted snapshot might well result in confiscation of the camera. Tourists had been banned from the sites for several years, having made a mockery of the rituals with their swarming presence, and local hotels could be fined for bringing tour groups to the burial sites. But our group consisted of students eager to learn, not tourists looking for souvenirs.

Finally, we reached the top and were better able to view the proceedings. Below, we could see eight monks sitting cross-legged in a semi-circle on a large flat stone. Their chants could barely be heard, and they were close to completing the burial rituals that had been underway since daybreak, the time that bodies are transported to the sky burial site. Unable to resist, I slid my camera out of my pocket and, just like one of those hotel tourists, took a quick shot of the maroon-robed monks before they rose and began walking back down the mountain to a waiting van. No one apparently noticed and I was able to maintain possession of my camera.

With the monks now absent, we made our way down to the large, flat stone. I had come voluntarily, but at this point found myself with some reservations. What were we going to see at the burial site? Something repellent, even nauseating? But all we saw around the stone were bits of hair and some other small detritus. Nothing could be seen of what took place on the top of the stone but some ash, perhaps the result of a small fire at the end of the ritual. I observed four sledgehammers attached to the rock by sisal rope and four hollowed-out indentations that apparently received the thrusts of the hammers.

What had occurred at this sacred site? Well, in a sky burial, the body is taken apart. The celestial burial master starts by essentially removing the skin. The intestines are mixed with *tsampa*, a mixture of roasted barley flour and yak butter tea. The bones are crushed. The work is done with good humor, even laughter. A jovial atmosphere is necessary to ward off the darkness of death, freeing the deceased.

Afterward, come the vultures. This is where the sky burial gets its name. It is in the sky where the body will ultimately go, now a part of the soaring birds that have come to know what these rituals entail and patiently wait for when the people are gone and the remains of the body are accessible. Like the water burial, the lifeless body is bequeathed to the living.

Farther on down the mountain was another site, this one for women and children. Only men received their burials on the upper rock. We walked down, past the lower site and I remember thinking, *please don't let me die in Tibet!* But, in time, I would come to consider their ritual and wonder how strange our own funerals might seem to the Tibetans. And fundamentally, is there a difference between being consumed by birds or being consumed by worms? Both Christianity and Buddhism hold that the being who inhabited the body is no longer there anyway. Giving back to the earth might not be so crazy after all.

It's interesting, the many things I would learn about Tibet, this strange world on the other side of the earth. But there were even more interesting things to be learned, things I had not anticipated learning, things I had not known needed learning. Yes, I would learn about Tibet. But the surprising part of my time there was how much I would learn about something else entirely. The surprising part was how much I would learn about me.

CHAPTER 2

McLeod

"Home is the nicest word there is."
—Laura Ingalls Wilder

When you grow up in a small farming community like McLeod, Texas, you don't ever really think about places like Tibet. You have no idea that entire cultures exist apart from your own. For years, the ways of McLeod, the ways of my family, were all I knew.

Our house was built in 1934, eight years before I came along. My parents had moved back to the community, then called Good Exchange, where both their families had lived for years. They moved from an oilfield location called Pine Island, about twenty-five miles away in Louisiana, where my father worked as a pumper, one whose job it was to monitor and maintain active oil wells. It was while living there that he lost a thumb on the job. My parents were married in 1918 when my mom was sixteen and my father was thirty. They had their first child in 1920 with the second, a son named Olin Sanders, coming along a year and a half later. It has bothered me as an adult that Olin was rarely mentioned in my early life. He had died of diphtheria at the age of six, long before I was born. Back in the 1960s my mother retold the story to my older brother of what the experience was like for her as Olin lay in his hospital bed near death. She said that with a smile on his face he raised up both arms, as if he

5

were about to be ushered into Heaven. She wept while telling this, a sadness that would be with her always.

My parents had bought some farmland in the Good Exchange community from Daddy's parents and siblings. Oil was soon discovered there and that was how they were able to build their very large brick house before the fifth child was born. The community grew by leaps and bounds. New people moved in and a post office was built. My parents donated the land for the post office, henceforth called the McLeod post office, leading, forevermore, to the proper name of our community: McLeod, Texas.

I would be the last child born to my parents, twenty-two years after the first ten. "Cheaper By the Dozen" was not to be. An older sister often told the story of my father's reaction upon my arrival at the hospital. "It's a girl," he said. "Let's go home." I can imagine that the reactions of my older siblings were even less enthusiastic. The family home was becoming more crowded and everyone's workload, especially my mother's, was becoming heavier. I would be the third baby in diapers at this time and the clotheslines were never empty.

Initially, growing up in our little corner of the world was magical. There were few responsibilities for a young child. But time would change this as tasks started to be assigned that became progressively more difficult and time-consuming with each birthday. My first household job was washing canning jars. My hands, so they told me, were just the right size to reach inside. Things proceeded from there. Nevertheless, there was plenty of time to be a kid. The call of the outdoors drew us younger siblings beyond the fenced yard. Fields and woods served as our playgrounds, and with trees and rocks that were better than any playground equipment money could buy. We were limited only as far as our imaginations would take us. Later, our bicycles gave us almost unbounded freedom.

Many times, I'd walk or ride the half mile to Grandma Walker's house. My maternal grandmother, lovingly called "Mother Walker" by the community, lived alone and her door was always open to us. Of course, no one locked their doors back then so strictly speaking her door was open to anyone. I liked to visit her at certain times of the day. Back then, a popular Dr Pepper advertisement advised drinking the product as a pick-me-up at ten o'clock, two o'clock, and four o'clock. Grandma took this seriously. I made sure to be there at those times for we rarely had soft drinks in our house.

If I happened to wander into Grandma's home at breakfast time, she'd offer me whatever she was having. But it was never the food that I yearned for. It was her "Flogers" coffee. On other occasions, we would sit in front of her fireplace and crochet. Grandma would be making yet one more doily (the only thing she ever made, as far as I could tell) while I'd be crocheting nothing much more than a long line of stitches that never became anything. This didn't matter to me. What mattered was sitting with Grandma in front of the fire feeling a sense of contentment, feeling "crizzy," my word for cozy. Along with "Flogers," I was building quite a lexicon, even though Merriam-Webster might not have recognized it as such.

In later years, I would marvel at how much my grandmother's nurturing meant in my life: her simple values, her abounding love for family and the Lord, and, greatest of all, her faith in God. She gave me hugs that I never remembered getting at home. Not that my parents didn't love me, but they were understandably busy. And for my father's part, he was old enough to be my grandfather. When we became teenagers, he could not relate. The music of my generation was not to his liking, something he was always quick to let us know. And, unfortunately, his inability to relate never got better. Years later, home from college, I would witness him shooting to death a stray dog under our dining room window, knowing my sister and I were present but never thinking twice about killing the dog in front of us.

Nevertheless, Daddy was a good man. There was no swearing in the house nor alcohol, save for an annual fifth of whiskey that a friend of my father's would drop off every Christmas. Daddy kept it in a cabinet and brought it out only when he'd contract a cold, putting some lemon with it and using it strictly for medicinal purposes. Daddy sure enjoyed his colds, we used to say.

But Grandma was the influential one, the counselor, the wise woman of God. At first, her faith resonated with me more than otherwise due to the fact that I was not unfamiliar with the Bible. When I was five, and the only one of the brood not in school, I had to entertain myself. One way I attempted this was to try reading the Good Book, starting with Job because, with only three letters to the title, it seemed the least intimidating. I would run back and forth from the living room to the kitchen asking Mama what each word of the Book of Job was and how it was pronounced. It must have driven her crazy, but in time I was to know of Job's relationship to God, his big farm, the number of his children (ten, one less than ours!) and the number and names of his animals. The name of one of his animals, however, I kept to myself. In our King James version, donkeys were referred to as she-asses, and in our house, we didn't use that sort of language. At any rate, when Grandma heard of my theological interest in Job, she invited me to attend the next meeting of the Women's Missionary Society, conveniently held in her home every month, and recite the verses I had memorized.

Grandma's spiritual influence would culminate in me freely accepting Jesus into my life five years later at the age of ten. It happened under a tabernacle at a Baptist camp near Lone Star. The camp cost twelve dollars, but my parents didn't have it to spare. Grandma paid the fee, a "widow's mite," as the Gospels might call it. At that camp, with child-like faith, I began the greatest adventure that I would ever know. "All things are possible, only believe," went a song that I learned then, and it would prove prophetic later on in life. God had a plan. I like to think Grandma's sacrificial mite was repaid many times over.

Somehow, in my early childhood days, perhaps because I was the youngest and a girl, I learned a toughness that would serve me well years later in life. Mama would many times retell the story of a train trip I took with her to Denver when I was five. My favorite place in the car was where the water cooler was. I was intrigued by the pull-down, funnel-shaped paper cups. At one point, as Mama told it, another girl about my age invaded my space at the cooler. A natural defense mechanism apparently kicked in for I stretched my three-foot frame as tall as I could and warned her, "I'll schlap the debil out of you!" I don't imagine Job would have approved, but the incident certainly seemed to say something about my willingness to stand up for myself.

By my junior high years, I was helping Mama in the kitchen more and beginning to experiment with baking. Most of my knowledge was by observation for Mama didn't have much patience for actively teaching me. In fact, most of my experimenting came after Mama would be finished in the kitchen for the day, when I wouldn't be in her way. The process of cooking intrigued me ever since I was a little girl and would get up early to observe Daddy mixing milk, eggs, sugar, and flavoring before he went out to milk the cow. Put in a slow oven, the concoction would magically turn to custard by the time he returned to the kitchen with a bucket of milk.

But Mama was the primary chef. She cooked most everything from scratch, including biscuits, at least until canned biscuits came out. Then she promptly announced she would no longer be making biscuits the old way. Mama assumed other roles, too. As needs required, she could be carpenter, electrician, plumber. She made our clothes, even formal dresses for the girls. Laundry, on the other hand, was the province of my father, not that it was especially complicated. He'd run the clothes through the wringer in the washroom in a large out-building, using cold water since hot was unavailable in the building, and then hang the clothes out to dry. That structure also housed a single-car garage and a smokehouse. Many mornings, Mama would send me out there with a knife to cut down some link sausages for breakfast. Years later, long after the days when the building was used to cure meat, you could still smell the smoke.

My high school years had many of the limitations one would expect in a very small country school. The parents of most of those in my class of eleven didn't follow their children's academic pursuits very carefully, if at all. Like my parents, they were too busy making their livings. We had football and basketball, but beyond that, we created our own diversions whenever we were bored, which was much of the time. One rite of passage for the teen years was the swiping of a watermelon from some farmer's patch. It didn't matter that several of our fathers grew watermelons; it was about the excitement of stealing and not getting caught.

When high school graduation finally arrived, Grandma was seriously ill, and was sent to the closest hospital around, in Shreveport an hour away. Mama and Daddy visited her on graduation day and barely made it back in time to see me and my ten classmates receive our diplomas. Then came the traditional week-long senior trip to South Texas, which began just as soon as we could change out of our graduation gowns. A bus was packed with our luggage, and we were joined by chaperones—a teacher from the high school and his newlywed wife, which turned out wonderfully for us as they kept more or less to themselves the whole time. We rode that bus all through the night to New Braunfels, near San Antonio, where we stayed several days. Then it was on to Houston and then Galveston, before returning to McLeod. At the end of the trip, after being carried to our respective homes, our high school years were officially over. That would be the last time that I would see most of those friends for a long time, or in one case, ever again.

For the summer, I applied at a large Baptist assembly in New Mexico for a six-week job. College students mostly filled the available positions, including dining room workers, which is what they hired me for. I went there on a bus, only the second time I'd ever traveled alone, the first being an all-day train trip. Mama and an older sister put me on the bus in Shreveport and cautioned me to sit behind the driver. At Albuquerque, I had to change buses, which meant working my way through the station to find the bus going to Santa Fe.

The job wasn't the best one in the world, but when we had free time, there were sports to participate in and we were also allowed to attend some of the assembly meetings. These were also attended by missionaries on furlough. Their work interested me intensely and I had a great deal of respect for them. Grandma, with as little money as she had, would give to missionaries, mostly to the Lottie Moon Foreign Missions offering, named after a Southern Baptist missionary who had spent forty years in China from 1873 to 1912. I've tried to picture in my mind how Grandma would react to knowing I would one day be where Lottie Moon was.

Meanwhile, however, Grandma grew more ill. She died while I was in New Mexico, the first death of a close relative I had ever known. My grief knew no bounds; I was far from home and alone in that grief.

After New Mexico, attending university was pretty much expected. A couple siblings followed other pursuits, but eight of the living ten children chose college, even if just two-year programs. Twenty years prior, two sisters had gone to Baylor University, and now two more of us sisters would be there, a senior and, me, a freshman. Another sibling was in college elsewhere, meaning three children requiring tuition and room and board at the same time, something I still don't know how my parents pulled off.

Unfortunately, my lackluster high school performance would prove to make my first year a challenging time for me. Mama at least took some interest, sending me an encouraging Bible verse, Philippians 4:13: "I can do everything through Him who gives me strength."

I took it to heart but nevertheless left Baylor for East Texas Baptist College, now East Texas Baptist University (ETBU). My grades improved a bit and I made friends. But a lack of self-confidence slowed me down.

From where did this come? Underneath, I apparently had strength. This was pointed out to me in high school when my basketball coach, Coach Thomas George, once observed that I was a different person on the court than off the court. For some reason, however, I was not, outside of the basketball court, able to fully be myself. It was as if I were constrained somehow. By expectations? By fears of what others thought? By the limitations of a small town? Who can say. All I know is that later in life, for a few wonderful years, I would find a place where I wasn't afraid to be me.

CHAPTER 3

ALONE ON THE MOUNTAIN

"You never know what's around the corner. It could be everything. Or it could be nothing. You keep putting one foot in front of the other, and then one day you look back and you've climbed a mountain."
—Tom Hiddleston

"Get both feet on the ground!"

"Can't," I said, voice trembling.

"Just do it," Drew said. With about ten steps remaining for me to make it to the top, where Drew stood shouting down at me, I had become panicked. The grade had become much steeper, seemingly straight up. And my heavy backpack made it feel like something was pulling me backwards. If there were only something to hold on to, something for a toehold, but there was nothing but pebbly sand and short, dry vegetation.

I was paralyzed. Drew unloaded his packs and began to inch down toward me. It was a struggle for me just to lift my hand toward Drew's outstretched arm, but he finally managed to pull me to the top where my racing heart began to finally slow down. It seemed like it had taken all day to climb Bumpari Mountain. In reality, it had been a mere three hours.

We were four English teachers, two of us women, Mina and me, who taught at Tibet University; and two young men, Drew and Scott, who taught at another nearby school. It was Good Friday and the guys had met us at the university in the early afternoon for the mile walk to the base of the mountain. After crossing over a bridge guarded by armed soldiers at each end, we'd followed the Kyi Chu River, known more commonly as the Lhasa River, which required us to walk past a PLA military installation—a place with a threatening array of weaponry of the People's Liberation Army of China, including tanks with barrels pointed across the river toward the city of Lhasa, the administrative capital of Tibet and the one-time home of the Dalai Lama.

As we passed near the base of Bumpari, three young soldiers sitting atop a boulder greeted us with shouts of "Hello." "Hello," we said back, and we continued on. As the oldest in our group by about twenty-five years, I soon found myself pulling up the rear of our hike. The other three had wasted no time in putting distance between the base and themselves, so it was not surprising that they didn't hear someone calling out to us from behind. I turned around to see the three Chinese soldiers marching my way. I called up to the others. Drew shouted that he wasn't coming down, but luckily Scott and Mina came back down to see what the soldiers wanted.

I hadn't been in China long enough to not be intimidated by someone wearing a PLA uniform. Later, I would view most of the soldiers as uneducated, homesick young people who wore cloth shoes and sloppy camouflage fatigues, as these three did. The body language of these soldiers appeared friendly enough, but I wasn't quite sure about their words. I was not yet accustomed to the sharp tonal language of Chinese, which to me always sounded angry. To my relief, all they wanted was to offer to help us take our backpacks partway up the mountain, an offer I took them up on.

Eventually, they bid us goodbye and I took my pack and was soon climbing higher and higher. Now I had to watch my footing for some of the larger rocks weren't always embedded securely in the ground and stepping on a loose rock could mean disaster. In the meantime, the altitude and stifling sun were doing me no favors, slowing me down with frequent pauses to catch my breath and sip some water.

At last, the summit was near. But it was my misfortune to let fear take hold. Fortunately, Drew pulled me up those last ten feet and I was flooded with relief to be standing safely at the top. Without a doubt, this mountain climbing experience would be my first and last. Strange to think that I was the one who had suggested the overnight excursion, the one who had always been afraid of heights.

Before setting up our little camp, we gazed at the exhilarating vista of the Lhasa valley with the river now far below. The moon soon began its rise over the far mountains, a purplish dusk settling over the dazzling panorama before us, creating blurry shadows of the rocky peaks. If I needed a reminder that I was not in McLeod anymore, this was surely it.

The plan was to spend a cozy night in a four-person tent. In short order, we discovered that this was not to be. Drew's agonizing groans following his desperate rifling through his backpack made this clear to us. He had forgotten the tent poles. And it was not going to be an idyllic night of peaceful sleep under the stars, either. This was still March. It was not unusual to see snow at the top of the highest peaks. There was a good chance that by morning, our camp would be covered in it. I had seen the snow appear at the tops of the mountains many times from my classroom at the university. I would watch from the window as clouds approached the summit of a mountain that had no snow, magically envelop the top, and then pass by having left behind a pure white iciness. Indeed, it was this very phenomenon that had me so intrigued by the mountains, the reason why it seemed important to climb one, to reach the summit where I had seen those clouds. And besides, how can one go to Tibet and not climb a mountain? Bumpari wasn't exactly Everest, but with an elevation of 14,250 feet, it was more than respectable. Bumpari would become my Everest.

Each of us carried in our backpacks some of the essentials we would need for the night. The others brought firewood for two meals, along with other necessities. My contribution was a container of yak stew and water. I had my sleeping bag, too, but it was one that a former teacher had left behind, and it had seen better days. I had my doubts as to its ability to keep me warm during the night. I had counted on the tent. When finally it was time to sleep, I positioned myself as close to the dying embers of the fire as I dared and yet I still shivered through the night.

Morning came early for me. Thankfully, there had been no snow, but it was frosty just the same. The others seemed warm and comfortable in their sleeping bags, and probably not waking up anytime soon. Wanting company, I began making a little noise to see who would stir first. Soon, everyone had crawled out of their warm cocoons and we were drinking hot coffee, thanks to the last of the firewood.

After taking pictures of the sunrise over the mountains around Lhasa valley, we packed up to begin our descent. Drew and Scott and Nina had decided we would follow a switchback path the locals used which required one to descend half running, half slipping. Some called it foot surfing. It's almost impossible to stop once momentum takes over. I could see myself tripping and rolling over a steep drop-off. And so a dilemma. Go with the others, or go an alternate way?

In the end, I knew there was no way I could traverse the steep path. And even if I could, I knew that the others would get farther and farther ahead of me and eventually be out of sight, leaving me to whatever might happen. Remembering the various gullies on the way up, I made my decision to locate one and follow it down as far as it went. The safe way, so I thought.

I let the other three go ahead while I went in search of a gully, finally finding what I needed: a "safe" gully. The problem was, it didn't begin at the top, but rather about thirty feet down, and it was a very steep decline to get there. I arrived the only way I could—scooting down on the seat of my pants. Then came the next problem. The start of the gully was not where it looked like it had been from my view up above. Instead, it was a sheer fifteen-foot drop below me, with no way possible to get down to it. Now I had to turn around and go back the way I had come, a route that, from my angle, seemed twice as steep as it had coming down.

At times, one is forced to do what one sees as an impossibility. One of those times had come for me. I knew that the longer I allowed myself to become paralyzed by my predicament, the more likely it would be that I would fall into full-blown panic mode.

It's interesting to consider where bravery comes from. How often is it sourced in fear? My fear conjured up courage that morning. That courage inspired a streak of bravery. The bravery led to action. I had, in other words, no choice. If I wanted to get down that mountain, I needed to be brave.

Drew's exhortation from the day before—get both feet on the ground— popped into my head. I knew that would be the only way I could make it back up. That and prayer. Fervent, desperate prayer. I began to climb, feet on the ground, with little to hold on to, but small, dried, prickly growths. Because of the altitude, I had to stop for quick rests to catch my breath, having then to work through my fear all over again.

The sun was unrelenting and my thirst unquenched; I had no water left. My progress was slow, coming in small increments. But with my adrenaline pumping double-time, I finally made it back to the top. From there, the isolation I felt was palpable. I was alone on the mountain. But there was no time for self-pity. I was on the hunt again for an "easy" way down the mountain. My sense of direction was practically nonexistent by then as the sun was at high noon, and, besides, I had meandered around so much trying to find the gully that would, hopefully, serve as my deliverance. Then I found it. There were huge boulders, loose rocks, and uneven footing, but it would have to do.

I started down. Now my fear was breaking a bone and being unable to move with no one coming to my rescue until too late. At least the special dinner with the US ambassador to China, James Lilley, and his wife, planned for that evening, gave me some hope that I'd be missed.

I continued on. Time passed slowly as I negotiated my way around boulders, having to scoot partway because it was too dangerous to walk upright. At last, the gully ended in a desolate field. And just as I was trying to decide which direction to go, a miracle occurred. The same three young soldiers I had met the day before were walking toward me. One of them took my backpack and led me to the exact place where we had first seen them.

I politely declined their insistence that I rest there. All I wanted was to get back to my apartment, to rest, bathe, and get ready for the dinner. Shortly, a huge tractor and trailer came down the road with six Tibetan men riding in the back and heading in the direction I wanted to go. After thanking my angels with a nod of my head, I allowed two men to grab my hands and pull me up into the high trailer, and off I went.

My tractor "taxi" stopped near a broken fence at the back of the university and the kind men lowered me to the ground. I wondered what tale they would tell their friends and families about this hitch-hiking foreigner. Between some bushes, I found an opening and stepped through and was hit with a strange sense that I was entering a portal into another realm, totally different from which I'd just come. Students were out and about, doing what they did on any given Saturday—playing basketball, huddling with friends. Children were everywhere. As I trudged across campus, I seemed to be invisible to them all.

It was a relief to finally reach my apartment, which had never felt so warm and comforting. The first thing I did was open a can of Jianlibao, a favorite orange-honey soda, drinking it quickly to slake my thirst. Then I took off my filthy shoes and socks and fell onto my bed. Later someone knocked on my door to inform me that the dinner with the US ambassador and his entourage had been postponed until the following evening. With thankfulness and a smile on my face, I could finally rest from the day's ordeal.

CHAPTER 4

TIBET CALLING

"The call is the expression of the nature from which it comes, and we can only record the call if the same nature is in us. The call of God is the expression of God's nature, not of our nature."
—Oswald Chambers

Graduation from college in 1964 could and should have been the launch pad to some type of career. Most female graduates would choose both career and marriage. I felt ill-prepared for either. Ultimately, I would choose marriage and a new kind of life in Michigan, which, coming from McLeod, was like experiencing another culture. My Texas accent was as much a novelty to the natives as their accent was to me. In order not to call attention to myself, I dropped the ubiquitous "ya'll" from my vocabulary and eventually replaced it with "you guys," but it would still take years for me to not feel like an outsider.

And it's no wonder. A few months after moving to a very rural part of the state, I began my "career" as a substitute teacher at three elementary schools that were part of a consolidated school district. Upon my arrival for my first assignment, the area principal introduced himself and then, referencing my hometown, laid this unseemly observation upon me: "I was really expecting you to be barefoot." I was too aghast and hurt to think of a quick and appropriate comeback.

Without the benefit of proper teacher training, I did manage to learn quickly. The principal's comment came to mean nothing to me in time, but it did show something of *his* character, and I decided that my young students would become my measuring stick as to my worth as a teacher. One day, while a group of students were in their reading circle, a little boy blurted out, "You sound just like a real teacher." That was all the confirmation I needed.

I was hired to teach second grade for the second semester at my own village school, but still found myself from time to time feeling the outsider. At a parent/teacher conference, a mother told me of the exchange she had with her daughter after I'd begun teaching. When the mother asked her where her new teacher was from, the little girl replied, "I don't know, but she's from another country."

Eventually we moved to the small town of Mount Morris, where our two sons joined us—Michael Jon on December 26, 1966, and Joel Robert on December 24, 1969. These two birth dates were a reminder that when I was about six or seven years old, I would beg my mom to give me a real live baby for Christmas. My family told me after Joel's birth that I'd finally gotten my wish.

Years passed. Outwardly, things seemed normal. But in the secret places of my heart, I was diving deeper and deeper into an unfathomable unhappiness. Midlife realism and the increasing awareness of passing time helped me face the fact that my only hope for a meaningful, fulfilling life was to end a marriage that had been dying a slow death. I knew that middle-age could be a lengthy, joyous, liberating, and pleasurable period of life. But if spent in the imprisonment of an outworn, outgrown, and loveless marriage, I was not likely to experience any of those, save lengthy. The eventual divorce proved to be the greatest liberation I could have hoped for, an essential step for my growth.

Growth spurts, however, can be awkward, and so it was with mine in my forties. I returned to East Texas Baptist University where my oldest son was now enrolled and where my youngest would be soon joining us. The students were my children's ages, and some of the instructors and professors were younger than me.

By this time, my goals, values, and expectations had changed from what they had been. And they would eventually change again. But now, they were mine and nobody else's. I put all my energy into being a good student. Life wasn't all pleasant during the few years that it took to get my degree in secondary education with a major in English. I found myself suffering from "maltuition." The shoestring I was living on was way too short. But through it all, I willed myself to keep a bright outlook, using prayer as my conduit.

Each day before I left my rented house, I'd turn the water heater off. When I needed a loaf of bread, I'd search pockets and anywhere else I thought I could find stray pennies. When I was able to wrap fifty pennies, I went to a small grocery store outside of town, being too embarrassed to pay with a roll of coins at a store in town where I might run into someone I knew.

One month, I needed to pay the electric bill, but my financial spigot was at the dripping stage. It wasn't a large amount, but it was more than I could pay. Then, an epiphany. What good was the engagement ring I had packed away? That ring went full circle for I took it back to the same jeweler where it was purchased. Considering the humble size of the stones, it wasn't worth a lot, but it kept the power on for yet another month.

In the second week of December 1988, Joel was called up for Marine boot camp. I was sad to see him go, but this was something he'd wanted since he was twelve. He packed many of his things in a chest in my bedroom. One of those items was his alarm clock. The Marines would be the only alarm clock he'd need. The first morning that alarm clock was in the chest, it went off. As I was about to turn off the ringer, I was hit with yet another epiphany. What a wonderful reminder of Joel, I thought. I decided from then on that I would use that time every day to pray for him. And so I did. Joel would eventually serve twenty-two years in the Marine Corps, including two tours in Iraq, before retiring at his final duty station, Pensacola Naval Air Station, leaving the Corps with the rank of gunnery sergeant.

Meanwhile, Mike graduated that same year and eventually earned an MBA. Then he became a CPA and moved to Chicago where he was employed by a large downtown bank.

Graduation day approached in the spring of 1989 without me knowing what I would be doing afterward. One day, in the campus library, Mrs. Brooks, the assistant librarian, asked me what plans I had for the future. Nothing had come together in my mind, but I told her that for a long time I could see myself being somewhere teaching an English as Second Language (ESL) class, some place in need of a Christian witness. I had felt the calling from my teenage years, and neither time nor distance had dispelled it. But where? It seemed to me as though a sky full of clouds had kept this place hidden from my view.

Then Mrs. Brooks asked the question that would forever change my life: "Have you ever considered China?" Well, no, I hadn't. China was a long, long way from East Texas. The first time I remember thinking of China was when we kids were digging a deep hole and believing that if we dug deep enough, we might be able to get to that mysterious land. Mrs. Brooks gave me the name of a young man who had gone to southern China to teach for the summer and he, in turn, gave me some helpful information including which organization I could contact.

The organization was a Christian sending agency and after mailing away for information, I received a quick reply along with pamphlets that detailed qualifications, financing, and cities in China where placements were made at various universities and high schools. One place in particular caught my attention: Tibet. This is the place on the other side of the clouds, I thought. A place far, far away. A Buddhist culture of which I had no preconceived notions of what I might encounter.

All of this from the very beginning was bathed in prayer, knowing for certain that the Heavenly Father would by necessity be my tour guide.

The moment was one I had been waiting for. During my youth, our small church served as both spiritual and social avenues for me. I was there any time the doors were open, but it was when I was in eleventh grade that I felt "the call of God." (Probably this coincided with the watermelon stealing.) But what did "the call" mean, exactly? Whatever it meant, the years that followed were rather murky as to how I was to answer it. The freedom to choose a path, however ill-advised my choice might be, was mine to make, and one might think that wrong choices automatically doom one to a certain, permanent path in life. But I know that the call of God knows no time constraint. There is a time for everything, so Ecclesiastes tells us, and my time of regrets and unhappiness could not change what had already been put into motion. My time came when it was preordained to be. No matter what *I* considered my abilities and inclinations to be, they would not factor in. The call was God's call.

And so there I was. Headed for Tibet.

Now, the only thing I knew about Tibet was from a sixth-grade social studies textbook where I had read that the Buddhist spiritual leader, the Dalai Lama, was given two automobiles by the British, even though the leader was only twelve years old. Why would this seemingly insignificant account remain in my memory? Another time that I heard something about Tibet was after my oldest sister was in India near the Tibetan border in the 1950s, right at the time the writer Lowell Thomas Jr. was there. Thomas was one of the first Americans to gain entry into Tibet and would write articles and books about his travels, introducing the area to many in the West.

Later, my sister would say that she never would have believed that, some forty years later, her little sister would actually live there.

In the meantime, waiting for everything to be worked out, I took a job at a middle school for a semester. I was keenly aware that I needed ESL training, so I enrolled in one night class and a Saturday class at Stephen F. Austin University in Nacogdoches. Enrollment in those classes ended up being a life saver for me, giving me the basic tools I needed to be successful. Ultimately, however, my education would come from Professors Trial and Error. Especially Error. But for the time being, I was now ready to answer the call.

I'd read that Tibet tends to cast an inexplicable spell on you. I was ready to find out. With a meager budget, an English-Chinese phrasebook, some ESL training, and a newly procured passport, it was now, "Lhasa, here I come!"

McLeod family, 1943

McLeod, Texas-1947

Grandma Walker enjoying a Dr Pepper at a picnic

Sky burial site behind Sera monastery

Sledgehammers at sky burial site

Mina and author on top of Bumpari Mountain

Soldiers on mountain

CHAPTER 5

THE ROAD TO LHASA

"Live by a compass, not by a clock."
—Unknown

I met my teammates for the first time in California. There were over a hundred new and returning teachers receiving the three-week training, including four of us going to Tibet—me and my eventual climbing mates Drew, Scott, and Mina. This would be Mina's second year, so she would act as our guide until we'd become acclimated to our surroundings. In California, we underwent intensive ESL instruction and training on a variety of topics including basic knowledge of the currency (renminbi), Chinese words and phrases, and culture, culture, culture. For us females, an experienced traveler gave instructions on how to negotiate the dreaded "squatty potty." This was definitely a closed session, with lots of hoots and laughter. Everything we were learning was all theory, of course. Putting it into practice was to be the eye opener, and it was to be seen whether practice would make perfect.

There was a stark difference in the ages of our little team of four. I was forty-eight while the others were in their late twenties or early thirties. I obviously didn't fit into the idealized version of the youthful, adventurous backpacker. Far from it, in fact. But I fit in as best I could and worked hard to keep up.

After the training, we departed from Los Angeles International Airport for the fourteen-hour odyssey that would take us to Seoul, Taipei, and finally Hong Kong, the launching point for Drew, Scott, Mina, and me to our eventual landing in Tibet, via Chengdu, China.

Hong Kong's airport was named Kai Tek, and the experience of landing there was often referred to as the "Kai Tek Heart Attack." This came from the closeness of the mountains and the water of Victoria Harbor at the end of notorious Runway 13. Coming in over the densely populated, six-story apartment buildings, pilots were required to use sight landings. Upon seeing "Checkerboard Hill," an orange-and-white painted marker above a park, the pilot, coming in at 200 miles per hour, needed to veer right, making a 45-degree turn. These hair-raising landings could be even more breathtaking if there was a change in wind velocity.

Dicey arrival notwithstanding, the lights of Hong Kong, a city that never sleeps, were a welcome sight to behold. Weary, we were happy to board the bus that would take us to our accommodations, the YMCA International House. The rest of the group would take off the next day for Beijing and their eventual teaching destinations. We Tibet four spent an extra day in Hong Kong, taking in the sights of the "Golden Mile," as it was known at the time—the main thoroughfare of restaurants and shops, filled with people. We went down to the harbor, too, and at one point we took the subway, a sardine can of humanity. It was my first time in a foreign city.

The next day we went back to the airport in what we thought was plenty of time for our flight to Chengdu, which, nevertheless, we almost missed. The problem was that the Chinese airline weighed our bags and told us our luggage exceeded the limits. Mine was fine, but the others were too heavy. Or so the airline said. We, of course, had no way to disprove the claim. Drew's suitcase presumably weighed a hundred pounds. The limit was sixty-five. An hour of haggling later, we ended up paying $300 for the airline to accept the bags.

Then, going through security, the problem was not one of weight, but of bulk. It seemed our bags were too big. It was back to the counter, which, unfortunately, had been vacated by then. Eventually, we were able to find another airline employee who walked to security with us and vouched for the bags. Then came another little fly in the ointment. Somehow, I set off the metal detector. A security guard asked me to empty my pockets and I found myself mortified when I drew out a knife. It was a Tibetan knife that Mina had given me so that I could tape up my carry-on bag. I'd completely forgotten about it. After being frisked, the security guard gave the knife to another guard who scrutinized it closely before deciding I was apparently harmless and handing me the knife back. We made it to the gate with mere moments to spare, and, finally, we were on our way.

After another lengthy flight, we landed in Chengdu, the capital of Sichuan Province and the home of spicy Sichuan food. Under leaden gray skies, we deplaned a distance from the terminal into the heat and humidity. In years to come, I would know that I was in Chengdu by those same gray skies and the peculiar, perpetual smell of coal. What startled me on that first trip was the intimidating presence of armed military guards posted near the plane. Not exactly a welcoming sight.

We were met by a US consulate driver who held a sign with Mina's name on it, as she had wired the prior day that we would be coming through. The teachers the year before had been invited to stay as guests in a wing of the Jin Jiang Hotel, which at that time, was the home of the consulate. We got the same invitation and were graciously provided rooms at no charge.

But it was not much rest for the weary. The next morning at 6:30, it was off to the airport again for our flight to Lhasa. Luggage was a hassle once more, this time because you had to move your bags along the conveyor belt to security yourself, and ours—thirteen pieces in all—were in a bit of a heap. Finally, we made it to the crowded bus that took us out to our 727. Once aboard, we learned that having a seat assignment on a Chinese airline didn't mean a whole lot. Other passengers had taken our seats. The flight attendant's response was to advise us to seek other seats, which we did, unfortunately getting separated in the process. I ended up between two men, one of whom had his bare foot propped up on the tray table picking his toes. Meanwhile, it was hot and muggy and rainy. Worse, we sat waiting to take off for quite a while before, owing to mechanical problems, we were made to deplane. Then it was back to the terminal on the crowded bus where we sat for six hours before another plane became available. To the airline's credit, they did provide a boxed meal, even if the contents remained unidentifiable to me.

Those six hours provided us with many cultural insights. As the crowd of people waiting flowed out into the hallways, we were forced to find room to sit on the filthy floor with our backs to the wall, sharing space with wads of spittle and little children going potty wherever there wasn't a body occupying a space.

When it was time to board the second plane, Drew and Scott and Mina and I fought to be among the first on. I grabbed the window seat in a row ahead of the others. Then a Chinese soldier came along, showing me his ticket with a seat assignment for the seat I had taken. I told him that from my earlier experience, I had learned that seat assignments didn't really matter, but, not understanding English, he said nothing and continued to stand there. Scott had earlier advised putting my nose to the window if anybody came looking for the seat, and that's what I did. I heard the soldier grunt and then he sat beside me in the center seat, another soldier taking the aisle seat.

Most of the trip to Lhasa was cloudy, but over Tibet, the clouds parted every so often and I was able to catch a glimpse of the mountains, covered in different hues of green velvet. Rivers flowing through them made for a beautiful scene. And seeing the terrain made me understand why the airport was so far from the city. There was no flat space for miles and miles.

When we finally landed, I turned to the soldier beside me and said, "Thank you," in Chinese and indicated that this was my first time visiting Tibet. He grinned a broad grin and I assumed all was forgiven.

Mina had wired our school letting them know we'd be arriving that day, but no one was there to meet us. We walked down a long, dusty, dirt road to the terminal, nothing more than a shanty, with our hands full with our heavy carry-on bags and all of us experiencing the effects of the high altitude, me more than anyone. When we got to the terminal, I was put in charge of watching over the carry-ons while the others went in to retrieve the rest of our luggage.

From the airport, we were lucky to catch the last bus out for the one-and-a-half-hour ride to Lhasa. I rode in the back with Mina, while the guys were in front holding down our luggage, and very quickly learned that the back of the bus was not the best place to be. My fanny came off the seat with every big bump, and there were plenty of big bumps. By the time we arrived, I had a splitting headache. Again, no one was there to meet us. Fortunately, Mina happened to spot a former student who was waiting on a bus. He went to alert our schools and before long a big van drove up to take us to our new homes.

Our first stop was to drop the guys off at the academy where we met some officials who apologized profusely for not having met us. They had not received Mina's wire. They provided us a welcoming drink of Jianlibao, the cola that would become my favorite. From there, I was delivered to my flat, still with a headache and now feeling dizzy and nauseous as well. The smells and noises didn't help. Someone was playing Tibetan opera very loudly and the smell of the outhouses adjacent to the apartment made me sick. Worse, an hour after our arrival we were told that we were to eat with the dean of the foreign language department, and right then. I wasn't up to it, but I forced myself to go nevertheless.

I managed to eat a little at the dinner, but it was difficult with a nauseous stomach and with our hosts insisting we eat everything. If I failed to try a dish, the person seated next to me would graciously place it on my plate. The "it" was always something unidentifiable. Having only recently left behind fried chicken, mashed potatoes, purple-hulled peas, hamburgers, and pizza, it was way too early to be plunged into such a gastronomic nightmare. My stomach would have to incorporate new foods in small increments. Mercifully, we didn't stay long, and I returned to my flat and went right to bed.

The next morning brought more loud music, this time blaring from a loudspeaker. It was the students' wake-up call, complete with exercise music, news, and the national anthem. It was still dark and it seemed very early, but it was actually eight o'clock. I felt better after having gotten a little sleep, even though the sleep had not come easily. I had read that high altitude affects sleep and would experience this firsthand for quite a while after arriving in Lhasa.

That morning we were all anxious to go out and explore and the guys came to our school to join us for the walk to the Barkhor, the Tibetan "old town" that circles the Johkong temple, the holiest temple of them all. According to religious custom, you walk clockwise around Barkhor Street. Our visit served as a quick introduction to Lhasa. I saw everything and smelled quite a lot too—nomads, dogs (scores of them), goats, cows, chickens, all loose. I noticed that nearly everyone knew the English greeting "hello" and liked to try it out on the English-speaking foreigners.

Nomad women came up to us trying to sell their jewelry—lots of topaz and turquoise, probably fake and overpriced. Little kids approached us begging for money. We ate at a Muslim restaurant and had noodles with yak meat on top. Dogs and flies were everywhere, inside and out. I knew enough not to try to kill any of the flies, however. As believers in reincarnation, the local Buddhists imagined a fly might be someone's mother.

I found the Tibetan women to be rosy-cheeked and pretty, many in colorful dresses. Mina, whose mother was Colombian and father was Ecuadorian, could be mistaken for one and she received plenty of stares from people trying to figure out exactly what she was. In fact, people thought nothing of staring at strangers. They would stand in their doorways to get a glimpse of foreigners, but they were always quick with a friendly "hello."

The entire time we were exploring Lhasa, it was never fully out of my mind that mere months prior, the government had cracked down, expelling virtually all foreigners. Martial law had been imposed. The occasion was the thirtieth anniversary of the Tibet Rebellion. China had annexed Tibet in 1950 and in 1959, Tibet had revolted, resulting in hundreds or perhaps thousands (nobody knows for sure) of Tibetan deaths and the fleeing of the Dalai Lama. The anniversary brought demonstrations and the demonstrations brought police and government soldiers, 60,000 in all. Clashes left at least a dozen dead and, shortly after that, all the foreigners had to go. Why? Tibetans would tell you it was to prevent outside witnesses from seeing what came next. It is believed that hundreds of demonstrators were killed but, even now, solid numbers are hard to find.

Martial law lasted thirteen months and was lifted just a few months before our arrival. Foreigners were allowed back, and there we were, walking around Tibet's capital, soaking it all in, wondering what it must have been like a year before. And wondering what the next year would bring.

⸺⧓⸺

The following day, we went to our school. I was introduced to my class monitor, Renchen. I found him to be a little shy, but he and all

35

of the students were curious about their new foreign teacher. I was to begin teaching the following Tuesday—two classes of second-year students for speaking and listening. Then a week later, a freshmen class. Once a week, a video session with both. My students were on the path to becoming English teachers. Mina's, tour guides.

The next few days were spent getting better acquainted with Lhasa. The four of us walked to a restaurant where, once again, I found myself with a dish of yak meat, this time on rice with a few cubes of potatoes in a broth. The meat was too tough to eat, but I managed okay with the rice and potatoes. This restaurant, like most of the restaurants around Lhasa, was no more than a small room. There was little light except what came in through the doorway, which was always kept open except at night when the door was closed and secured with two by fours. Most places had dirt floors, dogs hanging around under the tables hoping for scraps and cheap food.

At one point, Mina and I went to the big market. Under one roof were all sorts of meat in various stages of dress, and unpleasant odors wafting in the air. Under another roof were copious amounts of produce—cabbages, onions, green peppers, eggplants, long pink radishes, garlic, potatoes, melons, fruits of all kinds, watercress, carrots, and some foods that were new to me. Besides this market, there were grocery stores, but most were nothing more than small cubicles where you walked up to a counter and ordered what you wanted. Sugar was in short supply as was liquid dish soap. I saw Coffee-Mate and Fifth Avenue candy bars, which reminded me of home.

Our apartments were located on the ground floor of a two-story building with Tibetan neighbors and an abundance of cute kids. At some point, Scott had stopped by and given a few of the kids balloons. Soon, they were flocking at my door. Some would ask, "What's your name?" even though they had no idea what it meant. Tourists had asked them the question so many times that they simply parroted it. Sometimes they'd say good morning in the evening, until

I would say, "Good evening," which they would then start repeating. But some things are universal, and I would watch the kids flying kites or hear them singing and realize how similar children are everywhere.

There were many more observations I would make in the first days and weeks of living in Lhasa. I'd had no concrete expectations of the place, and so I took everything in with an open and curious mind. But one thing presented itself to me very early. It was a strange land, full of new and different experiences, far from home and far from anything I had ever seen before. And yet I found myself drawn to it to such a degree that it became apparent to me that, as foreign as the place was, and maybe even because it was so foreign, I was clearly meant to be there.

CHAPTER 6

LEARNING LHASA

"Traveling—it leaves you speechless, then turns you into a story-teller."
—Unknown

I found settling into my Tibetan apartment to be an interesting experience. Once the peculiarities had been explained to me, I ventured a thought: *You ain't in Kansas anymore.*

A basic Tibetan apartment wouldn't be complete without what I came to call, per the local vernacular, the WC, for water closet. That designation seemed most appropriate. One couldn't exactly call it a bathroom, for no baths could be taken there. In the WC, there was a floor urinal with cold-water pipes on the wall in front, which, when grabbed, served as a lift. If one wanted to be tortured by icy-cold water, then one could straddle the urinal and turn on the shower, but this held no appeal for me. Instead, I took to filling a plastic kiddie pool with kettles of boiling water. Bath time came around once a week. The humidity was always low in Lhasa, so there wasn't a need for a full bath more than that. In the winter, I'd wear many layers, so who'd be the wiser? Because it was an ordeal to get ready to bathe, what with the heating of the water, I would use the bath water to also wash the kitchen floor. I simply sloshed bucketsful onto the floor, then swept the water out the doorway to the entry, and then outside. I multitasked before it was in vogue.

The kiddie pool concept also served my purposes for doing laundry. My teaching partner's apartment came with a washing machine, a two-sectioned, top-loader like a 1940s machine. Me, I had to wash everything by hand in the kiddie pool, and after a few months of wringing out clothes, my wrists felt as if they'd been permanently sprained. I dried my clothes on a clothesline set up in the spare room, but sometimes when I needed items to dry quickly, I took advantage of the courtesy of my neighbors who allowed me to hang my laundry outside in their fenced-in chicken yard. As you might imagine, this didn't exactly produce a Febreze-like fragrance to my clothes.

Another quirk of the apartment was the pair of needle-nosed pliers I discovered hanging on the wall above the small electric-coil tripod cooking element. I soon learned they were there for a reason—namely, for when the coils needed repair work. Which was often. There was a pressure cooker, which I would end up using frequently and what the electric coils were mostly for. But the pressure cooker required a bit of a learning curve. No one told me, for instance, that dried beans could produce sufficient gas inside the pot to explode. I discovered this on my own one evening. Beans shot out of the pot like gassed-up projectiles, some of them discovered days and weeks later in various nooks and crannies. It was a magnificent explosion.

The kitchen came with a small, pea green refrigerator. I was thankful for it, especially when I realized that most families in Lhasa didn't own one. The spare room served as my walk-in freezer in the winter. In the corner of the small kitchen was a deep, concrete-block sink, which would have been at the right height for a short person. This became a busy spot for it was not only where I washed my dishes, but also brushed my teeth, washed my face and hands, and, in general, became my morning and evening *toilette*. In the winter, I had to remember to keep the toothpaste in my bedroom or else it would freeze.

My south-facing bedroom came with a narrow bed with a mattress that felt like it was stuffed with straw. There was a small, square, electric heater, which kept the chill out of the air in the mornings, but the sunshine coming through the windows heated the room by the afternoon. A small desk, lamp, chair, and modest sofa completed the furnishings. The electricity was unreliable, sometimes going off during the day and most of the time for a few hours in the evening. Having a large supply of candles was a must, for it took several to read, to do my teacher work, or to write letters. Candles or not, writing letters was not easy in the winter with freezing cold fingers.

A small room just off the kitchen was where the yak dung stove was located and where I had been supplied with a nice burlap bag full of fuel. I didn't use the stove until I cooked some of Thanksgiving dinner with it where I discovered that yak dung burns very hot and it was next to impossible for me to regulate the heat. But the good news was that, to my pleasant surprise, the dung had very little smell.

Eventually, I would acquire a roommate of sorts. A student would give me a semi-wild cat as a gift. That feline created a lot of havoc for me and I don't know why I put up with it. I named her Samantha, but I called her a few other choice names, especially when I was trying to sleep and she would leap on the bed with fierce intentions. I never knew when Samantha would jump out from under something and grab a hold of my leg. (One thing in her favor was that she actually used the squatty potty.) After about a month, to see if she had any other place to go, or maybe to test her loyalty to me, I cranked the window open a little, giving her the freedom to come and go, half hoping she'd find herself better digs, but she always made her way back to my place. When I would leave Lhasa for good, one of my students would adopt her.

As I was settling in, there was much of Lhasa to discover. Perhaps what Tibet is most famous for is a certain resident who no longer makes his home there. I speak, of course, of the aforementioned 14th

Dalai Lama, born Lhamo Thondup. The Dalai Lama is the spiritual leader of the Gelug school of Tibetan Buddhism and, like all the Dalai Lamas who came before him, believed to be the incarnation of the Bodhisattva of Compassion. He was enthroned as the Dalai Lama in 1940 at the age of five, and assumed his duties ten years later, just after the Chinese occupation of Tibet. After the 1959 uprising, the Dalai Lama was forced to flee Tibet for India and has lived in exile ever since, still the Tibetan spiritual leader, and, of course, a much-admired, Nobel Prize-winning religious leader of the world, more or less the Pope of the larger Buddhist community.

Naturally, then, one of the first things we did in Lhasa was to visit Norbulingka, the palace and park that served as the summer home for all the Dalai Lamas from 1780 up until the 1959 exile. Mina had tutored one of the caretakers, Pemba, the person in charge of the palace library. Presumably, Pemba was a monk, but he didn't dress the part. Mina referred to him as a plainclothes monk. Pemba took us on a tour, giving us access to parts of the palace off-limits to tourists.

First, however, we had to stop in his very spartan quarters where he insisted on serving us tea. Yak butter tea. This is just what it sounds like. It's made from tea leaves and yak butter, along with salt. I had a sip out of politeness. The truth is, I had tried yak butter tea a couple of days before and it gave me diarrhea. Diarrhea would become a common thing for all of us as we tried to grow accustomed to the local cuisine. We took to calling it "the Big D." After the yak butter tea, we took our tour of the palace, seeing many interesting things, including the rotted remains of what were, at one time, beautiful automobiles that had been gifted to the Dalai Lama from England, but had since sat unused and unmaintained. These were the cars I had read about years before in my fifth-grade social studies textbook. (The unexpected journeys in one's life can be magical considering where and when they begin.) After the tour, we sat outside of the gate enjoying small, tasty apples from a very old tree.

Besides Norbulingka, we visited the aforementioned Barkhor street, a sacred place for Buddhists, but also a large market selling traditional Tibetan artifacts along with fruits and vegetables and meats, plus clothing and other goods.

For my part, I spent a lot of the first few days gawking at the scenery, mesmerized by the mountains. The city was surrounded by them, the ones to the north capped with snow. One time, Mina and I walked the bridge over the Lhasa River and found a spot from which the view was especially spectacular, and from every direction. I had to keep reminding myself that I was not in some dream, that I was actually in Tibet. Though I would gawk less and less as the days and weeks and months wore on, the sense of wonderment I felt owing to the majestic backdrop of this land would never leave me.

One characteristic of Lhasa that I also could not fail to observe, even if I tried, was the plethora of beggars around town. Some were Buddhist monks with their traditional begging bowls. According to legend, the Buddha was offered a golden bowl while he was meditating under the Bodhi tree awaiting enlightenment. Some monks now use bowls to collect alms, signifying their non-attachment to the material aspects of this world. But most beggars were poor or old or disabled. Or children. Ragged and dirty children were everywhere, forever tugging on our clothes, even hanging off of us. You'd walk away from them and find yourself literally dragging them behind you. Not all were begging for themselves. Sometime a parent would send a child out to beg while they remained hidden.

One day, I managed to commit a terrible faux pas in my attempt to give alms to a beggar. Mina and I walked the Lingkhor one day, another sacred path like the Barkhor, but this one a five-mile outer circle encompassing all of Old Lhasa. The path wasn't easy in places, but we saw old ladies managing the task and if those grannies could do it, so could we. And we did. But not before I approached a group of tired grannies resting on a rocky outcropping beside the trail.

Surely these were beggars hoping to receive alms. I dropped a few coins into the cup of one of the old women, only to have her rise and take a swat at me, then snarl something that I imagine wasn't necessarily appropriate for such a sacred path. I didn't need to know the language to understand that this was no beggar. In fact, I had just dropped my coins into the woman's yak butter tea. Red-faced, I mumbled an apology and Mina and I wasted no time hiking onward.

Besides beggars (and non-beggars who looked like beggars) another thing one couldn't fail to observe, and, in fact, needed to watch for: excrement. Dog poop was everywhere. So was the poop of other animals, including the human animal. Puddles of water were not necessarily just water. Occasionally, you might be walking along and someone would fling a pan of dirty water out of their door. Of course there were flies everywhere.

In March, there were dust storms, sand catapulted by strong winds coming from the desert of northwest China. These storms came in March of every year, as predictable as the swallows finding their way back to San Juan Capistrano. Not that I'd ever learned from past experience. Inevitably I'd go out and be caught by total surprise by a dust storm. Many Tibetans wore masks, but I'd have to find a doorway or shop to escape the stinging grains of sand. I usually wore a knit, long-sleeved turtleneck top which I'd pull up to cover my nose, and that would have to do.

While my mind was adjusting to all the new and alien things I was seeing and experiencing, my stomach was trying its best to adjust to the food. There would be no more yak butter tea for me, but there would be mo-mos, a dumpling filled with yak meat and vegetables and the ever-present garlic that a lot of Tibetan dishes were spiced with. There were pickled vegetables and bone marrow soup. And there were some food items that I simply couldn't bring myself to try and which would remain forever unknown to me.

In fact, I took to feasting on noodles, something I recognized, something that didn't give me the Big D, and something economical. Initially, I faced something of a conundrum. What kind of noodles? There was no shortage of Muslim noodles, Tibetan noodles, and Chinese noodles, each with their own characteristics.

Muslim noodles are a special kind of hand-pulled Chinese noodles made by Chinese Muslims. The noodle is very thick, with a consistency of an undercooked noodle. In a Muslim restaurant you can't eat pork or drink alcohol, but where they lack in swine and wine, they make up for by dishing out plates of hearty, chewy, succulent noodles. Tibetan noodles are made of wheat flour, which tastes a bit raw. Generally, they're cooked with yak meat and some people will add a few spoonfuls of Tibetan chili sauce. Chinese noodles vary, but yao mein was my favorite, a thin egg-and-wheat noodle.

When a person is hungry and on a limited food allowance, it probably doesn't matter which noodles to eat. Nevertheless, I found myself gravitating to the Chinese noodles of a certain restaurant. This restaurant became my favorite by checking several important boxes. For one thing, it was conveniently located. Plus, there was always very little wait time. Importantly, there were no dogs camped out under the tables waiting for a slippery noodle to escape my chopsticks. The chopsticks themselves factored into the decision because this particular place gave you an option—wooden, disposable chopsticks hygienically wrapped, or the re-used plastic ones that I had often seen other patrons chewing on. Naturally, I chose the former.

I liked the ambience of the place, too. It was casual, with a few small tables placed at open, curtained windows, each providing a perfect view of the happenings in, on, and beside the laid-back two-lane street. Being able to listen to the street noise was part of the appeal, as well. If you put it to music, I imagine you'd need a range of instruments to represent it all, from a cello to a violin, piano, saxophone, and the occasional rumblings of a kettle drum. Tying the visual, aural, and gastronomic experience together was the restaurant's main noodle chef, a forever smiling and laughing Han Chinese gentleman. I would sometimes eat in his establishment twice a day, and for pennies. After a while, I imagined that he kept a table by the window unoccupied, just for me.

It was one thing to look out of a restaurant window and observe and listen to the street activity. It was another thing to jump right into it. The traffic patterns took a little time to get accustomed to, but this task became easier once I recognized that there *weren't* any traffic patterns. Everyone and everything simply merged together into a serpentining flow that was generally very peaceful. No road rage in Lhasa! The only hot-rodders were the surrey-with-the-fringe-on-top tricycles, known locally as pedicabs, an inexpensive means of transport. Time for them was money and woe to the man or beast that got in their way. With bells ringing, the race was on when a pedicab jockey scored a passenger. One could count on an exciting ride and it was always amusing to witness a tourist's maiden voyage.

I negotiated the streets on foot and on bicycle. Beijing Road was one of three main streets running east to west, and the one I typically biked down. Most of the businesses along this street were small specialty shops. One sold butter and flour. The butter, called "Beijing butter," was the real deal and was cut and portioned from a large block which was sensibly covered with paper to keep the flies off. Another establishment along Beijing Road was a restaurant I frequented that served curried potato chunks, and yak meat over rice. Potatoes in any form were a favorite of mine, right up there with noodles. The "potato restaurant" was located on the corner of a short street leading to the Barkhor and was large enough for three tables and a few dogs that were always around to clean the floor of dropped food. We took to classifying an eatery by the usual number of dogs present, figuring that the dogs knew all the best places. This was a "four dog" restaurant.

On one corner of Beijing Road was a large Tibetan furniture business that produced colorful cabinetry of red, blue, green, and yellow, of all sizes, with many pieces displayed near the street. The not so unpleasant odor of sawed wood and lacquer would alert one that the shop was nearby. Every home I visited had more than one cabinet. Their Buddhist altars seemed to demand them. Even though I dreamed of buying one—knocked down for shipping—it was never to be, my lack of money the deciding factor.

Farther down the street, located on Middle Beijing Road, was a small restaurant I would eventually visit called the Drunken Celestial Being. On that occasion, we teachers invited some of the aides of the US Foreign Relations Committee who had come to Tibet on a fact-finding trip. I didn't notice any celestial beings hanging around the place. Nor did I notice a single dog. So this restaurant's ranking would be a "no dog" restaurant. Or I suppose another way of saying it is that no self-respecting dog would deign to enter.

Bicycling the streets was manageable during the day, but something of a risky proposition at night. After a while you learned where the open manholes were and the other traffic and road hazards, including a pack of vicious dogs that I made it a point to steer well clear of. I knew these dogs. Individually, in the daylight, they were a picture of innocence. At night, a posse of ferocious beasts.

The night rides were out of necessity. Times, for instance, when I would accept a dinner invitation from Americans or Canadians who were in Lhasa on official business—US consulate personnel, researchers from academia, and others. Over a two-year period, I would amass quite a selection of business cards. If it wasn't too late, some of the shops would still be open and I'd feel less alone as I pedaled along, the lights from the shops keeping me company. Only after I'd become more familiar with my surroundings, would I venture out later at night. By then, I would not be burdened by the many "what ifs." Fear of the unknown would not keep me in.

Besides dinners, invitations often came for government-sponsored celebrations. National Day of the People's Republic of China was October 1. There was a ceremony and we were given a print-out in English so as not to miss any of the all-important remarks given in Chinese by some all-important ranking member of the military dressed to the hilt, complete with his all-important sunshades. I don't imagine the remarks changed very much from year to year.

Mina and I attended the National Day ceremony for two reasons. First, our school expected us to. Second, and what we considered a more important reason, it gave us the chance to have something different to eat, something, for once, besides noodles or potatoes. A benefit of having foreign expert status was being invited to the buffet tables immediately following the notables. Of course, it was still a "name that dish" scenario, but to my delight, we came across a large tray of cut-up, bone-in chicken breasts. Of course, presentation is everything. To make sure the entree had eye appeal, the chicken chef had carefully placed chicken feet around the perimeter of the tray. I almost broke out in song to the tune of "These Boots Were Made for Walking": *These feet were made for walking.* Then: *You invited me here, this banquet to eat, but all I got were these chicken feet.*

I soon had a favorite spot for tea in Lhasa. It was a small place where they'd serve the piping hot liquid in a small glass with no handle. The recipe was simple: black tea, sugar, and dried milk. I have no idea why anyone would serve a hot liquid in a handle-less glass, but I suffered through the mild burning of my fingers mostly for the smile and wave of the boss of the establishment, "Grandpa" as I called him. His domain was a corner near the front door. How he could track from there each glass consumed would always remain a mystery to me. And his snaggle-toothed smile would remain a treasured memory.

A favorite place for many of my female students was the ice cream parlor and they'd invite me along occasionally. Ice cream—*bing ji ling*—was served as a tiny scoop and consumed with a tiny spoon.

The serving was expected to last for a considerable time. In the US, most of us would have put it away in one bite (one swell scoop?). The place was definitely not a "House of 49 Flavors." You had your choice of vanilla or chocolate. And it tasted like sweetened, non-fat ice milk. Out on the street you could buy ice cream from a cart (sans the traditional music of the iconic American ice cream truck). This was *wa wa bing ji ling*—baby ice cream, and it was served on a stick and was in the shape of a panda, consisting of vanilla ice cream with chocolate features.

The Muslims did a booming business just off the street grilling shish kabobs of lamb and the aroma was intoxicating even from a distance. At first I wasn't sure I'd want to eat any kind of meat, especially meat from a street vendor. But watching them spread the thin strips of meat on a stick, sprinkled with spices and placed on a grill, was enough to make even a vegetarian swoon. The grilling brigade set up several narrow, elongated, four-legged grills and kept the 'bobs moving. The heat from the charcoal kept the flies away and the meat retrieved from a big box appeared to have been refrigerated. For certain, this became my favorite street food once I'd fought through my finicky food phase.

On one of my routes to the Barkhor via the alleys, I'd pass one of four mosques in Lhasa, this one the "Great Mosque," located in a vibrant part of the city with many businesses. Most of the time I noticed animals across the street, possibly waiting to be slaughtered as many of the Muslims were butchers. Sometimes I'd hear the call to prayer. Every morning from my apartment at Tibet University, I would hear the loud sound of a male voice, which I came to assume was a Muslim making the morning prayer call.

From time to time, it was necessary to go to the post office, either to mail letters or to retrieve packages. It was always a shoving match at the post office, with nobody properly queuing up at the windows. It was shove or be shoved. One time a letter for me had been opened and no doubt read before it reached my box at the university. Some ex-pat employees of the local Holiday Inn had this happen often. This was the government checking the letters for unacceptable content. Sometimes the letters even had notes penciled into the margins, no attempt made at all to hide the intrusion.

Mailing packages of any size was a hassle because after the contents had passed inspection, you practically needed a needle and thread to sew the contents back up into a package again. The same thing happened when you were on the receiving end. When you were notified of a package, you had to go to the post office with another container to put the contents in, such was the rough treatment of the original package during its route as well as the harsh inspection process. Once I received a *National Geographic* that had been examined page by page. This was shortly after the Tiananmen Square demonstrations and one page had the now-iconic photograph of a man standing before a line of tanks. Before I could take the magazine with me, the postal employee made me tear the page out and rip it up in front of him. I made large tears so that when I got back to my apartment, I was able to tape the page back together again.

Early on in my time in Lhasa came the afore-described climbing of Bumpari Mountain with the others. I had thought I'd given up climbing after that experience. But one of the sites I frequently passed was Chokpori Hill, 12,221 feet above sea level and with a view of the Barkhor, the Jokhang Temple, and at a short distance, the Potala Palace. The Potala Palace, a museum today, was the Dalai Lama's winter home from 1649 until 1959. It rested on another hill over 300 feet high and was useful in orienting oneself as it towered over everything. At one time, hundreds of years ago, a beautiful temple sat on top of Chokpori Hill. Eventually it was turned into a medical college, but during the 1959 uprising, it was destroyed. In the 1980s, the debris was cleared away to make room for a large, fenced-in television tower, a painful vista now. The medical college/temple had been important for the Tibetans in a visual, religious, and practical way.

At any rate, Chokpori Hill stood there begging to be climbed and one day the call was too much for me to ignore. So up I went. The upper half, with the TV tower was fenced off, which was just as well. I didn't need to climb any farther and, in fact, had probably climbed too far as it was. When I turned around to go back down, it was Bumpari all over again. Déjà vu! Slippery rocks underfoot filled me with fear, and for a while I stood in place contemplating my situation.

And then, there she was.

An elderly Tibetan woman wearing sneakers climbed up to me, smiled, and, saying very little, held my arm and walked me safely down. A guardian angel? In this magical land, why not?

CHAPTER 7

THE STUDENTS OF TIBET UNIVERSITY

"Jobs fill your pocket, adventures fill your soul."
—Jaime Lyn Beatty

Having become at least somewhat familiar with my apartment and surroundings, it was time to meet my students. These were second-year students, members of the class of 1992.

Tibet University, with an enrollment of several thousand, had been officially established just a few years earlier, in 1985, although Tibetan communist cadres had held informal classes since 1951, and the Teacher's College was already in existence. My class consisted of twenty-eight students, eight boys and twenty girls. I wondered if they knew how nervous their new American teacher was. When I entered the classroom, the students all stood, surprising me by the action. It took me a few seconds to react, to motion for them to take their seats. How long would they have stood if I hadn't done so?

Once they sat back down, I couldn't help noticing the expressions on their faces, so serious, so expectant. To break the ice, I turned to the pock-marked chalkboard and printed in large letters SMILE. When I turned back around, there were twenty-eight smiling faces, followed by laughs. My nervousness went down a notch.

I introduced myself, then told the students how they could address me, which was as "Mary Laoshi"—Teacher Mary. I knew that Chinese/Tibetans would have trouble sounding the *th* in my given name.

They could also call me "Miss Mary," I told them. (Months later, I would receive a Christmas card from one of the students, trying hard to use my real name and addressing it to "Mrs. Mary Dith.")

But for any problems they might have had pronouncing my name, those problems didn't quite match the problems I had pronouncing theirs. My attempts were met with groans and laughter. Fortunately, they already had English names from the year before, so that took care of roll call for the time being. As I became more fluent, I'd use their Tibetan names. Tibetans have no family names, but use two words with two syllables each, such as Dawa Lhoma. Or a syllable from each word might be combined for the name. Unlike the seemingly infinite number of American names, the number of Tibetan names is limited, with most used for both male and female. The meaning of the names is of great importance. I learned this when a student invited me to her home during Tibetan New Year. The family had a puppy that didn't yet have a moniker, so they asked me to give it an English one. I made a little ceremony of the occasion and proclaimed the puppy to be henceforth known as "Fido." To my surprise, they asked what it meant. Thinking quickly, I said, "Fierce protector." They were thrilled with the choice.

Looking out at the class, I observed that most of the students were sitting next to best friends. But what surprised me was that two of them were boy-girl. In China/Tibet, pairing up with the opposite sex was unheard of, especially at this time. Spencer and Catherine were a rarity. I would notice that they were always together, and it seemed as if they didn't have any other close friends. I'd be invited to Catherine's home and find Spencer there. I'd be invited to Spencer's home and find Catherine there. Both of them were good students. Catherine was quiet and somewhat shy, but Spencer was a self-assured, polite young man who looked and acted older than any other boy in the class. If there had been a yearbook with superlatives for seniors, he would have been listed as "Most Likely to Succeed." He was a natural leader. I was amused by his line of reasoning on one of the tests on verbs: *bleed/bled/blood.* Years later, I would remind him of this and we'd have a good laugh.

The Chinese-English Language Department was not unaware of this couple, for at the beginning of the second semester, they were required to sit apart, which they did, even if it was just a single table that separated them. For my part, I never saw anything between them except innocent friendship.

A few days into the new school year, the department threw a party. Nobody had told us about it, but one night around nine o'clock, a student came knocking on our doors to tell us to come to the teaching building to join the festivities. The party was held in a long room with first-year students sitting at tables lining one wall, and second- and third-year students lining other walls, with administrators and teachers sitting in front. Some students presented Mina and me with long, white scarves, called *katas,* as a welcoming gesture.

Then we were seated at a table where unshelled sunflower seeds and wrapped hard candies were piled. This would be repeated at future parties, and I began to believe that no party would be proper without these table favors. Students served us hot sweet tea (tea, milk powder, and sugar), a drink that would appear almost daily in my life in Tibet.

The dean of the foreign language department, Jian Ting Feng, a non-English speaker, was the wife of the president of the university, Tse Wang Jigme, and he and other officials from the school came to join the party. It was common at parties to have entertainment with songs, poetry, and, on this occasion, a male student doing a break-dance. The lights were dimmed and a few couples began to dance—male-female, male-male, and female-female. This was not at all unusual in China. As a matter of fact, it was a common sight to see couples of the same sex holding hands—even embracing. All part of the culture. Meanwhile, I noticed that the first-year students rarely moved from their seats, too shy and embarrassed to say or do anything. Mina sang "New York, New York" as her contribution, and even though I'd thought to follow with "The Eyes of Texas," I decided it would be best for everyone if I just gave a short speech. After a few hours, the party was, thankfully, over.

Back in the classroom, I was presented with a problem that concerned me at first. As it happened, the textbooks and workbooks had been provided by the British Council a few years before. I imagined how tangled things could become: British texts, British pronunciations, British spellings, taught by an American with a Southern/East Texas accent. To make it easy for everyone, I decided to accept both British and American versions of the language. I needn't have worried. After two years of being my students, these kids would eventually get it all sorted out.

The students had come to the university from all over Tibet with very different academic levels. A few male students were very inefficient with English, which made me question their placement. These were students who were supposed to become middle school teachers, after all, which, in China, corresponds to high school level in the US. But I accepted the challenge of trying to bring them up to speed.

I had the students keep journals in English as an ongoing assignment and I learned a lot about most of them from this exercise. I never had to wonder what the weather was like on any particular day, because that's all some of them had to say. Several students wrote that I seemed very kind. Apparently, I reminded them of their mothers even though, they were quick to note, I didn't seem old enough to have kids their ages. (Naturally, I loved them from that moment on.)

"Hillary" was the American name of the most athletic of the female students. She was always smiling and laughing, and I found her journal entries to be some of the more interesting and pleasurable to read:

On 12 September, 1990   cloudy

54

I hold my books go to the classroom this morning. I look around. I discovered foliage became yellow. I feel cool. I know this implied meaning that the winter will come. The time passed very quickly. It's good say, "Time and tide wait for no man."

On 21 September, 1990   shining
Our basketball match is end. I think it was relatively savage. When we play basketball is a skilled and cooperative sport. As you shoot at the basket, you should brush past basketball board near the basketball stand. You should estimate with your eyes if you far away. We should grab the rebound and make a shooting in a match. We must grab scoring opening. You should shake your hand when your opponent shoot basket. Such as you affect her (him) shoot at the basket. You should check your opponent drive shot in front of her or (him), and lest referee tell you foul. Additional: You should look at hoop shooting again if you faraway.

It would be an interesting year. Becoming accustomed to one another would come incrementally. I tried to make them laugh to put them at ease, and I laughed at myself for the mistakes I made. I loved all my students, but some, hampered by a relative inability to speak English, would remain forever shy, preventing me from getting to know them better. For the ones who did communicate with me verbally, imperfect as their English might have been, I could see improvements not just in their language skills, but in their self-confidence.

During the first weeks of class, still looking to get my bearings in this strange world, I asked many questions about a variety of things, sometimes with more success than others. For instance, some days there would be no electricity and I'd ask why. "It's Thursday," would come the reply. It wasn't unusual to get responses like this, short and lacking vital information.

There were some things about the students, indeed the people of Lhasa in general, that I never became accustomed to. The most repugnant to me was when a student would bring a wad up from the "deeps," lean over, and spit it onto the floor. Then, to make it disappear, use the sole of a shoe and spread it around. Not wishing to embarrass anyone, I would politely explain some of the ways that cold germs were spread around. Like spitting, for example. Speaking of colds, I noticed right away that Kleenex had not yet made its appearance on the shelves of the Lhasa shops. The only alternative seemed to be the crepe-like, Pepto-Bismol-pink toilet paper. This was sold in all shops and used in restaurants as napkins, in addition to the more familiar use.

It was really no wonder that colds and the flu seemed so prevalent. I noticed when I was out and about that there was hardly a child in Lhasa that didn't have snot running from the nose. Handkerchiefs were used by some people, but the men mainly blew their noses into the air. The spitting was ubiquitous on the streets, which I learned to dodge while riding my bike. Sometimes I'd hear someone up ahead clearing his throat and I'd have to ring my bell.

Worse than the spitting, however, was the public urination. For the most part, this was men. Fortunately, they'd typically turn toward a wall. I'd heard of the Berlin Wall, of course, and the Great Wall, and the Wailing Wall. In Lhasa, they had the Peeing Wall, which was essentially any wall that was handy. Not that the men always bothered with a wall. More than once I was shown the waterfalls. But it wasn't just the men. Women who wore the traditional dress would occasionally squat, their long dresses acting as their privacy screens. Little children, on the other hand, would go anywhere and anytime.

Meanwhile, back in the classroom, I continued to get to know the students, helped, if not verbally, by the always-entertaining journal entries. Hillary's continued to hold my attention.

On 8 October   shining
My dear teach. You correct student's papers. It's very in earnest and careful. I am express my heartfelt thanks.

On 16 October   shining
I was later this afternoon. So I miss lesson. It's twenty to four when I was get up. I was flurried. I want to went, but I was worry. What should I do? I know, foreigner's time concept is very strong. This is very good habit. I reproach myself, but my friends reproach themselves, too. They said that they not called me. It's proved profound friendship. At last, I had to went to study room.

On 6 November   cold
Weather is getting colder and colder, so in these days, we miss family very much. We want to come back my hometown. Fortunately, there is football [soccer] match in our school every day. I like play football, but I have not chance, because a lot of girl doesn't like this sport. Maybe, this sport is very savage. Sometime I wanted play football very much. My instep became itch. It's very terrible. So I went to court and play football with boys. I cannot take into account what some people said.

Rachel was another student whose journal entries were always delightful. She was especially artistic and one day came to my apartment, where I gave her some of the carrot cake I had baked and we looked at some family pictures I had set about. She described our time like so:

Today I went to my foreign teacher's house to give a picture to her. This time is my first time went my teacher's home. Oh, when I went into the house my Teacher was very busy. She was making cake. She lets me take one. Oh, that was a very nice cake with pleasing smell. That very sweets, and including dry grapes and walnuts. I hope one day I can make cake like that. There are a lot of pictures in her house. I like the very lovely girl. She's only eight years old. She looks like Tibetan girl and I sure that she was very happy. I envy her, because now I have a lot of trouble like adult. I miss my no troubles time.

My teach told me that standing in front of the cookery the older woman is her mother. She looks very kindly and health. I wish many happy returns to her. From a lot of pictures, I learn my teacher have a very warmly family, and she own a lot of happiness. I very very envy my teacher.

Another entry:

Today I went to my teacher's house to send film to her. I find my teach just very busy to cooking. I hope I can do something help her. I saw some dish and bowl need to wash, so I began wash them. Teacher told to me, she likes cooking, but she doesn't like wash. Oh, so am I. I don't like washing too, but I felt very pleasure to help my teacher. I think her very busy to teach us knowledge, and busy to do a lot of things.

When my teacher will learn me how to cooking, a visitor came in, and hope my teach help him. I have to say good by to them, but I felt very pleasure. I like went to my teacher's house. Because I can learn a lot of thing by her. And I know this meet either a friendly visit and a study chance. I speak very poor. I hope I can speak more than last term.

Reading the journal entries of my students was a perpetual source of entertainment. What in the world were they going to write next?

Tibetan New Year, 1991. Neighbors came calling.

Dalai Lama's old car at Summer Palace, 1990

Little "monk-ee" at outlying monastery

Yak Hotel

Prostrators in front of Jokhong Temple, Lhasa

The "Vireity-Shop"—Lhasa's one-stop shop

CHAPTER 8

FAVORITES

"In the classroom of friendship, we take turns being teachers and students, constantly learning from one another."
—Anonymous

Another particularly interesting student of mine was Meghan, "the girl in the pink hat," which is the way I would refer to her before we became better acquainted. I could spot Meghan in any crowd with her pink hat sitting atop her head, the short brim adorned with a swath of tulle. She was fashion personified in our classroom and the only one who daily wore a hat. No matter what clothing she was wearing, that hat set it off. Few female students owned a variety of clothing. Fashion didn't have the status as in other parts of the world, that particular form of commercialism having not yet reached Tibet. Besides, nobody had the disposable income to spend on unnecessary items.

Megan's initial greeting to me was nothing less than startling: the girl stuck her tongue out at me. She was the only one of my students to greet me this way, but, as it happens, the sticking out of the tongue is a traditional greeting in Tibet that dates back to the ninth century. Long Darma, the Tibetan king at the time, was thought to have had a black tongue, which people took as a sign of evil. So, to prove to new acquaintances that they were not evil, people started sticking their tongues out at each other when they met. Very few people continued the practice. And, in her pink hat, there was absolutely nothing about Meghan that I would have thought to be evil.

Olivia was another student who stood out with her personal style. Olivia was a very pretty girl with a pretty smile. I thought of her as "the artsy one" of the class. She was always experimenting with new ways to style her hair, more times than not showing up to class in braids. She wore unique clothing and possessed a self-assurance that many of the other students didn't have.

A journal entry:

It seems that today is a lovely day: The sun is shining, there're white clouds in the blue sky. The flowers in the garden haven't withered yet, but leaf of the tree begin to turn yellow and fall down. After a few days, we'll go to some middle school to practice. Maybe it'll be a good experience, but I don't want to go. I think I'm not suitable to be a teacher.

And yet, her attitude about student teaching improved dramatically once she did it. The students in her class all did their student teaching in various middle schools and Olivia would write glowingly about her positive experience. Some of her classmates, on the other hand, would write about not liking their students, or even discovering that teaching was not for them.

I had a very good time during this practice. I taught Senior two in No. 1 middle school which isn't very far from our University. At first, I afraid that I couldn't undertake teaching Senior 2, it might be a little difficult for me. Later, I began to accustom to teach. The children in our class are very lovely. I loved them gradually.

Most students in my class are Tibetan, so they don't like calling me "teacher" in Chinese, they also called me "teacher" in Tibetan. Many of them lived in Barkhor, they know a lot about Tibetan customs more than me.

When I had to leave, they required that I don't leave them. When I said goodbye to them, when some of them called me "elder sister," I couldn't help tearing. I cried. Maybe you'll think that's funny. When I left, they presented me a lot of gifts, all of them wrote, "Don't forget me, teacher."

When springtime blossomed in Lhasa, I decided to have my picture taken wearing my Tibetan chupa, a traditional dress that the foreign language department had presented to me at the prior Christmas party. My intuition led me to ask Olivia to accompany me to Norbulingka to be the photographer. We walked around looking for the best backgrounds, but it was Olivia who staged the shots and it couldn't have worked out better.

The students continued to entertain me in various ways. Or shock me. One day, I had them write a paper on the subject of "puppy love." Write about your first experiences, I told them. One student was especially forthcoming, surprisingly so:

My First Puppy Love
My first puppy love is when I was going to English school. We make date on Saturday evening and sometimes go to cinema or dance, but my parents didn't know any thing I was making date with my boyfriend. After five months we make love. I tell parents everything.

I've held onto a lot of my students' papers over the years and only recently, re-reading them, did I discover that the girl in question was not, in fact, writing about *making* love with her boyfriend. The error was one of penmanship. What I now realize is that she actually wrote, "After five months, we *maybe* love." I needn't have been so shocked after all.

One of my favorite students in the '93 class was a young man I named Kenneth. Kenneth was small in stature, wore clothes that seemed to hang from his frame, and most of the time was in need of a haircut. But his outward appearance would not define him. He was much more. One of my many regrets was that I didn't ask more questions about his life before he left home for Tibet University. On one of our walks to the Barkhor, he gave a very brief sketch of his life in his village near the western border with Bhutan. From what I remember, he went to live with a family who was not related to him.

Kenneth had a remarkable command of spoken and written English. His accent was not of the usual accents that I heard from other students, but more of one coming from close to India—precise enunciation that indicated a British connection. Like the other students, he was the personification of politeness, but he had a level of a genteelness like no one else. From where did this come? I'm sure I'll never know.

While on one of our walks, we passed some hanging *thangkas*, banners with beautiful colors and religious figures. I asked Kenneth what he could tell me about the meaning of the various banners, but he said that he didn't know, that he wasn't Buddhist. Surprised, I asked him what he was, and he came back with, "I'm nothing." I regret that I didn't delve into what his philosophy might have been.

I could tell that Kenneth was a dependable young man, a take-charge kind of person. Recently, after unpacking a box of treasured items from my time in Tibet, I came across a tape that I'd made of the class a week before I was to leave Lhasa for the last time. Kenneth's voice brought back wonderful memories. I miss him.

An entry from Kenneth's journal:

Sunday is the best day in the lives of students. Every Sunday we do everything we want to. Some of us go out to watch movie, because from all kinds of movies we'll learn a lot and at the same time it will open our horizon. Some of us to go to teahouse. We are not only drink tea, but also talk about a history and news of the world. Some go out to around a market and do some shopping which we need. Some of us always play game of electron to see if they are clever. We will spend our happy Sundays by doing all kinds of thing.

Zara was another unforgettable student. Her name meant "radiance," and I described her as my "Tibetan daughter." In class, she was initially reserved, but as time went on, she became bolder around me. She told me that her English-speaking skills weren't especially good and that she hadn't made the progress that she'd hoped for in her first year at the university. She seized every opportunity to speak to me. It wasn't long before I could tell that she possessed a servant's heart, for she frequently volunteered to help me in any way.

Zara's parents and brother lived close to the university, so she invited me to visit the family on numerous occasions. She looked just like her mother and was every bit as hospitable. I was welcomed to Zara's birthday party and was able to see who her best friends were from our class and from her middle school. When I went back to the US for the summer, I asked Zara to stay in my apartment to cat-sit Samantha. She was happy to do so.

One student who stood out to me perhaps more than any other was Renchen or Ryan. Each class at the university selected a student who would act as their representative to the appropriate department. From time to time, the monitor would consult with the department about various concerns, whether they were about the class or the teacher, although I always suspected that the monitor's primary job was to provide an evaluation of the teacher. Renchen was the student for the '92 class. He was two years older than most of the other students, seemed more mature than the others, except for Spencer, and was a sweet, adorable person.

Renchen came from Shigatse, the second largest city in Tibet, where he spent two years working in a department store. But he wanted more from life, which meant that he needed more education. His father was a retired headmaster at the local middle school and encouraged Renchen to apply to Tibet University. During Mao's Cultural Revolution, he had been dismissed from his job as a teacher and sent to a rural area far from his home to work with farmers, living with meager food rations and long hours of work. The Revolution, lasting from 1966 to Mao's death in 1976, was a movement aimed at purging any vestige of capitalism from the country. Farmers and laborers were glamorized. Intellectuals were sent into the fields to work and the universities were shut down. The government prohibited the Chinese people from studying anything that wasn't part of Mao's communist ideology. When, finally, Renchen's father was able to go home, he was ill and underweight.

Renchen wrote about it in his journal:

When my father was a boy, he went to a Tibetan style school in Xigazi, where he studied Tibetan, maths, Buddhism and art. At that time, only nobleman's boy could get education. He never learned Chinese. When he graduated from school, he went to a village to be a teacher. After several years, he got married with my mother, soon they moved to Xigazi. Because my father was respected for his Tibetan literature, he got a very good job, but in 1966 all the Chinese people were suffer from the CULTURAL REVOLUTION, my father lost his job, for he was a Buddhist during these times. The life was very hard. After seven years, he got a job as a teacher. Now my father is a school headmaster. When I reminded him his early times of the life, his eyes full of tears and told me his story.

A frontline student of history, Renchen's father believed in the power of education. After taking an entrance exam and being admitted to study in Lhasa, Renchen was placed in the English department where students would eventually become teachers. Students didn't choose their field of study; the school chose. Renchen was then designated the class monitor and would fill that position for three years.

I found Renchen to be unusually polite. (Then again, the entire class exhibited unusual politeness.) Whatever I needed as far as the running of the classroom, Renchen was always willing to help. His best friend, Paul, was from his hometown and they had been friends since primary school. Paul's spoken English was poor, so during the two years that they shared a table, Renchen helped him with his lessons. At times too much so. This was the case with other students, as well. What they called "help" was what anyone, anywhere else, would call cheating—allowing someone to copy off your paper during quizzes. I tried many times to appeal to their better selves that this was another form of stealing. Before quizzes, I'd go through the same speech about keeping their eyes on their own work, especially to the girls with long hair, which I noticed they used as a way to hide their roving eyes.

There was one afternoon class that met once a week. Some of the boys would come to class late, having spent time in a nearby tea house. It was customary for late arrivals to knock on the classroom door, then when it was opened, to ask permission to come in. One day a group of five, led by Renchen, was rather late, so I decided to teach them a lesson. They knocked but I ignored it. They knocked again and I ignored that too. Meanwhile, the other students were watching intently to see how this was going to play out. I continued with the lesson until, finally, I heard Renchen's voice from out in the hall pleading, "May we come in?" I opened the door to five embarrassed boys, including a repentant Renchen. They were never late again.

Alas, I was late myself one morning. I had music playing, my watch batteries were dead, and my clock never seemed to have the correct time. Sometimes technology isn't well-suited for the cultural circumstances one finds oneself in. What I was listening for in my apartment, perhaps unconsciously, was the dependable ringing of the gong outside. The gong was hung from a tree not too far from my apartment with a hammer of sorts hanging next to it. It would ring out multiple times a day to call students to class. Either it didn't ring that morning, or I didn't hear it for the music I was playing. Somewhat unwittingly, I had come to depend upon it. It had become so commonplace to me that it had no conscious bearing on my life, until it did. Until that moment, I hadn't even been curious enough to find out who struck it. At any rate, I gathered myself together and made my way to the classroom, ten minutes late. Naturally, everyone was seated and the door was closed. Now it was me knocking and, to much laughter from within, asking, "May I come in?"

From time to time, Renchen and his friends would invite me to walk to the Barkhor with them. It was interesting to observe their personalities outside the classroom. They would laugh and carry on. They attempted to teach me some Tibetan phrases that they said were guaranteed to keep the hyper beggars away, but I didn't intend to use the phrases. They would roar with laughter when I'd practice them and there was no telling what I was really saying.

Renchen wrote about the Barkhor once in his journal:

Yesterday evening I went to the Barkhor Street to buy something. I met two American tourists and had a talk with them. They bought a small plastic ball which had written the map of the world on it. They asked to the people at the street what was it, but most of them don't know. They think the world is flat.

69

Some of the better English speakers from all the departments were able to teach in a nighttime English school located near the Barkhor and founded by a disabled young man named Losang Bandian. When Losang was three years old, he had contracted a high fever that resulted in infant paralysis. But at the age of twenty-three, he had established the school, which had grown to about 700 students. The money the teachers made there wasn't much, but it was good experience for them. Renchen invited me to observe his class one evening. Of course, he asked me to give a short speech, which I was happy to do.

Renchen would always be one of my favorite students. But in some ways, they were all favorites. It was a classroom full of polite, sincere, and respectful young men and women. They were special. I sensed this almost right away and for all the time I would spend with them and beyond, that sense would never leave me.

CHAPTER 9

RIDING THE RAILS

"Traveling alone will be the scariest, most liberating, life changing experience of your life. Try it at least once."
—Anonymous

I would have loved to have taken the plane to Guangzhou. Even a crowded plane. Even with a middle seat assignment. A two-hour flight only as far as Chengdu would have to suffice. From Chengdu to Guangzhou, I would be relegated to a berth on a train.

My January trip from Lhasa to Hong Kong would be to attend, for the first time, the required annual conference of my sending agency. The conference was always scheduled to coincide with the separate Chinese and Tibetan New Year's, which were held according to the ancient calendars. Mina left Lhasa by Land Rover with a few others who'd rented the vehicle along with a driver for a trip to the Nepal border. She would travel on her own from there to Kathmandu and other places before meeting up with me in Hong Kong. A seasoned backpacker, Mina was comfortable with her way of traveling.

Me? I had to travel as cheaply as possible. I had not been able to raise enough funds back home to entirely fund my first year in Tibet, and my school salary was not enough. It was a train journey for me, and it turned out not to be a simple one. If it had not been for a new acquaintance in Chengdu, Xiao Li, I would not have been able to navigate the North Train Station there. She was the take-charge per-

71

son I needed. Her English wasn't great, but she found the foreigners' waiting area for me to await the announcement for departure.

That announcement eventually came crackling over the tinny speaker, but I couldn't understand a word of it. Soon a woman in uniform came to me, glanced at my ticket, and motioned me to follow. We walked a long way down the platform, past army-green cars with old gold trim, until the woman ushered me up the steps to my sleeper car and to the door of my compartment where I saw my sleeper-mates—all male. Oh no, I told the woman. This I will not accept. I said it with an expression and a tone that I hoped would come across as though it were a religious no-no. The woman accepted my proclamation and escorted me to another car where the compartment was empty. With my luggage stored snugly under the bottom bunk, I took in my home for the two nights and days I'd be aboard.

The Chinese rail system was the primary means of transportation in the country at that time, with air travel outside the financial realm of most Chinese. It was geared toward the mass's financial health by offering various classes: hard seat, soft seat, hard sleeper, soft sleeper. Hard sleeper compartments consisted of six berths. Soft sleepers consisted of four berths, and the berths were bigger. Oh, and to cram more people in, there was also Standing Room Only. For me, it was soft sleeper, which was something like the equivalent of flying first class. Besides the bigger beds, there was no sharing of boiled water; each passenger had their own thermos. Not to mention the homey lace curtains on the wide windows. What an unexpected decorating touch. And each pillow was covered with a small, terry-cloth towel.

What the beds lacked were ladders to climb to the top bunk. To get there, I had to place my stocking feet on the end of the lower bunk mattress, then heave and struggle to make it safely to the top. Once there, I spied the compartment's only loudspeaker—right above where I'd lay my head. But I'd not get the full impact of my discovery until later. To complete this personal space was a hook and nightlight. All the comforts of home. I imagined my loft accommodation as my cocoon, where I'd dine on my snacks and fruit, then brush away the crumbs before turning in (by turning over) as I'd fall asleep to the sounds of the clickity-clack of wheels on the rails. Reality would prove to be something else.

Not long before departure, a young Chinese man entered. Why would I have imagined I'd have this space to myself? I wondered what he was thinking when he laid eyes on me. What he did was to say "Ni hao" with a slight smile. He then chose the bottom bunk across from my top bunk.

My roommate spent much of his time outside the cubicle, either walking around or sitting at a small desk in the hallway reading, smoking, or both. I could see him through the glass door, just as anyone walking the narrow hallway could stare into the cubicle. The extent of my walking around was to locate the WC. As usual: follow your nose. The line was always crowded for the facilities, and it was clear that passengers from two cars shared it. The necessary room was plenty commodious but with spartan furnishings. When I finally made it inside for the first time, confidently locked in, I saw quickly how things worked. Besides a simple, metal sink attached to the wall with a small mirror above it, there were two holes in the floor with outlines of feet on each side to help those who might have problems aiming, which I imagined was everyone given that there was nothing to hold onto to steel oneself against the continuous swaying and jerking of the train. Why two holes? Who can say? Maybe for those who preferred having company while tending to business. There was no soap present and, sadly, I discovered it was purely a BYOTP state of affairs. Later, I noticed that about thirty minutes before each stop, the door was locked, hopefully with no one locked in. This was to prevent your business from polluting the area around the station.

By 11 p.m., the train grew quieter, at least in my car. Snoring was no doubt a problem for those who had the misfortune of being stuck with snorers. For me, it was the sudden blast of the speaker that caused me to shoot upright like a Chinese New Year's rocket. The beat of my racing heart slowly ebbed, but I couldn't rest for when the next time came. Earlier, I'd counted thirty-nine stops for the entire trip, each requiring at least one announcement over said speaker, if not more. There would be no sound sleep for me.

In the middle of the night at one stop, the door to my cubicle opened and in came in two young women—Westerners. One of them, I later learned, was from Denmark. The other I don't remember. They had met while traveling solo and had decided to travel together. Neither had any set travel plans—two independent women planning as they went. How I wished I were that adventurous—and brave. After they settled in, the car was quiet again—until the next stop.

The first morning began with an early, rude awakening. Without fanfare the door opened, and a female employee swept into the room while the train had stopped briefly at yet another station. She was a woman on a mission as she stepped on the bottom bunk, balancing herself with her one foot while changing out the window curtain. She must have been on the clock because she was in and out of there in seconds. I concluded that we had reached the "curtain-changing-station," and the curtains were to be changed no matter the time of day. Soon we were on our way again.

One's morning routine usually starts the same no matter where one finds oneself, and so it was that I was out of my bunk and on my way to the WC. Naturally, there was a line of passengers, but I tried to keep my thoughts on things other than why I was there. Shortly, out of nowhere, a girl of about ten attempted to break into the line in front of me. Without thinking, I brazenly stood my ground and pointed her to the end of the line. I say "brazenly" because by the glares I got from some of the others in line, my action was far from universally approved. She was just a child, they seemed to say. But I was in no mood for making exceptions.

As the train kept chugging along, I noticed that the male member of our compartment continued to spend more time outside it than in. Who could blame him? How would I feel if I had to be in that small space with three Chinese men? We acted kindly toward him and inquired about his plans, but I cannot remember what he told us other than Guangzhou was his destination.

At every stop there were vendors trying to sell their wares, mainly food, to passengers through the opened windows. Time was a factor as there was a flurry of back-and-forth exchanges of food for money before the train departure. One of my young women compartment-mates thought it a good idea to step off the train at one of the stops. She assumed she'd be able to make it back by the time the train departed. We called out to her to hurry as she sprinted back and boarded just as the train began moving. She came back with her purchases, but not with the change she was due. Lucky seller.

We finally arrived in Guangzhou by early afternoon the second day. I was tired, but happy to get off the train. The ladies were planning a trip to Macau the following day and would be looking for transportation to Hong Kong and a place to stay. I'd been instructed to meet some fellow teachers at the White Orchid Hotel, located near the Pearl River. From there, our organization, always intent on using our donated funds wisely, chose the cheapest way for our group to cross the maritime border between China and British Hong Kong—an overnight ferry.

Somehow, my phrase book failed me. Also, being an amateur traveler didn't help, which resulted in my making a huge mistake. I got in the wrong taxi. I quickly learned that there were Chinese taxi drivers who could not be trusted. A savvy person would have first looked to see if the taxi had a valid license displayed on the dash. This one did not. And the meters in those taxis were bogus. I was an unsuspecting foreigner about to be taken for a ride. Figuratively and literally.

It was too late by the time I realized the driver wasn't going where I wanted to go. Had he misunderstood the directions I had given him to the White Orchid Hotel? He drove me around. And around and around. Ultimately, he drove to a secluded area near the river with nothing in view but old, shabby buildings. He drove slowly, so slowly that I was afraid he was going to stop. I couldn't let that happen. If I had seen another taxi, I'd have bolted but there was no other car or person in sight. In fear, or maybe panic, I yelled at him to drive out of the area, which he did, eventually dropping me off on a tree-lined street with a McDonalds nearby. In the end, I suppose the driver must have gotten me close to the hotel, because I didn't have to walk very far before coming face to face with two young women from my group. I calmed down but picked up an important travel lesson in the ordeal: I was not ready to travel solo in strange lands.

That night I found myself reunited with all the fellow teachers I had met at training in California, ready for our slow boat to Hong Kong. Boarding time was 9 p.m. at the wharf on the Pearl River. A boat employee led us to a lower deck that contained a large area with bunk beds in rows, and not two-bed bunks, but bunks that were three beds high. Unlike the train, there were at least ladders to access the upper bunks. I chose a "penthouse" bunk at the very top. Thankfully, there was a "lights out" time so that everyone could be assured a decent night's rest. The gentle rocking of the boat and the hum of the engines created a soothing environment, and I slept well, but found myself awake before the 6 a.m. scheduled docking time. Many of us were awake, allowing us, in the daylight now, to see the natural beauty of the Pearl River Delta, and then the magnificent skyline of Hong Kong as it came into view. So many tall buildings competing for such limited space.

After docking, we gathered our belongings and headed for the queue to be processed, and soon I was on a sidewalk of a lively, bustling Hong Kong street. In my younger years, and not so long after the end of World War II, Hong Kong was regarded as a place that exported cheap, poor-quality products. "Made in Hong Kong" was not exactly a ringing endorsement. But this was a different Hong Kong now—a glitzy and glamorous bastion of modern capitalism.

We teachers were advised not to let the plethora of wares of this stylish city entice us to foolishly spend our money. Having come from a place of socialism—with its scarcity and complete absence of any vibrancy—it would have been tempting. But, seeing as how I had little money, temptation was not a problem. If I felt poor, and at one with the masses of China, imagine how I felt viewing the shiny objects in the flashy store displays. My only planned purchase was a purse to replace my old one with a broken strap. It wasn't easy being one of the have-nots.

Our organization reserved space for all of us in the small hotel where the conference was held. The hotel was decent, and the conference was worthwhile, with an abundance of positivity and valuable training. We heard from teachers about their positive experiences and about some not-so-positive experiences. Everyone had some of both, and it was nice forging closer relationships with the attendees. But soon enough, it was over, and we were on our own again.

This of course meant finding new accommodations, at least for the night before our journey back to Tibet. Mina stayed that night, too, and so off we went to find a cheap place to stay. Of course, she would be flying back, while I would once again be journeying by train. Mina knew of a very inexpensive hotel on Nathan Road, a strip known as the "Miracle Mile." This was in an area called Tsim Sha Tsui located on Kowloon across the harbor from Hong Kong Island. The hotel was called Chungking Mansion and was known as having the cheapest accommodations in all of Hong Kong.

It was also thought to be the most infamous slum. I naturally didn't expect the hotel to be a glamorous "mansion," despite the name, but I still expected a sort of colonial-style manor, perhaps with high ceiling fans swooshing overhead, and old, wooden window shutters looking out over the streets below. In reality it was a huge, drab, water-stained concrete block building with noisy air-conditioning window units dripping onto the streets below. And through the large entryway, we found not a traditional hotel, but a kind of city within a building. Traders of different nationalities, mostly Easterners, were enticing tourists to buy watches and electronic wares. Most of course were rip-offs and knockoffs. Beyond the traders were shops, business offices, private apartments, and cheap rooms more suited to backpackers than to average tourists.

We had heard that the Chungking Mansion was a frequent destination for the local fire brigade. This bit of information does not make for a good recommendation. Nonetheless, we had made up our minds to stay there, though we committed to finding accommodations no higher than the second floor, allowing us a quick escape if needed.

Somehow, through the bedlam of activity in the building, we located the elevator and found the guest house. All the choice rooms had been taken by the time we arrived, so we had to settle for bunk beds in a dormitory-style area, and we each took top bunks across from each other. By the looks of our beds, the thin coverings might have been decades old: dingy, dirty, ripped.

Soon enough, the room started attracting more guests. A woman came in and chose a bottom bunk down from ours. Then came a big surprise when several men came in. Whoa! We hadn't thought of this possibility. But this would not be our greatest surprise. The woman, probably in her forties, and appearing "well-traveled," stood by her bunk and proceeded to strip naked in order to change into something more comfortable. It didn't matter to her that it was a co-ed dorm.

Additional guests came in with their own unique ways of making us feel uncomfortable, and we soon decided to spend the night in a nearby, twenty-four-hour McDonalds. Later, we would read from a former guest of the Chungking Mansion that we had apparently missed one of the more endearing attributes of the place: a bathroom that was the epitome of efficiency. Where else can you (theoretically) brush your teeth at the sink, take a shower, and sit on the toilet all at the same time? Close quarters, indeed.

Sadly, my time in Hong Kong came to an end. The city was endlessly fascinating, but it was just as well; I couldn't afford another day. It would be a subway/train to the border, then a train to Chengdu. But of course, nothing was simple. The border crossing was chaos. I followed the crowd to a gate where a certain number of people were allowed through at a time. There was a lot of pushing and running, and I wasn't even sure I was in the right place. The uniformed man operating the gate held in his hand a rather effective "persuader" for crowd control—a truncheon, iron or rubber, I couldn't tell, but it was enough to keep the unruly masses from rushing the gate.

When I couldn't tolerate the pushing and the closed-in feeling any longer, I left the insane crowd, feeling sick to my stomach, and steadied myself against a wall. I'm sure I looked sick to anyone who bothered to look at me, which, in time, was someone in authority who came to my aid and took me to where foreigners went through the border processing. It was a great relief to leave the throng behind. My protective angel was wearing an official uniform, but with no visible wings.

Once through, now in the train station, I was again a part of the mass of humanity, everyone trying at once to buy train tickets. All along one wall of the cavernous, high-ceilinged space were ticket windows. Above each window was a sign with Chinese characters presumably indicating what tickets were issued there. Eventually, I made it to one of the windows, not under my own power, but rather shoved there by the crowd. I retrieved my passport and said "Chengdu." Whatever the Cantonese word for "wrong window" was, I got the message. But what *was* the right window? There was only one thing to do: leave and try to find someone who spoke English who could tell me what to do.

Pushing and shoving against the flow took all the strength I could muster to get outside, but I finally made it. Across and down the opposite side of the street I noticed a travel agency with a few window signs in English. Inside, a helpful person told me which window back at the station I should go to: "Number 7." So, back to the beginning. Once back in the station, I decided to take advantage of the crowd, positioning myself where the pushing, shoving, impatient mass of people would more or less lead me in the direction of Window 7. With some newfound courage, I did my share of helping them get me there.

At the window, arms from behind me were reaching over my shoulders with paper IDs in hand for last-ditch efforts to be the next one served. This was not a bad strategy as the workers behind the counter never seemed to care who was next. They'd grab a paper from anyone. I was squashed against the counter, which made it difficult for me to get anything out of my purse. After I finally thrust my passport under the nose of the counter person and shouted, "Chengdu!" she indicated that I had come to the wrong window and pointed to the adjacent window.

This was too much to take. I stood my ground and said firmly, "No!" To my relief, she handed my passport and return, paid reservation to the adjacent clerk. This, however, caused the pushers to become especially agitated by the few moments of delay, so they pushed harder against me. When I finally had my ticket and everything red-stamped, I had to keep it in my hand, for I could not get it into my purse. It was difficult even to turn around. The only thing I knew to do was to let out a blood-curdling scream. "Get me out of here!" Another angel recognized the English, and with his truncheon in hand, raising it at anyone in his way, made his way over to me and led me out, scattering the pushers as we went.

Once outside and sitting on a bench waiting to board the train, I vowed to never again travel during Chinese New Year. Meanwhile, loudspeakers were constantly blaring out announcements that I could not understand. Shortly, I noticed a scrambling horde of waiting passengers hell-bent on boarding a train. As I watched the spectacle race past me, one woman motioned for me to get up and join in. But why? Why was everyone running when we all had tickets with seat numbers? Maybe the better question would have been, why would I ever think it would work that way? Squatters were apparently commonplace. When I found my car with the soft-sleeper compartments, I was thankful that at least no squatter had claimed my space. But then I saw my fellow compartment-mates: three Chinese men!

Knowing there was nothing I could do about the situation, I resigned myself through a quick attitude adjustment to make the best of things. My Chinese "uncles" appeared to be in their sixties. We exchanged tentative, polite nods and I could tell that these men were sizing me up without letting on that they were doing so. Just as I was with them.

With my luggage stored under the bottom bunk, I hoisted myself up to my upper-bunk home for the duration of the trip. It all looked the same as on the preceding trip: bedding the same and *that blasted speaker above my pillow* waiting to drive me crazy.

Foodwise, I was all set. I had shopped for an array of finger foods and sweets, and even brought along a small paring knife for use with apples and cheese. If I needed more variety, I could always put the window down at any stop and do some "window shopping." But without the two young women who added much-appreciated companionship on the outbound trip, time moved more slowly. On one of my walks through the various cars to break the monotony, I came upon the dining car. Looking it over, I decided to order something for lunch, maybe rice and vegetables. At least I had learned the vocabulary for this. While sitting alone at my small table, a cook removed a cover from a straw basket nearby and held up the contents: a skinned dog!

So much for the dining car. Back in my compartment, I tried to read, then, tired of that, I dipped into my snack bag and cut off a chunk of cheese to have with some crackers. The time continued to drag, and the blaring of the speaker was driving me to madness. A light sleeper, especially with three men in the same compartment, I couldn't even pass the time with sleep. The speaker would not allow it.

Something had to be done.

At one point, with all the uncles out of the compartment, I took out my paring knife and unscrewed the metal screen covering the speaker. I looked fruitlessly for a wire to disconnect, then decided to stuff the large terry-cloth pillow cover over the squawk box. In the meantime, the uncle from the bottom bunk across from me returned and instead of being a disinterested observer, became quite interested. So much so, that he left the compartment and came back shortly with a male train employee who didn't take kindly to my attempted re-engineering of the speaker. Nobody likes a snitch, and I shot the uncle a dirty look. The employee ordered me, in English no less, to cease and desist, and stood by while I reattached the screen to his evident satisfaction. What he didn't see was that I left the pillowcase in place.

Everything was fine until we pulled into the changing-of-the-pillow-cover station. As before, with the changing-of-the-lacy-curtains station, a woman employee swept through the compartment and made the exchanges, all except for my pillow cover, of course. Befuddled, she said, conveying by her tone, that I must be holding back pillowcase No. 36. With up-turned palms and a shoulder shrug, I was able to successfully end the speaker cacophony caper. I've often wondered since how many years passed before that towel was discovered. Is it stuffed into the speaker still?

Finally, the train pulled into the Chengdu station. I soon found a registered, legitimate taxi (I was learning), and was delivered without incident to the Traffic Hotel, a haven for backpackers looking for a cheap, clean place to stay. Just down the lane was the Flower Garden Restaurant, a quasi-Western establishment, and a place in the coming years that I'd come to know very well. From Chengdu, it was back to my Lhasa home. My train adventures were finally, mercifully, over.

CHAPTER 10

CRUISIN' THE BARKHOR

"Better to see something once than to hear about it a thousand times."
—Asian Proverb

The Barkhor. As mentioned, it's a circular pedestrian street surrounding Jokhang Temple. But it is more than this. In fact, the street has given name to the district so that when one speaks of going to the Barkhor, they could be referencing the street, or the general area, which includes the temple, a public square, and many narrow streets and lanes. Legend has it that Barkhor Street itself was created from the trodden paths of thousands of Buddhist pilgrims visiting the Jokhang Temple after its completion in 647 AD. They all walked clockwise around the magnificent structure until a path was formed, which was ultimately paved with hand-polished stones. The stones remain to this day and pilgrims still stroll around the temple in a clockwise fashion.

Two- and three-story buildings line the Barkhor, old buildings of natural materials like stone and clay and wood, but colorfully painted. Everything is adorned with symbols of Tibetan Buddhism or Chinese script or both. The structures house shops of clothing, handcrafted souvenirs, jewelry, antiques, and religious artifacts. There are restaurants and cafes and tea houses. The smells of cooked food and incense fill the air. Monks in deep maroon robes stroll reverently, and share the space with tourists, nomads, merchants, pilgrims, and more tourists. There are countless stands along the route—food vendors or locals selling prayer wheels or scroll paintings.

Above all else, there is constant activity.

To forget all her worries, forget all her cares, Petula Clark had "Downtown." Me, I had the Barkhor.

It was a mere fifteen-minute walk from my apartment and often I'd be accompanied by students or fellow teachers, although frequently I'd amble to the Barkhor myself, sometimes for a bite to eat or some tea or just to people-watch. There was never a dull moment.

Initially, the myriad alleyways of the area were a puzzle for me to figure out. I would lose my way and never know exactly where I might end up. It could be onto a main street or somewhere on the pilgrim path. The alleys were like spokes on a wheel, with some being offshoots, making it easy to become disoriented. Wandering around, I often feared I'd suffer the same sort of fate as Charlie in the old Kingston Trio song, the man who "never returned," doomed to "ride forever 'neath the streets of Boston." Only I was doomed to amble forever the alleyways of Lhasa.

Eventually, I became familiar with the area, using landmarks to tell me where to turn—a corner, for instance, where the grain merchant set up shop. The alleys were a microcosm of what one would see in the open areas but more condensed: more dogs, more dog poop, more dirty water puddles to skirt, more flies, and more children, and all with less space to navigate through.

Along many of the alleys were the walled courtyards of two-story complexes where multiple families lived. One day as I was walking near a courtyard, a child approached me holding a washbowl, then attempted to splash me with its contents, which I was able to (mostly) avoid. The playful child residing inside me decided to give chase to the retreating, very surprised, child who made it back to his courtyard, but where I noticed a water spigot with buckets handy, one of which happened to be full of water. I grabbed it and let loose on the child, while some of the residents looked on in disbelief, but nevertheless laughed at the antics of the foreign woman running around the courtyard chasing a child with a bucket of water. It was a veritable water-splashing festival, and I knew how much Tibetans loved their festivals.

Whenever I exited an alley near the wide-open plaza near the Jokhang temple, I would always find entertainment from men playing musical instruments, typically surrounded by a circle of onlookers. At times there could be two or three musical venues at once, all vying for small coins appreciative spectators would toss into the circles.

From there, I'd walk around aimlessly, absorbing the vibes from the crowds of people either milling about, or on their way to somewhere. Once, a young man brushed by me and said, in perfect English, "I am not free!"

At that time, pictures of the Dalai Lama were taboo, even though tourists would sometimes bring some to give away. I don't think there was ever a time I went to the Barkhor when someone wouldn't come up to me and say, in broken English, "Dalai Lama pic? Dalai Lama pic?"

People came to the Barkhor from all over Tibet—nomads from the smaller towns, beggars (scores of them), old people, young people, the able-bodied, the disabled, and more snotty-nosed children than could be counted. As for the beggars, I gave only to the disabled or the elderly. Dirty and often wearing ragged clothing, many children begged, but most of them were begging for their able-bodied parents who were often times standing nearby.

The sight of the most pitiful of the beggars often caused my heart to be heavy with sympathy, and also with wonder. The destitute Buddhists along the path accepted their plight, believing their lot in life to be the consequence of their reincarnated selves, or else believing that the material nature of the universe was to be eschewed.

Or maybe some of both. I wondered if they ever thought about a better life. Did they think about the people who were giving them alms? Were the givers gaining merit for their own spiritual path? If so, what did the beggars have to give?

Perhaps the most pitiful sight I saw in the Barkhor was in the middle of a short, mostly pedestrian street leading to the bazaar. There, a mother, who had just given birth. She was lying on a flattened piece of cardboard, her head partially hidden by a large scarf. The baby was wrapped in a dirty cloth. Women were hovering over her trying to get a glimpse of the baby, while she was eyeing the people around her. Had someone been there with her in her hour of need? My instinct was to help her, but I'd heard from someone wiser than me that it was best to let the local culture take its course and not to interfere—especially as a foreigner.

There were, of course, lighter times when I enjoyed walking the Barkhor along with the merit-seekers. On one occasion, I approached a shop and was surprised by the loud music I heard playing from a cassette tape inside, a female vocalist singing "Amazing Grace." I imagined a Christian tourist must have given the tape to the shop owner. The Barkhor Bazaar was forever delivering surprises.

One favorite place to hang out in the Barkhor was the Barkhor Café. Other than the foreign-run Holiday Inn, this was the only place where one could order a plateful of french fries. We would sit and people-watch from the second-floor partially-roofed, half-moon balcony drinking Coca-Cola from a can and enjoying those wonderfully golden fried potatoes. McDonald's had nothing on this place. From the balcony we watched the happenings on the square in front of the Jokhang and beyond. Sitting in the sunshine during the winter months made for an especially relaxing afternoon.

Not far from the café and located at a corner of the plaza was a small outdoor tea house. It was widely agreed that the café served the best chang in town. You were lucky to get a table there; the cramped second-floor balcony establishment had just three of them. The woman who ran the café and the maker of the home-brew was a tiny, seventy-ish individual who represented the epitome of quiet efficiency. Her husband, Tashi Cering, shared the small house and balcony with her, but did not appear to be involved in his wife's endeavors. Instead, he was an intellectual who had an interesting past. Reputed to be a communist, he had spent time in the US attending several schools. He had taught in Tibet University soon after it had become that entity, and was, at this time, working on a Tibetan-Chinese-English dictionary.

On one of the coldest of mornings, our "gang of four" went to the Barkhor to see the sun rise in the east of Lhasa from atop the Jokhang. I'm still not sure how we made it inside because the temple was not officially open for everyday pilgrims. Perhaps we had a monk or gatekeeper with us. In any event, there we were standing on the roof not far from the Wheel of Life.

There's something magical about early mornings everywhere, but the early morning at the Barkhor was a different kind of morning, with a different feel. Pilgrims and circumambulation walkers were already there, as were Tibetans catching the buses nearby that would take them to outlying monasteries for the day. The faithful were already burning their juniper offerings, and combined with the frosty morning, the haze created an otherworldliness that would stay with me always.

Unfortunately, the Barkhor was not only the scene of normal and ritualistic activity, but also of rioting and mayhem. This was usually precipitated by the arrest of Tibetans who had shown their nationalistic zeal by waving the forbidden Tibetan flag, chanting anti-government slogans, or plastering posters all over. The result would be that many were arrested, injured, and even killed. Monks and nuns usually started the melees. The Barkhor police station was a favorite target of rioters. Early on in my time in Lhasa, I saw the threatening machine gun that rested on a tripod atop the roof of the police station. Eventually it was taken down in favor of a camera.

That was not the only camera around. One time I was skirting the perimeter of Barkhor Square on my bicycle, heading toward a department store (think 1940-ish) when I heard a loud, startling noise from the crowd. Then, as if on cue, the crowd began rushing toward the circular path. I stopped my bike, not understanding what I was witnessing. Soon, the crowd came back, surrounding and heckling a plainclothes policeman who had a Tibetan man in handcuffs and was heading toward the Barkhor police station. What prompted the crowd to react? A camera on top of one of the buildings filming the crowd, apparently a familiar sight that was set up before an arrest to catch those who misbehaved. Luckily, my camera was tucked inside my jacket. I'm sure it would have been an offense to take it out and start snapping pictures. At best, it would certainly have been confiscated.

One warm Sunday, our gang of four decided to take a stroll to the Barkhor and we walked down the usual alley we'd taken many times on our way to the Barkhor Café with the intention of sitting on the balcony people-watching while having our usual Coca-Colas and fries. But something was different, and it occurred to us suddenly that there were no tourists around. No people at all, in fact. Scott and Drew eventually returned to their apartments but Mina and I decided to hang around a little longer. I wasn't feeling particularly well and feared a bout of the Big D might be in the very near future.

Shortly, three men in suits approached us, pointing their fingers at us and brusquely ordering us to leave. Mina asked them for their IDs and they became furious but then they showed cards in English indicating they were with the Public Security Bureau. Then they asked for our IDs. We both showed them the university badges we were wearing, but this did not satisfy them. We could have picked them up anywhere, they claimed, even off the ground. Mina fished her residence card out of her backpack. I usually didn't carry mine—a mistake. Then the men told us again to leave. Immediately. Mina told them I was feeling sick, to which they replied that Mina should go and they would take me to the hospital. Mina said she had no intention of leaving me. By that time, my Big D fears were coming true and I hurried off to find a bathroom.

While I was away, the men said all manner of rude things to Mina and interrogated her with questions. "You're teachers," they said, "what are you doing at the Barkhor? Why are you here?" When I returned, the men said they would take us back to the university and would give Mina her ID back. But when we arrived there, they refused to return it to her. In fact, they refused to let us out of the car and said they were taking us to our "leader." When they wouldn't stop, Mina opened her door at which point they stopped and Mina and I got out.

Mina ran off to get our foreign affairs officer while I waited for her. The men, meanwhile, went off to the university president's home to report us. When Mina and the foreign affairs officer came, we three walked to the president's home where we saw the men talking to the president's wife, Jiang Ting Feng. They rose immediately when they saw us coming and again began pointing their fingers at us. Whatever version of events they had been telling Jiang Ting Feng, she seemed upset by it all.

The next day Jiang Ting Feng, the Han Chinese vice president, and the foreign affairs officer met with the PSB office, which presented them with a couple copies of a booklet of laws for aliens living in China, a booklet Mina and I had never seen before. To this day, I do not know what "law" we transgressed, but Mina and I were made to write self-criticisms to take to the PSB, a good, old-fashioned Cultural Revolution punishment, coupled with monetary fines—100 yuan for me and 150 yuan for Mina, about twenty bucks. I've often wondered if anyone had ever bothered to read our "confessions."

And if so, would they have appreciated my concluding sentence? "I hesitate to reiterate for fear of deviating from the virtual path of rectitude, but, in a word, I be wrong."

The whole incident only confirmed what I had felt and would continue to feel for the entire duration of my stay: in the Barkhor, and indeed in all of Lhasa, there was never a dull moment!

CHAPTER 11

CELEBRATING LHASA

*"A mind that is stretched by a new experience can never go back
to its old dimensions."*
—Oliver Wendell Holmes

That New Year's celebration where I named the dog was quite an event. As it happened, about an hour after I arrived, a film crew from the Tibetan TV station came to tape a segment to include in a documentary about Tibetan New Year, and how one family celebrates. They chose this particular home because the family was well known. The father was the director of the Tibetan theater, the mother was a retired singing and dancing instructor, and the eldest daughter was a famous singer in Tibet.

Everything was staged for the shooting of the celebration. The crew even brought along five of their own people, all dressed in traditional Tibetan dress to round out the party. Although they weren't expecting a foreigner to be present, they were more than happy to include me as well.

A trio played instruments while everyone danced and the eldest daughter sang. They gave me a part to play, too, namely to perform the ceremonial barley beer offering. I disliked the stuff but what choice did I have? The older sister offered me a full glass of the home brew. I was expected to take three sips, with the glass being topped off after each. After the third sip, I was to down the entire glass without stopping. With all eyes upon me, and to much applause, I managed to accomplish the task, chugging the contents and turning the glass upside down afterwards to show that the deed had been done. Mere moments later, I felt the effects. My head was fuzzy and I found myself laughing and talking much more than usual. This is what happens when you're not used to drinking alcohol. Meanwhile, the hosts kept pouring red wine for everybody, including me. It was customary, for such a celebration, to stay for not one but two meals, which I did, leaving for home happy, stuffed, and admittedly a little tipsy.

There were other celebrations throughout the year. I happened to be there for the fortieth anniversary week-long celebration of the "Peaceful Liberation of Tibet." This of course was an unintentionally ironic name for the Chinese movement to take control of the region. Nevertheless, a celebration is a celebration. Soldiers gave free haircuts and government stores held their versions of sidewalk sales with clothing at half price. It was truly awful clothing, but better than what some of the poorest wore. We teachers heard from a couple of incognito reporters that there was to be a big demonstration against the government, but it didn't happen. That's how martial law began in 1988. The only incident we heard about was an old monk getting arrested for carrying a Tibetan flag in front of a temple. Because the government was fearful of trouble, we were told to not go out alone for the week. Finding appropriate escorts wasn't always easy and we felt like we were being treated like children.

The Foreign Affairs Office invited foreign residents to a dinner during the big week held at the Holiday Inn, where we were treated to a ridiculous pre-meal speech that extolled the virtues of Chinese rule. We didn't applaud, which was rather obvious to the others there. Some Taiwanese journalists were in attendance as were the people from the Nepali consulate. They were at a table with Scott and Drew, and Scott kept them laughing. He said he didn't want to spend his evening with people who were somber, so he entertained them by telling them about his search for a Khampa woman for a wife. For their part, the consulate members tried to convince him to find a Nepali wife instead.

A TV crew was at the dinner and we made the news. By then I was getting used to being filmed. First the New Year's dinner and now this. And there would be more multimedia coverage. It seemed somebody was always making a documentary about Tibet. Mina and I were each filmed in our classrooms, though what became of the footage, I never did know.

Besides the celebration for the "Peaceful Liberation of Tibet," there were plenty of other events that had me concluding that Lhasa was quite the party town. It seemed I was always off to one social event or another. One Saturday night the government of the Tibet Autonomous Region (TAR) invited us teachers to a large banquet at the Holiday Inn, a buffet dinner where they sat us at large, round tables of ten. A rather formal affair. We were greeted at the front door by an official and escorted to the dining room. There, we met other foreign experts working in the area including two UN tourism experts, the Nepalese consulate officials and wives, a couple with the "Save the Children" program, and a German couple from a leather factory. The food, courtesy of an Austrian chef, was varied and the desserts were spectacular.

Shortly after that, I attended a university Language Department banquet where I sat through twenty-two agonizing courses. Very little of the pig was left off the menu on that night, I can tell you.

A few days later, we were all invited to the TAR Public Security Bureau's mid-autumn festival. This was held in a big hall with dancing under strobe lights. Students from the Tibet School of Arts entertained with Tibetan dances.

Then, just a couple of nights later, there was the university president's intimate banquet for eight. Again, twenty-two courses, including some sweets—glutinous rice balls, filled pinwheel cookies, sweet rice, and cherry soup. Some of the food offerings were duck, stomach, lungs, eel, rabbit, chicken (I ate a lot of this), and one huge fish on a platter with reddish sauce. The cook made sugared walnuts, too, which I found to be delicious.

Scott, Drew, Mina, and I sometimes had our own celebrations, like American Thanksgiving Day. We held it on the Saturday of Thanksgiving Week, given that Thursday and Friday were, naturally, class days. After our Friday classes ended, we all went to the big market to shop for our food, leaving with two chickens, sweet potatoes, potatoes, walnuts, pumpkin, green onions, and fruit including apples, tangerines, bananas, and persimmons. That Friday night, I made sweet potato pudding with walnuts on top, pumpkin pie, and a double batch of yeast rolls. Early Saturday morning, I fired up the yak dung stove, adding a few small logs, and the rest of the cooking resumed. The apartment smelled divine and everyone swooned upon entering. A good meal and a good time were had by all. We ended the day with some hot apple cider.

Shopping at the big market was fun, but buying from the street vendors was even more so. I learned how to dicker. The vendors asked for an initial price, which I always refused. We'd go back and forth and then, unsatisfied, I'd turn to leave, at which point I'd almost always get one more price concession. I got so good, that sometimes a crowd would gather to watch the negotiations. Locals would occasionally follow me into the small sidewalk shops, prompting me to wonder if the proprietors should give me a commission.

Although the campus was typically abuzz during the week, it often felt like a ghost town on Sundays. Many of the students would take the day to visit family if their homes were in or near Lhasa. Others would go to the cinema, go shopping, or spend the afternoon in a teahouse. For us teachers, after spending a few hours on Sunday mornings together listening to taped sermons, singing some songs, praying, and eating lunch, often in my apartment, we would usually go our separate ways.

On one Sunday afternoon, I rode my bicycle across the long bridge that spans Lhasa River with the intention of sitting on a retaining wall high above the river. There, I'd planned to study Chinese vocabulary and listen to music while taking in the mountains. It wasn't long, however, before I heard children yelling "hello" to me from the bridge. A few moments later, four of them came over and I motioned for them to sit. I gave them each a Tootsie Roll someone had sent me from the US. I made it a point to carry small candies around in my pack for such occasions.

I asked the children simple questions in Chinese, for "simple" was all I knew. At one point, the wind gusted and took away the fabric hat of the littlest of the group, a sweet little boy, sending it into the river where it got caught on some concrete and became waterlogged and, unfortunately, out of reach. We tried to tie poles together to fish it out, but with no luck. The boy sobbed, afraid of punishment, I imagined. I got on my stomach trying to reach the hat as best I could without creating a situation whereby someone might have to fish *me* out of the river. I noticed that soldiers stationed at each end of the bridge were watching, but they didn't budge. And so the hat was lost. I walked the kids back across the bridge, giving each a turn riding on the back of the bike. People passing would smile at the foreigner with four kids in tow. Then the kids headed back to their housing unit, which, by the looks of it, told me they were very poor.

It was too early to go back to campus, so I headed for my favorite teahouse, where the owners and I were fast becoming buddies. We sat around a table drinking sweet tea and cracking English walnuts (Chinese walnuts?). A middle school girl and neighbor looked through my Chinese phrase book and then the most unusual conversation began, some of which was pantomimed. Several young men came over and tried out their English. One wanted to know if I danced.

One woman wanted me to have my picture made the following Sunday evening wearing her Tibetan dress. Of course, I said okay. In the meantime, the electricity went off and we all sat and visited by lantern. Just another lazy Sunday afternoon in Lhasa.

The request to dance was not as odd as it might seem. I learned early on that the Tibetan people love to sing and dance. In fact, the '92 and '93 classes held a party and it wasn't surprising that it was a dance party. The revelry was held in one of the classrooms, which necessitated pushing the tables against the walls. On the tables, they put the standard fare—unshelled sunflower seeds, hard candies, and cookies. They served sweet tea and chang, which is barley beer. I passed on it, even though I'd bravely chugged it at the New Year's party.

All that week, I had told the students that someone needed to teach me to dance, but, since nobody was volunteering to do so, I jumped out on the dance floor and did the best I could. Before long, the best of the boy dancers came along and led me through a waltz, dipping me at the end, making for a flamboyant finale. Then I joined the students in a traditional Tibetan circle dance before calling it a night around 12:30 in the morning. A third-year student told me the next day that he'd passed by the building at five o'clock and music was still playing.

Sometimes, students would come to my apartment for a visit or accompany me to the Barkhor for an outing. One day I took four of the girls to the Holiday Inn to have a look since none had ever set foot inside. Here, they enjoyed their first elevator ride, and by the expressions on their faces and the sounds they made, you would have thought they were on a rollercoaster. After a few round trips up and down the three floors, I had to get them off before we were run out of the place.

The students were always fun, but I found some of the faculty members to be fascinating. Yang Chen was a professor in the de-

97

partment of history/Buddhist studies who spoke excellent English. I don't remember where exactly I met her, but I do remember that we connected almost instantly. One day, she invited me to visit her in her office. When we entered the room, the first thing I noticed was an entire wall of glass-enclosed bookcases containing Buddhist history and scripture. As was the custom, she reverently approached the case of wooden-covered books and pressed her forehead to the glass.

It was a short visit; we didn't sit. As she was showing me Buddhist thangkas—scrolled religious paintings—a fly decided to end its life by falling from the light fixture onto Yang Chen's desk. She used two pieces of paper to scoop it up, then took it carefully to the windowsill to aid it in the process of reincarnation. That's what I imagined, anyway.

Yang Chen invited Mina and me to her parents' home for a visit and dinner. Yang Chen and her six-year-old daughter had moved in some time after Yang Chen's divorce. Their house, not far from the Barkhor, was an old, traditionally built Tibetan house, surrounded by a high wall with a heavy wooden door with ancient-looking hinges. It must have been a nobleman's house at one time, possibly handed down to Yang Chen's family. It was not clear to me how the family figured into Lhasa's history but, surprisingly, the house had escaped the destruction of the Red Guard, the paramilitary student movement guided by Mao in the late 1960s at the start of the Cultural Revolution. The Red Guard destroyed many symbols of China's pre-communist past.

Yang Chen's mother had studied in India and spoke excellent English with a precise English accent. She pronounced each word distinctly and typically punctuated her remarks with, "you see." Her father gave no indication that he knew English. The most honored guest at the dinner was, according to my hosts, a former living Buddha—the reincarnation of a spiritual master. He was a friend of the family and someone who had spent years in prison during the

Cultural Revolution. The bulk of the conversation was in Tibetan, with their most-honored guest doing much of the talking. When thinking about this gathering, I still wonder why I didn't ask more questions. Clearly, I was never journalist material.

Not long after that dinner, I happened upon Yang Chen's mother in the Barkhor. We chatted and in the course of our conversation, she asked me if I was learning the language. My answer would be the biggest faux pas of my entire time in Lhasa. I told her that I'd try to learn Mandarin, since everyone seemed to know that dialect. What happened next caught me by surprise. She literally spat out her condemnation of my choice. Mandarin, of course, was the official language of the Chinese, the government that had occupied Tibet. I regretted it immediately, but the damage had been done. Without knowing how to extricate myself from the tense exchange, I politely bid goodbye and walked away.

A few weeks later, I decided to visit her. Yang Chen came to the courtyard door and hesitantly invited me in. She left the room to tell her mother that I was there, but when she came back, she said that her mother was asleep and she didn't want to wake her. But I knew her mother didn't want to see me and that was that. My budding relationship with Yang Chen's mother had ended, leaving me saddened and with no doubt in my mind as to her feelings about the Chinese.

———◦———

At one point, March Madness came to Tibet University. Not exactly in the same prestigious vein as with US universities, but with just as much enthusiasm. Tibet University was the home of the Fighting Yaks. Women from all departments answered the clarion call to organize themselves, with short notice, into cohesive groups they would be proud to call teams for an intramural tournament. I was invited, or rather expected, to join the foreign language department's fledgling group of rag-tags. How could I possibly be a decent contributing member of this team when I still became breathless climbing two flights of stairs? But I joined nevertheless. Members came out of the woodwork, teachers I had never seen before. We needed a lot of practice, but there was precious little time for that. This would not be a brand of game that I was familiar with as a player on the McLeod High School team. I couldn't have known at the time I joined that I'd end up needing a first-aid kit, along with an inordinate amount of stamina to last even for a few minutes.

There may have been brackets, but more likely names were pulled out of the hat to match up the teams. When our team arrived at the court, I couldn't help noticing that our selected opponents happened to be a collection of the baddest- looking, out-for-blood females in the university. I tried to tell my teammates what they could and couldn't expect from me before they proudly paraded me out onto the court, the only foreigner clueless enough to join in. Mina had the good sense to be part of the cheering squad on the sidelines, since she'd never played the game.

Wouldn't you know that our opponents would choose the baddest of them all to guard *me?* The fun started almost immediately. "Big Bertha" didn't let anything interfere with her performance, like exhibiting any shred of mercy she might have had for someone of my age, or any real attention to the rules, which she apparently dismissed as trivial and bothersome inconveniences. And it didn't help that the referee was evidently of the same mindset. I began wondering if perhaps nobody had explained to him the proper operation of his whistle.

At halftime, I went to my corner to doctor my wounds and to tattle on Big Bertha to Mr. Li, the English section chairman. He delivered some sage advice to aid me in surviving the ensuing second half bloodbath: fight my way through, take a page out of Big Bertha's playbook whenever the opportunity presented itself and smile as I delivered every blow. I tried and I got in my fair share, but before the game ended, I took myself out, the quitter that I was, knowing, at least, that I'd given it my best shot and even shed some blood for the sake of our team.

CHAPTER 12

A CHILD IS BORN

"A baby is God's opinion that the world should go on."
—Carl Sandburg

On a cold, rainy summer night in Lhasa, a baby girl was born to a mother who had waited for nine months to give birth. Did the child's parents happily welcome her arrival? Was it a mother all alone? Who can say? But moments after the birth, everything would change.

Early the next morning, before dawn, a man out for his daily walk along the Lingkhor, came upon dirty, wet, rumpled clothing at the edge of the unpaved path. Curiosity induced him to walk nearer, near enough to see the clump of cloth move. What he discovered was a tiny baby wrapped in her dirty swaddling clothes. It was a miracle that the nightly pack of roaming dogs had not come upon this baby. The good Samaritan scooped up the little package and walked it to a foundling home. His good deed completed, he continued on his ritual walk.

Word spread in certain circles about this foundling. Because of apparent ignorance and wishful thinking, one childless Han Chinese couple applied for adoption and were allowed to take the baby home.

I heard about this "throw-away" baby from a young man who had begun attending one of my classes. His brother, who was the head of the Tibet Mountaineering Association, was the new father. Mina and I were invited to visit and we took turns holding the precious baby. But we immediately saw what the parents did not: the child was born an albino. Their blindness was due to ignorance and to unfounded ideas. The couple believed what they'd heard, that this was a western baby with a Tibetan mother. And it appeared to me that they welcomed the distinction that would come from their adoption.

The new parents asked Mina and me to give the baby an English name, and we were even invited to a dinner party where we would reveal it. The day arrived and we announced "Mina Elizabeth," our names. It was a happy evening, and Mina and I did not divulge what we knew. Later, we were to learn that the child's parents took her to Beijing, ostensibly because she was ill. In fact, baby Mina Elizabeth would die there. Was she really ill? Or were they trying to rid themselves of this poor albino child? I'll never know, and I think I prefer to keep it that way.

Baby Mina Elizabeth with new parents after having
been rescued from a street in Lhasa as an albino.
Is that a smile on her face?

Parking lot at Lhasa market

Temple complex on side of Medicine Mountain, Lhasa

Bridge over Lhasa River after snowfall

Young monk at fertility temple near Bayi

Drew, Meredith, Mina, and Scott at Victoria Harbour, Hong Kong,1990

CHAPTER 13

DRAPCHI

"Prison is a second-by-second assault on the soul, a day-to-day degradation of the self, an oppressive steel and brick umbrella that transforms seconds into hours and hours into days."
—Mumia Aby-Jamal

I made my way to the second floor's west wing as the time neared 2:15 p.m., the time that we'd agreed I'd make the clandestine drop. I was to slide the envelope under the door. It was after-lunch rest time for the Canadian consul who'd agreed to accept my toxic piece of paper and take it back to Canada. He'd cautioned me about his Chinese government "minder" who was in the adjoining room. No foreign officials were ever left alone during visits to any place in China. "Be careful," the consul had said.

I decided to take the stairs to the second floor, fearful that the elevator would make an unexpected sound as the doors opened onto the hallway. The least little sound would have come across to me at that moment as a wake-the-dead *BOOM*. Every part of my body was on high alert.

I walked briskly down the hall toward the consul's room, willing myself not to stop at the door, but rather to slow my gait and slip the envelope under. Unwittingly, I was not breathing. *Just keep walking...just keep walking*. Once the envelope had been delivered, my mission now complete, I went downstairs and exited the hotel, taking a deep breath once outside, getting as much oxygen as the Lhasa air would allow at that elevation. But I could not bring myself to stop shaking and I couldn't pedal my bicycle fast enough to get back to the relative safety of my apartment.

The mission began innocently enough when, a few long weeks before, I'd begun visiting Eddie, a student of mine who was hospitalized. I can't recall why he was in the hospital, but my interest was in keeping him updated with classwork and to show his family that I cared about him. In the hospital, I met his parents for the first time. They were a warm and friendly pair. I brought Eddie magazines, puzzles, and rice pudding. His mother was so grateful that she would later knit me a pretty wool sweater.

Eddie shared a large room with four other men, all but one who were ambulatory. The bedridden young man, according to Eddie, had been in Drapchi, a prison located not far outside Lhasa. He had been released because he was expected to soon die, something to do with his liver. It was standard practice to release to the hospital tortured prisoners who appeared close to death. That insulated prison authorities from blame. When a political prisoner died, the official line was usually that the individual committed suicide or that he or she had a serious medical condition unrelated to prison conditions.

I never knew why this particular prisoner had been sent to Drapchi. Possibly it had to do with the revolt that took place in late 1988. The revolt resulted in martial law, which lasted until March 1990, just months before I arrived in Lhasa in August. Even Eddie, as a young teenager, had been caught in the riots. The gates of his house, which was located in a work unit, had been closed, locking him out, but in desperation, he managed to climb over a wall to get to the safety of his home.

The Chinese government never seemed to offer a reason for imprisoning anyone. Indeed, they often claimed that there were no political prisoners. In fact, political prisoners made up most of the prison population. Non-violent activity inconsistent with official ideology was often labeled "subversion endangering state security," or regarded as "plotting the overthrow of the state." Failing those accusations, there was always the catchall "disturbing public order."

One day at the hospital, I found Eddie's parents with tears in their eyes. They had been listening at the prisoner's bedside while he had recounted the tortures he'd experienced. Eddie later told me of even more of the cruel punishments that the man had suffered. His jaundiced pallor was a result of being tortured, beaten, and poked with a steel truncheon.

On my next visit, I carried a few magazines with pleasant pictures for the man to look at and maybe give him something with which to pass the long hours. I also carried him a dish of rice pudding, as I'd done for Eddie. The pudding was an entirely new taste for him I was quite sure.

Afterward, back in my apartment, I thought about all Eddie told me concerning the cruelty taking place in Drapchi and even the names of a few prisoners whom the young man knew had died from the torture. I decided at that moment that someone needed to know what the local officials were covering up.

My next visit to Eddie was for an entirely different purpose than bringing him up to speed on his classwork. I intended to give him a new assignment. When I entered his room, I noticed books that he'd been paging through, large books that his parents had brought him. What surprised me was the genre; they were art books, one being Christian-themed. In fact, Eddie asked me about my religion. He wanted me to tell him about Jesus and what my God had done for me. I told him I had a small book written in Chinese that explained the events of my holy book if he wanted to know more.

"My father told me that I cannot read or have an interest in other religions," Eddie replied, "because a person can have only one belief system." That of course would be his family's belief in Buddhism. I told him that he should be respectful of his father's reasoning while he was still living in his father's home. After all, I knew that his father's admonition had been repeated in various ways in pretty much every culture. I'd heard it put like this: You cannot sit in two chairs, for if attempted, you will fall through the crack in between. But I also told him to always keep an open mind to all areas of knowledge. And I knew Eddie was the sort of person who would do just that.

I turned our conversation back toward the prisoner patient, ready to give Eddie his new assignment. Fortunately, his parents weren't there. His roommates came and went from the room. I wasn't sure if any of them knew English but to be safe, we kept our voices subdued. Eddie needed to understand what I was asking him to do and I made it clear that he should discuss it with his parents. He seemed to have no reservations about what I was asking.

What I wanted were the names of the prisoners who had died from their torture, the dates, and the circumstances. Eddie was to find out the methods that were used, especially on his roommate. More than once, I stressed that he was not to write *anything* down. This would be much too risky. We would meet once he was back home and he could pass along the information to me verbally.

For Eddie, the stakes were high. He could be put in prison for the same thing that many prisoners were accused of. For me, I'd be kicked out of China, never to return.

Several days later, rested and recuperated, Eddie returned to class and we made plans for me to visit his home for the debriefing. For the particular work unit where Eddie lived, it was necessary for me to be met at the gate. A non-resident couldn't just walk in, which said a lot about what the unit was all about.

Eddie met me at the gate and walked me into his home. The few times that I'd seen his mother, she always had a smiling face. This time was different. Her face was grave without even a hint of a smile. The atmosphere was tense as if everyone was waiting for an avalanche to come crashing through. She drew the curtains closed as if to prevent this very thing from happening.

Eddie led me to a small room where he would reveal what he had learned in that hospital room. I was dumbfounded when I saw the piece of paper in his hands. He'd written it all down—every darn thing!

On the paper were the names, ages, and possible dates of the deaths. There was both physical and psychological torture, especially aimed at monks and nuns. Their religious beliefs were abused, and long-term solitary confinement was common. They were made to disrobe in front of one another. Other common torture methods and cruel treatments at the hands of the soulless guards and staff included electric shocks delivered by cattle prod to the genitals and other sensitive areas; beatings with metal rods, sticks, and rifle butts; exposure to extreme cold and heat, with the prisoners often left outside in winter with no shoes and little clothing; aerial suspension or restraint by rope in painful positions; mock executions; urinating in a victim's mouth; and no medical treatment for sores and infections. Withholding fresh water was common, forcing the prisoners to drink out of latrines or, in some cases, to drink their own urine.

That poor soul in the hospital bed told Eddie that the worst treatments he'd received were from the Tibetan guards, who were even more cruel when they'd been drinking. It seemed that the only hope for the prisoners was that they would meet a quick death.

All of this was on the sheet of paper Eddie gave me. I knew the information had to get to someone. I also knew that I wanted to rid myself of that piece of paper as quickly as I could. And that's why I chose the Canadian consul. The university was a natural stop for many Western visitors and they would often take us to dinner. The Canadian consul was the first Westerner I'd interacted with after receiving the paper, the first person I could safely dump the paper off to. Over dinner, I'd quietly mentioned it and he'd given me the instructions that I followed.

What became of the paper after I slid it under the door that day? I'll never know. I have often wished I had handed it off to an American. The US ambassador to China at the time was James Lilley and Lilley had been critical of the Tiananmen Square crackdown. He would have been the perfect candidate. After all, it wasn't long afterward that he had come with his wife for that dinner that I'd almost missed because I'd been struggling, all alone, to get down the mountainside that day. Nevertheless, I did learn that Lilley had visited the prison at one point. Somehow, a couple of the prisoners had managed to slip some information to him about the conditions.

What did the Canadian consul do with my information and how interested was the Canadian government in human rights abuses in Tibet at the time? Who can say? For me, the larger matter was that I needed to do *something*. Truthfully, I would have liked to have done more. The stories of torture sparked an anger in me that I feel to this day. The people who administered the torture were animals. Worse than animals; no animal purposely tortures another. The torturers possessed what I have heard described as "leprosy of the soul," and if I was naïve about what one human was capable of inflicting upon another, my naivete died in those days.

Much later, from Hong Kong, I would call Amnesty International, but I hung up before I could get anything out, too nervous about providing information that, in some way, might be traced back to Eddie. Even now, as I write this decades later, I am careful, using a completely made-up English name for him.

Delivering that page to the Canadian consul would be the extent of my involvement and walking down that second-floor hallway of the Holiday Inn did not warrant any special feelings for myself at that moment. However puny my efforts might have been in the grander scheme of things, I had to make an attempt to reveal the unspeakable, inhuman cruelty that had been heaped upon those poor souls imprisoned at Drapchi prison. Since then, whenever I contemplate my discovery of what went on there, I try to remember Romans 12:19: *Vengeance is mine, saith the Lord.* At the time, I suppose my ultimate aim, though not entirely clear to me then, was to honor those prisoners, to recognize the lost humanity and lost hope that that single piece of paper represented.

CHAPTER 14

CHRISTMAS AT THE PLA HOSPITAL

"Adversity draws men together and produces beauty and harmony in life's relationships, just as the cold of winter produces ice-flowers on the windowpanes, which vanish with the warmth."
—Soren Kierkegaard

Oh, the fun of rough travel. Early one morning, an old pilgrim bus left from near the Barkhor Bazaar with roughly fifteen post-menopausal American women on board and it would prove to be the beginning of an interesting day. I was invited to accompany the tour, a group of ladies who were associated with a museum in Southern California with an interest in Tibet. Their leader was a spry eighty-year-old who was making her fourth trip to Tibet. Our congenial Tibetan guide that day was a much sought-after guide named Renchen (not to be confused with my student) with an excellent reputation. He had lived in India for some years and hadn't learned Chinese, but his Tibetan and English were excellent.

We made our way to the first place of interest in Yarlung Valley, which was at a lower altitude than Lhasa. It was a two-hour trip over a very bumpy gravel road with very bad shock absorbers. And even in the middle of October, the sun made it a hot trip. We had to make a trade-off: open the windows and eat dust or keep the windows closed and suffer the heat. We opted for the former but, at last, we were free of the bus when we arrived at Yumbu Lakhang a medieval-looking castle reputed to be the oldest building in Tibet. Of course, the castle was located on a small mountain and only a few of us made it to the top, huffing and puffing all the way.

Renchen informed us that the Tibetan race originated in the Yarlung Valley and that the first king descended from heaven and came to this place to rule. Near the site were four sacred peaks and in one of those peaks was the "Monkey Cave" where the Bodhisattva Chenrezig, in the form of a monkey king, mated with an ogress to create the first Tibetan people. A bit different from Genesis 1, to be sure. Back on the bus, we headed to Tsetang, the third largest city in Tibet where we spent the night after a decent meal and hot showers.

The next day would prove to be another cultural extravaganza, a trip to Samye monastery. Getting there was another rough experience, but the ladies on this tour were tough and up for the challenge. The first leg in getting to the monastery was crossing the Yarlung Tsangpo river, named Brahmaputra once it flows into India. Our bus left the main road and arrived near the shore of the river where a few Tibetans were waiting to cross, loading what looked like sacks of grain or flour into flat-bottomed boats to take to the monastery. Our group was distributed to several boats, each of which had a small motor to ferry us across. As we relaxed against the sacks, we had a wonderful view of the river flowing around the many sandbars. In an hour, we arrived at the opposite shore, but not before having to wade our way to dry ground.

Then came the next leg of the odyssey. Once ashore, we waited for half an hour for the next means of transportation to the monastery—two large dump trucks. The only other people on shore were a few Tibetan men, one of them sitting on a tractor. Then it happened. One of the ladies had to *go*. There certainly wasn't a WC anywhere, nor even any bushes. Our sister was getting desperate. What to do? Then someone came up with the idea of making a circle around her as a shield. Even still, the man on the tractor wouldn't stop gazing over at our group, probably wondering what we were doing. I walked over to the tractor to get the man's attention, pointing somewhere to avert his gaze. Finally, it was over. You do what you have to do.

The trucks arrived and we struggled to climb aboard for the thirty-minute trip to the monastery. And, oh, what a trip it was. Huge bumps would practically send us airborne as we held on tight to the sides. It wasn't a road, but more like a track.

Fortunately, the glittering roof of Samye's main temple soon came into view. There were willow and poplar trees in abundance, four holy mountains stood to the east of the monastery, and far off to the south from where we had just come were sand dunes along the Tsangpo. Barley fields alternating with plots of yellow and white-blooming rapeseed contrasted sharply with the barren hills. Renchen explained to the group that if it weren't for irrigation, the Samye Valley would be a desert.

There were many small temples, but we spent most of our time in the main one. Renchen told us many facts about the history. Samye was the first great Buddhist monastery in Tibet, founded around 775 AD. It was built as a three-dimensional model, or *mandala*, of the Buddhist universe. A lot of the buildings were destroyed during the Cultural Revolution, but money from the government and other sources helped renovate many of them.

The interior of the temple's ground floor was lit by candles and had a very old, musty atmosphere. I imagine a person susceptible to allergies might leave the place with clogged sinuses. We were allowed in the kitchen, which had a hole in the ceiling over the fire pit to draw the smoke, and we used the boiled water from the thermoses to prepare our dried noodles. Dried *anything* was the sustenance of travelers everywhere out in the wilds like us.

Mid-afternoon, we headed back to Lhasa, non-stop, reversing the path of our adventure: teeth-rattling truck ride, slow trip across the river (fortunately nobody having to go), and then a hot and dusty bus ride. We made it home safe and sound. But little did I know that breathing in all that dust would later result in a real life and death adventure.

It was close to Christmas, and winter in Lhasa is a time for many Tibetans from other regions to come to the little city, some on pilgrimage, some to buy and sell, and some for other reasons. While the local population increases, the tour groups decrease or stop altogether and tour agencies have very little to do. Along with the reduction in the monetary resources of the tour guides, their communications in English drop off, too. One tour agency, wanting to keep the guides sharp, asked me if I would offer re-fresher English. They were willing to pay me, so why not?

The first few classes went well except for my fits of coughing, sometimes bad enough to where I'd have to excuse myself and leave the room. Then, halfway through one class, my coughing became so incessant that I realized I could not go on. The leaders were sympathetic and drove me back to the university.

The next morning, as I slowly walked to my university class, a woman from the language department took one look at me and pointed me back to my apartment. Renchen took over the class that morning while I returned to bed. I was determined, however, to make it in for my afternoon writing class. So that I didn't have to talk and burden the students with my coughing fits, I gave the class a longer than normal free-writing session. Then I played the sounds of an approaching rainstorm in a forest and told them to write about what they heard. While they did that, I sat in a chair, which was about all I could do.

Shortly, I noticed two Westerners standing outside the door. I went out to see what they wanted and they told me they were bureau chiefs in Beijing for two European newspapers. They were in Tibet incognito and asked if they could talk to the students, assuring me they would introduce themselves as tourists. I let them come in and the students seemed to enjoy the exchange. But before they left, they noticed my condition, remarking that I needed to see a doctor. Then they called the Holiday Inn to request the minibus to come for them and for me and soon I was on my way to see the doctor at the hotel. He sent me home with a packet of colorful little pills, which, having no idea what they were, I could not bring myself to take. I crawled into my bed and covered up with my blanket and comforter, trying to keep warm. Unfortunately, my little table-top heater had given up the ghost some days before.

By the next day, my condition worsened. I now had racking coughs and pain. Mina checked on me every few hours and at one point left a bottle of Tylenol on the table beside my bed. After she left, I tried to get the cap off but didn't have the strength and I had to wait until she came back. Mr. Li, the English section chairman, became aware of my condition and contacted a female doctor from Denmark who was with a medical non-profit organization. She came to my room several times to check on me, once bringing a mister to add some needed moisture around my bed, but the mister didn't help. Meanwhile, my fingertips and the area around my eyes were turning shades of blue.

The next day, a Sunday, Mina came into my room and found me crying and in a great deal of pain. "Get me out of here!" I said to her. "I'm going to die!" Mina ran out of the room to find Mr. Li and he in turn went to get the doctor. Upon her arrival, they made sure that I had on all the warm clothing that I could put on and then it was off to People's Hospital Number 1 and what passed for their emergency room. Once there, I was x-rayed, whereupon the technician told the Danish doctor that he couldn't see anything. It was no wonder; the doctor could see that the machine wasn't working.

Then we went to a room filled with other patients to be examined by a Chinese doctor. I reluctantly raised all my tops to allow him to use his stethoscope to listen to my lungs. His diagnosis? I probably had the flu. The hospital didn't want me for a patient (lucky for me), so Mr. Li said he would try for the PLA hospital, which was located north of the city.

When we arrived at the gate of the People's Liberation Army Hospital, the driver was directed to the VIP building up a hill from the main building. Mr. Li went inside to see if I could be admitted. Soon he came out with a tall, good-looking army doctor who told me they would take me. I went to a room, crawled into bed, and was soon covered by two soft, surprisingly pure-white comforters. (Whites usually don't stay white in Tibet.) Soon they gave me oxygen and within half an hour, my normal color returned.

In a little while, a nurse came in and hooked me up to an IV. Apart from someone bringing me hot tea, no one bothered me, except for when I needed to become acquainted with my own special VIP WC. A nurse helped me and the IV stand to get there. Once inside, I had to wade through some water on the floor to ascend the toilet, and I say ascend because the toilet rested on a cement block. It resembled a Western toilet at first, but upon closer examination, I could see it had no seat and became, consequently, nothing more than a glorified, raised, squatty potty. For all the time I would spend there, the WC would have water puddled on the floor and remind me much more of the kind of grimy restroom you'd expect to see at a bus depot or highway gas station than a restroom in a hospital, and in a "VIP" room to boot!

That night was a restless one. My coughing continued to be painful. In the morning, two nurses came to get me and we walked down the hill, through the newly fallen snow, to the main hospital for an x-ray and a blood test, the latter of which almost caused me to pass out. Walking back up the hill, we met two Tibetan women from the university, one being my neighbor who had brought mo-mos. I couldn't eat anything more than toast, but I thanked her for her kindness.

I was diagnosed with pneumonia that day and it became clear that I'd be spending Christmas in the PLA hospital. A course of three injections of penicillin a day began. My nurse was very good at administering them for she did each injection slowly and used her fingernail to lightly scratch around the needle. I concluded that her process was designed to alleviate the chill of the solution and this was confirmed when a substitute nurse dispensed with the more comfortable procedure and instead drove the needle immediately home, plunging its contents all at once. My scream left no doubt in the mind of this Nurse from Hell how I felt about her methodology.

Meanwhile, the cook sent in a dish every day, and I could always observe him peering around the corner to see if I would eat it. Sweet fellow, but I couldn't possibly eat most of what he sent, including meat mo-mos that oozed fat. For the most part, I stuck with toast and tea, although after a few days, I was finally yearning for a change. When a few nurses came into my room for no other reason than to rifle through my things, I showed them my Chinese-English phrase book. I turned to the food section and pointed to the food I thought that I could eat in the future. Things like mashed potatoes, white-meat chicken, noodles in broth, bean curd, spinach, and more, to a total of around ten items. One of them dutifully wrote down my choices.

Truthfully, I think the nurses might have come in to visit with the *laowei* (foreigner) to try out the little English they knew. They'd make attempts and end up giggling to themselves. This became my entertainment.

The very next morning, they brought me the food I'd requested. All of it.

A server swept into the room with a big, round tray with all ten choices on it. The chicken, the noodles, the mashed potatoes—everything. How could I tell her and the cook that it was all a mistake? The poor cook had probably set his alarm extra early to get this colossal breakfast tray ready. And of course, there he was, peering around the corner to see if it was to my liking. I managed to force down what I could.

Every few days, in the university car with a driver, Mina came to visit me. Other days were lonely, with no one to break up the time except my nurse who came into my room three times a day with that needle. I began walking down the hall every day for some exercise. Early one morning I happened to look out my front-facing window just in time to see two men carrying a large bundle covered with a white cloth. This seemed strange for an instant until I realized someone had died overnight and these men were collecting the body in preparation no doubt for a sky burial.

I did have a few interesting visitors in my time at the hospital. One was Andrew, a former student and now tour guide. He brought with him a woman who was a doctor from England. She turned out to be an angel, sent to plot out my stay in Hong Kong. It would soon be time again for a conference there, but, of course, my illness prevented me from doing any planning. Because of the difficulties of traveling and the spotty scheduling of Chinese transportation, it would be a trip that would last for more than a month. Not to worry. This visiting angel had all the details worked out. First, I would stay in the home of her sister and husband who were Lutherans associated with Friends of China. They wouldn't be there, but she gave me the phone number and address of someone who had a key to their house. Then she gave me a phone number of a Christian retreat house, a cottage on Cheung Chau Island, an hour's ferry ride from Hong Kong Island.

A second angel to come see me was a man I'd never formally met—Tashi Cering, the Barkhor chang maker's husband. He came because of his association with Tibet University, but also because he'd had many American friends help him while he was in the States. This dear man offered to loan me plane fare to Chengdu. I would eventually pay him back from my last pay from the university after I would leave for Hong Kong, delivered to him by a Tibetan professor. We had a short visit in the hospital that day, but I would visit with Tashi again several times at the House of Chang.

A week before Christmas, my neighbor, Droga, brought a battery-operated tape player and a few white candles, explaining that she heard that people used candles on this particular holiday. All I needed then was to hear some bells and some carolers outside my window singing carols to put me in the spirit. But hark! What did I hear? Could it be that Santa had allowed Rudolph to find the way to Lhasa and then bravely rushed the gates of the PLA hospital? I swore I heard noises. Then what should appear coming through the door of my room? Not one Santa, but eight, all wearing Santa hats and singing, slightly off-key, "We wish you a Merry Christmas." As it turned out, these Santas were from the Holiday Inn, along with Mr. Li and a few of my teacher friends. Besides Christmas cheer, they brought candy canes and fruit.

Christmas day came with a dusting of snow. I had more visitors. This time it was some of my students. Several of them brought fruit (my room was beginning to look like a fruit market) along with Christmas cards, such that could be found in Lhasa, with sweet handwritten sentiments:

My dear teacher, On Christmas day I ask God as soon as you can left here. (hospital) And wish you happy. God Blessing you! Eddie

To Meredeas: I wish you overcome soon! From Nikky

Dear Meredith. I hope you are feeling better now and that you will soon been completely recovered. I missed you very much. I am looking forward to your quick return. Please get well soon. With kindest regards and best wishes for your good health. Your Chip.

Dear Meredith: MERRI CHRISTMAS! AND HAPPI NEW YEAR! Taking this opportunity I wish you have a speedy recovery. We miss you very much! Buddha Bless You! Your student, Spencer.

It was a most memorable Christmas.

Meanwhile, my coughing, though better, was not stopping, and each time I coughed, I was still racked with pain. The tall, good-looking doctor began to annoy me with his insistence that I could not be in any pain because of the regimen of penicillin. Yet he wasn't agreeable to my insistence on leaving before the new year, telling me that I should stay for two more weeks of therapy. The therapy consisted of hot packs laid upon my chest for about twenty minutes. But I had my way, and university officials came to sign me out on December 31. Because part of my contract with the school was that it would pay for any medical bill while I was in Lhasa, they would ultimately settle the hospital debt.

On my way out, I tried to find each person who had tended to me for what ended up being fifteen days in the PLA Hospital to say a warm "thank you." Walking outside felt like walking out of a prison. All I could think to say to the driver was, "Home, James."

CHAPTER 15

HONG KONG R&R

"I will love the light for it shows me the way, yet I will endure the darkness because it shows me the stars."
—Og Mandino

My body was weak, I had little strength, and I was down to 108 pounds. Home had never looked so good to me as it did on December 31. Outside of the surprise visits of the ex-pats and students, there had been nothing to like about the month. Looking back on my stay at the hospital, I can see now that there had been lessons learned: humility, gratitude for small things, thankfulness for the kindness of strangers, and the lesson of not judging a person by the uniform he or she wears.

It was almost noon when I walked through my door on New Year's Eve, finding my apartment only slightly warmer than the outdoors. The water left in a pan in my kitchen sink had become a block of ice, but there was heat in my bedroom from the sun coming through my south-facing windows. With curtains open to take advantage of the solar warmth, I crawled into bed. Later, someone brought me some noodles from my favorite noodle restaurant and Tylenol for the lingering pain that I was still experiencing on my left side and back. I was set for the afternoon.

Word spread that I had come home and at some point in the afternoon, I heard the murmurs of the little voices of the neighbor children who were perched on the ledge looking into my room. The head of my bed was next to the window, so I knew they were looking directly at me. I kept my eyes closed for I wanted them to maintain their relative silence. Knowing of their care and concern gave me great joy that day.

I stayed in bed for two days, then had to get busy with plans to leave Lhasa on January 4. There was that Hong Kong trip I needed to take. Mina was going too, but she was traveling on ahead, as usual, taking a drive to Nepal first where she would stay in Kathmandu and take day trips. The plan was to meet up with her in Hong Kong around February 22.

As always, the trip to Hong Kong went through Chengdu, but for two days, the daily flights there had been canceled due to weather, making it practically impossible to get on the first flight out. But then came Zara's mother to the rescue. She went to all the influential people that she thought might be able to pull it off. Finally, the director of the Tibetan Tourism Bureau took over. I'd met him once in a restaurant at the Holiday Inn called the Hard Yak Café. He told us he'd try to get me on the first plane out on a medical emergency, but that I should be prepared, even after arriving at the airport, for the possibility that I might not be successful.

Meanwhile, Mina sent a telegram on ahead to some teachers in Chengdu to ask if they would meet me at the airport and stay with me until the Dragonair Flight would depart three hours later for Hong Kong. Finally, a British gentleman we knew from the Holiday Inn contacted a friend in Chengdu to get my ticket for the Hong Kong flight and take it to the airport since one couldn't buy tickets there. All in all, a whirlwind of activity to get my trip all lined up.

The flight was scheduled for early in the morning and I packed the night before with the help of Zara and Mina. But Murphy's Law found its way across the ocean and landed in my apartment that night. The electricity went off and I had to pack by the light of candles. I was still weak and tired and in pain each time I coughed. And I was having trouble thinking about what I needed to pack for a month or more away from Lhasa. Zara and Mina helped all they could.

Morning arrived too soon, but the university car, still in need of shocks, arrived with Mr. Li. Zara and Mina came along to see me off. After we arrived at the airport, the others went inside and left me shivering in the car for what seemed like a long time. Finally, Zara came out to get me, telling me, "Miss Meredith, you have to look *very* ill." For me to get on the flight as a medical emergency case, I needed to *look* like a medical emergency case. So, I wrapped my wool scarf around my head and neck and with every bit of theatrics I could muster, I put on a show that might have earned me an Academy Award. Mina had to stifle her laughter.

While my bag was being inspected, someone escorted me to the bus which would take passengers to the plane. In case anyone was still watching me, I mounted the steps with much difficulty. Then an attendant helped me up the steps and saw me to my seat. Feeling as if I needed to remain in character, I continued to act like I was at death's door.

We landed in Chengdu in less than two hours, and I was told to stay seated until someone could help me deplane. Air China's plans were for me to go to the back of the plane and down a lift to the tarmac. There, a wheelchair would be available to take me inside. This was getting to be too much. By this time, I was feeling guilty anyway, knowing there was a passenger back in Lhasa I had bumped. I told the attendant I didn't need the lift or the wheelchair. I was capable of using the stairs if I were careful and went slowly.

Inside the old terminal were a few of the teachers that Mina had contacted. Little did I know that Mr. Murphy and his Law had deplaned before me. Packing by candlelight, and not being clear-headed about what I'd need going through customs, I'd forgotten a very important document, that being one that lists what valuables I'd taken into Tibet. It was a short list—a camera. The man with my Hong Kong ticket told me that I might not be able to leave the airport, but the crisis was averted when he explained my plight to the officials. I was able to clear customs. Oh, what joy filled my soul.

My Dragonair flight was not for three hours and I wouldn't think of having those teachers wait there with me for that amount of time so I insisted I was fine and they went on their way. But a couple of hours later, there was an announcement that the flight had been cancelled for that day. A man I had been talking with, a Hong Kong Chinese in Chengdu on business, told me the bad news. This was the first time that I'd been in Chengdu alone. What to do? Fortunately, the kind man invited me to share his taxi and he dropped me off at the US consulate located in the Jing Jiang Hotel where I asked the personnel if there was a vacant room on their wing where I could stay the night.

It might be remembered that this was the same place we had stayed on our way to Lhasa in the first place. Since then, I had met the consul and his wife when they had made a visit to Lhasa. At the Jing Jiang Hotel, this thoughtful couple not only offered me a room for the night, they offered me their room, complete with TV. "What you need is a little taste of home," the consul's wife told me. How right she was.

Dragonair left on time the next morning for Hong Kong and, upon my arrival, I was a relieved to see someone from my sending organization there to meet me. In fact, someone had even made a doctor's appointment for the next day to check on my progress from the pneumonia. After a fitful night of coughing and pain, I made my way by bus, using a map that showed me the way to the doctor's office. Gaining more independence is a fine thing in normal circumstances, but not what I was especially interested in at that time.

At any rate, after an examination of my respiratory system and a phlegm sample, I became aware that, as usual, Mr. Murphy and his Law were in attendance. It turned out that my coughing and pain were caused by thrush of the mouth, which, in turn, had been caused by almost fifteen days of penicillin. The PLA hospital never tested me to see what kind of pneumonia I had—viral or bacterial. I'd had viral. The penicillin had done nothing. So, I began a regimen to rid me of the thrush.

Finally, there was time to rest and recuperate. I had my room in the cottage on Cheung Chau Island that had been offered to me in the hospital, and I intended to make good use of it. I took the ferry to the island and made my way up a long hill to the place that would serve as my sanctuary for three weeks, a pleasant place with papaya trees in the back and flowers everywhere. After a week there, I was able to take short walks. Soon after that, I was going for longer walks, taking a trail down to a rock ledge where I could sit and look out at the South China Sea.

The operators of the cottage, a British couple, provided a cold breakfast every morning for anyone who wanted it and a home-made dinner every evening served family-style for those who made a reservation. A congenial older couple from Australia were there as volunteers. We were a happy family. I got much-needed rest and gained ten pounds. All was well.

CHAPTER 16

THE HAPPY NOODLE RESTAURANT

"Eating is a need, enjoying is an art."
—Unknown

There was no yellow brick road to my aforementioned favorite noodle restaurant. Like a lot of things I stumbled upon in Lhasa, I was lost on my bicycle when I'd first discovered the Happy Noodle Restaurant. Finding the Happy Noodle Restaurant, that is to say, was a happy accident. My funds were limited when I arrived in Lhasa and the noodle restaurant was a place I could be sated for small money. The noodles at this restaurant couldn't be beat for taste and variety of toppings. My go-to toppings were chopped green onions and peanuts. The blob of noodles rested in a flavorful broth.

Most of the time I'd bike there by myself. Upon my arrival, I'd point to what I wanted (my finger pointing was a substitute for spoken Chinese), take the bowl from the counter, and then find a seat. The owner was a funny young man and one day after I began eating my second bowl (being especially hungry that day), I noticed he and his worker started snickering while looking at me. Why was I the object of their fun? Maybe it had something to do with how I looked—big nose and slightly hairy arms. The Chinese had hairless arms. For all I knew they might have likened me to a monkey. But I continued with my meal, taking no offense. And for their part, they must have gotten used to my presence because it wasn't long before we didn't even have to go through the ordering routine. They'd begin preparing my bowl as soon as I came through the door.

For the longest time, I had no idea what the place was called. Finally, I asked a student to translate the sign on the door. With the cooks always laughing and friendly, I should not have been surprised: The Happy Noodle Restaurant. In time I learned the owner's name, Mr. Mao, and I began referring to him as Chairman Mao. His business didn't rate on our 1 to 4 dog scale, for Mr. Mao ran a tight establishment. I often wondered if maybe there really were dogs, but that perhaps I just never saw them because they were confined to the kitchen, possibly even stewing in a pot. These were not idle thoughts. Many Chinese did, in fact, eat dogs. But, whatever the dog scale, the noodles were good and, in truth, after the first few weeks in Lhasa eating at various establishments, I found my standards unconsciously dropping.

My usual place at the Happy Noodle Restaurant was a table out front by an open window. In a major city, a table that close to the street might cost handsomely, if available at all. But at the Happy Noodle Restaurant, it came with an inexpensive bowl of noodles.

There were, of course, many more places to eat and some were especially interesting. One afternoon, biking down Beijing Road before the predictable afternoon dust storm began, I stopped when I spotted a new sight—a plastic, three-sided food cart on wheels. There were several of these I'd seen on other streets—veritable moving feasts. The carts all looked the same so perhaps an entrepreneur had a franchise business going. With the help of a student on one occasion, I learned what delicacies were stocked in these stands: roasted pig's ears, pig scalps, pig innards, yak meat, and yak tails. Yum! Eating at the new food stand on Beijing Road would certainly have added variety and taste to my Tibetan diet. But I was not tempted. I was on my way to the Happy Noodle Restaurant, which I hadn't visited for a few days, and no amount of fancy menu items was going to prevent me from getting there.

Upon my arrival, I waved to Chairman Mao and his pal and wandered over to my streetside table. No more would I have to wait at the counter for my bowl of noodles. Not only had they started preparing my meal as soon as I walked in, but now they insisted on serving me where I sat. Frequent diner privilege, and fit for a queen! There were precious few luxuries in Lhasa, so I hungrily embraced them whenever one dropped into my lap.

While waiting for my noodles that day, I was entertained by two young girls playing a "jump-the-grid" game beside the street. They jumped, skipped, pranced, and argued, behaving as any young girls would behave at their ages. A growling Lhasa Apso, seemingly bewildered by the girls' swift movements, hopped about keeping pace with the girls' steps. Soon enough, my large bowl of steaming, fragrant noodles were served and I was happily indulging myself in this tranquil moment, sitting by a street in the heart of Lhasa, watching frolicking children at play, and thinking what a wonderful realization of my dream it was to be there, feeling at home and at peace. I slurped my noodles down (slurping was the norm in Lhasa) and I was in hog-heaven.

The Happy Noodle Restaurant became a place of great convenience to me. For what's a girl to do when she finds herself terribly hungry and sees that the kitchen cupboard is bare? Or has food to cook, but cannot bear to contend once more with the electric-coiled tripod cooking apparatus? It's not that I didn't have time to cook. In fact, lunchtime at most universities in China lasted for two hours. This was so because many families didn't have refrigerators. It was necessary to make trips to streetside meat and vegetable vendors to acquire the ingredients for lunch. Time was needed to buy the food, prepare it, cook it (typically in woks), eat, rest, and get back to work.

For my part, this seemed like an awful lot of energy to expend. Why go to all that trouble when there was a noodle restaurant only a short distance away? I made use of it sufficiently that had Chairman Mao made a frequent diner card available, mine would have been riddled with punched holes (probably made with a sharp-ended chopstick, or *quisai.*)

Sometimes on my way there, I would notice Chamba, a cute, smiling young man, slight in stature, whose duty it was to red-flag any vehicle whose driver was foolish enough to make even the slightest mistake when approaching his particular territory. Chamba, dressed in his impressive white uniform replete with important-looking ribbons and insignias, would step down from his concrete pedestal and write up the offending party. With his youthful, innocent face, Chamba's pad of tickets held most of his power. Who could fear him? Once I saw a driver attempt to bribe him with a pack of cigarettes. From my vantage point, I could not be certain as to whether or not Chamba took the bribe.

On that particular day, or maybe it was one just like it, I found my usual table at the noodle restaurant when, only moments later, a beggar zeroed in on me, ambling up to my table. It would happen from time to time that beggars would enter the establishment, but Chairman Mao was usually too busy to deal with them. This time, however, he snapped into action, not willing to allow one of his favorite customers to be harassed. I thought the world had come to an end when he let loose with a thunderous shout from the kitchen, then dashed out with his dripping ladle, fuming with rage and screaming foreign words to the beggar, who took his cue and promptly hightailed it out the door. I sat wide-eyed, almost too stunned to move.

Then, as quickly as the barrage of words and thunder had transpired, it abated. Chairman Mao was not one to get side-tracked by events. Soon, he was emptying customer's bowls of uneaten noodles into the bowls of the poor hanging outside the door.

It seemed there was always something new at the Happy Noodle Restaurant, a place of convenience and refuge, not to mention a grand place to slurp along with the natives.

Serious discussions, tete-a-tete

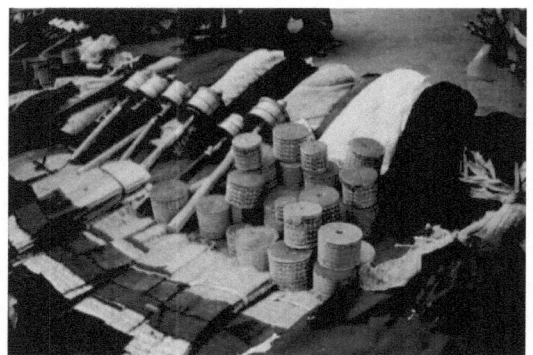

Merchandise in Barkhor market—prayer flags and
prayer inserts for prayer wheels

Coiffed at the market

A mountain view of Potala Palace

Yak, Yak, Yak

CHAPTER 17

THE POET

"Freedom is never voluntarily given by the oppressor; it must be demanded by the oppressed."
—Martin Luther King

One day, after lunch, Mina and I decided to take a walk along the Lhasa River. We did this from time to time and it never seemed to get old. Often it was the familiar, mundane, middle-of-the-day kind of walk, though pleasant. We'd sometimes see women out in the shallow water washing rugs, and other times we might see them washing sheep's wool, preparing it for combing, spinning, and knitting into sweaters. My neighbor knitted me a sweater after going through these steps. I watched some of the spinning in a small shack located inside the fenced chicken yard.

On that particular day, Mina and I came upon a young man standing on the raised path above the water, staring out in apparent deep thought. We must have disturbed his reverie as we got nearer, for after sensing our presence, he turned slightly and said "hello" in a hesitant voice. We stopped and replied with our own "hellos" and began a simple conversation after discovering that he spoke English rather well.

He seemed guarded, if not shy, in revealing much about himself. He told us he was a poet, and that he wrote about peace and freedom, which had us thinking that he could get into trouble with those topics, considering the political atmosphere of the city. For all we knew, he might have been an underground rabble-rouser, an organizer of street protests, or a spy for foreign diplomats. We might have come under suspicion if seen talking to him. Learning to self-censor was a valuable asset in a place with a heavy-handed political presence. By the time I left Tibet, I would see how the gradual tightening of social and political controls had insidiously crept in.

Before we left the poet to walk back to campus, I asked to see a poem he'd composed and he seemed happy to have me read one. I relived that chance meeting in my mind for the rest of the day, and, for the next few days, I walked down to our meeting spot. But no poet.

Eventually, I stopped returning to the spot thinking that meeting him again was not meant to be, or so I tried to convince myself. But there was something about him that I couldn't seem to get out of my mind. He was...different. Thoughtful. Pensive. I couldn't help but wonder how he spent his days.

Because it was near the end of the semester, there were classroom tasks to attend to before the almost two-month break for the winter holidays—both the Chinese and Tibetan New Year. With everything going on, I had little time to think about the mystery man and he slipped into the back of my mind.

Soon the break was upon us. Chinese New Year was one of the busiest times of the year, with millions and millions of people overburdening the transportation systems, mainly the train. Air travel at the time was beyond the means of most common people, but a necessary option for us teachers to be able to reach our destinations out of the country. But not much was easy in China; most everything had its unpredictable, time-consuming mishaps. Even the hour-and-a-half trip to the airport in the early morning hours could be something to write home about—the teeth-jarring ride on a bumpy, pot-holed road, the school's old sedan driven by a driver who knew only two speeds—fast and faster, curves be damned. Or the accident site of some poor soul's Jeep that had hit a high speed bump and catapulted down the ravine toward the river. On one occasion, four of us were on our way to the airport in a small, decrepit old bus. We had almost made it to the turn-off to the ramshackle terminal when the bus took its last breath. It was too far for us to get out and carry our luggage, so our gallant young men had to get behind the bus and push it the rest of the way. When nothing happened on these trips, it was a time for celebration.

I spent the break in Hong Kong that year as was typical. And there could be no greater extreme of culture shock than when traversing back and forth between Lhasa and Hong Kong. Hong Kong was a glitzy, glamorous city. After an amazing few weeks, it was back home. It wasn't clear to me when I began referring to Lhasa as "home," but by then, that was certainly the sentiment.

And I had certainly adjusted. I was reminded of this at the airport, waiting to retrieve my luggage. A young female tourist approached and asked if I could let her know how to tell the male from the female facilities, as she was in desperate need. I told her how I had figured it out soon after I'd arrived the first time. The sign that has one stroke of the Chinese character, resembling a male organ, denotes "male." The other sign, denoting "female," has two diagonal strokes, which look like crossed legs. After she stopped laughing, she said that she'd never forget this lesson.

Of course, coming home from the airport, there were the inevitable travel hang-ups. About halfway to Lhasa, we were delayed for more than three hours due to a dirt and rock slide. Men were already at work clearing the slide, armed with nothing but shovels. Eventually, they created a passable route and we continued on our way. All the familiar smells and sights of Lhasa greeted us upon arrival and my apartment never looked so good. Home at last.

A few days later, the students were back at school, ready to return to their studies, greeting their classmates, and making their ways back to their favorite tea houses. I made my way to the foreign language office, where no one spoke English, just to show my face and to collect any mail that might have arrived. And that's when I saw him. The poet by the river!

What could this mean?

What it meant was that he was there to sign up for several English classes, including the new writing class I'd added to an afternoon time slot, substituting it for a video class that hadn't been very productive. He could not have known about the change, but there he was registering for the writing class and I found myself looking forward to his attendance.

I was not disappointed. When the class eventually started, I learned right away of this man's enthusiasm for writing. In fact, he came to my apartment from time to time with his most recent poem in hand. It wasn't my intention to teach poetry construction, so I would gently tell him that if I rewrote his writings, they would no longer be his. I could see in his poems the depth of his emotions. His poems, as he had told us that day by the river, were all centered on peace and freedom. Those were all he wanted to write about.

In the months that followed, I came to know the poet quite well, though in an incremental way. I could not have understood what I was to hear from him all at once. As it turned out, he had learned English in India, following his escape from Tibet years earlier with others who were fleeing, a group of about fifteen, some of them children. They were escaping their homeland because China had turned Tibet into a police state where Tibetans could no longer freely study and practice their religion or assert their Tibetan identity in any meaningful way. The group traveled on foot over the Himalayan mountains, a trip that took more than a month.

The poet had grown up in a small village in eastern Tibet with his mother, grandmother, and a brother. He had lost his father to Mao's Cultural Revolution. In 1968, his father was accused by members of the Red Guard of some trumped-up charge and was made to spend months of detention in a cowshed, followed by years of hard labor a long way from home. The poet never saw his father again. His mother eventually became ill in both body and mind and died. The grandmother served as his surrogate anchor during those early years, encouraging him to leave the village when he was fifteen so that he might find his way to Lhasa and a better life.

He spoke with remarkable detachment about the destruction of his parents' lives. But whenever he spoke of the past, there seemed to be a hardness to his demeanor. I came to think of him as a member of Tibet's "lost generation," the youth who became unmoored by the chaos created by Mao.

My new friend was fearless, and determined to continue improving his life. But there would be no better life in Lhasa. Because of the Red Guard, there would be no schooling. The poet managed to find ways to sustain himself until, almost by fate, he heard of some Tibetans who were planning to escape to India by way of Nepal. It was with this small group that he would learn the life and death necessity of secretiveness, to be wary of strangers, to live in the shadows.

Planning for the trip had to be meticulous: what truck driver could be trusted to take them to the place where they would begin their almost thirty-day journey on foot? How much food did they dare take so that, if caught by the PLA, it would appear that they weren't going far?

But the planning was only the first of many challenges. The route from Tibet to Nepal required crossing the daunting Himalayas. The group accessed Nangpa La, a mountain pass running to the west of Mount Everest that starts near Tingri in south Tibet, leading to Cho Oyu, the sixth highest mountain in the world. At 19,000 feet, the pass was nothing more than a foot trail with dangers that included sudden storms, frostbite, and altitude sickness. It was a lonely path. There was nothing along the way but rock and mountain and snow. The hike was brutal and exhausting. When, finally, the poet's group arrived in Nepal, they were half-frozen and half-starved. But they were free.

Unfortunately, there would be more mountains for the poet to climb before he could feel safe. Nepal prohibited newly arrived Tibetans from remaining in the country. Many were picked up by police while attempting to travel through to India. This was the poet's fate. Worse, he was, by then, separated from his escape family. He was a teenager, completely on his own now. When he came to the attention of the authorities, they turned him over to the Tibetan Reception Center in Kathmandu where he was interviewed to determine whether or not there was a credible *prima facie* case for considering him a refugee. But the main purpose of the interview was to determine if he was really Tibetan.

That established, he was allowed to continue to Dharamsala, India, but he had to wait days for a bus. Then he left Nepal. But the poet had no valid papers, just an exit card that he surrendered at the border. He was now a man without a country—no papers to prove that he even existed.

I cannot trust my memory to relate much of what the poet said happened after he arrived in Dharamsala, the place where the Dalai Lama lived and presided over the exiled community. He must have felt some communion with the Tibetans there, although many of them were by then at least a generation away from their self-exile. Many had never lived in Tibet.

The poet was allowed to enroll in the schools and he studied Tibetan, English, and Chinese. For eight years he was there, living in student housing facilities that were, for all intents and purposes, homeless shelters. Lying in bed at night, he allowed his thoughts to wander. He tried to convince himself that he was home, but he longed for Tibet. He belonged to Tibet. His mind was forever chasing the long-cherished dream of a free Tibet. Hopelessness was not part of his character. He was convinced he would some-day see the land he left behind.

He was, in fact, encouraged to return to Tibet by others. The increasing presence of Chinese in Tibet, coupled with the persis-tent fleeing of Tibetans for India, continued to dilute the native Tibetan claim to the region.

In re-living his experience of walking through dangerous icy passes to reach India—his land seized, his monasteries razed, his prayers silenced—the familiar cry of "Free Tibet" from long ago came out of his repressed soul. He could not, would not, give up on his Tibet.

In the years away from his natal home, the poet had learned resourcefulness. Survival had depended upon it. He'd only made friends with those he could trust. Some might have thought him distant and aloof but, out of necessity, he had learned to be guarded. Even with his small circle of friends, he'd kept secrets, especially about his plans to return to Tibet.

For weeks, he played out in his head different scenarios for the trip through India toward the Nepali border. In his small arsenal of possibilities, there was a piece of paper that could be his means of transiting both India and Nepal. The poet never told me where he came by this travel document. I'd often thought about this and decided that I was glad I did not know.

With transit papers in place, the poet left India. Getting into Nepal was not a problem, but crossing into China was a different story. He was a returning escapee with what I presumed were forged papers. He told me of a premonition he'd had the night before he made his attempt to cross. A dream where he was questioned and detained. "We've been looking for you," said a man in charge at the border.

"Do you not realize that we will always find you, no matter where you try to go?"

The poet awoke in a cold sweat. He contemplated not going, but in the end, he knew he had to try. He could not stay in Nepal. When he arrived at the border he waited until a time when there was a horde of people in line to be processed, hoping the border agents would use less scrutiny. He stood in the Nepali line where he felt he had the best chance of being free of trouble. He had the transit paper of a Nepali and he had mentioned to me more than once that he could have passed for a Nepali.

A border agent who looked very much like the man in his dream—or was it just the poet's imagination?—paused over his papers for an agonizingly long time, inspecting them closely. The poet became certain that his premonition was coming true. He would be detained, taken away, thrown into a prison or worse. For one panicked instant, he contemplated turning and fleeing. He held himself together and, finally, the agent waved him through. He was free to continue. The poet walked across the long Sino-Nepal "Friendship Bridge," a rickety bridge over a deep gorge, toward Tibet, toward his beloved homeland.

Yes, the poet was free to cross, but what did freedom mean in Tibet? I had an uneasy sense as he related the story to me that he had never stopped having premonitions of being followed, of being watched, of being found. And it occurred to me that the poet was, in a sense, a symbol of Tibet, a metaphor for a free heart in a not-free place.

It was extraordinary to listen to this young man—now about thirty years of age—re-live his life up to that point. But over several weeks, he would have even more to tell me. He came to my apartment from time to time, not so much to talk about his poetry, which had gotten repetitious, but to suggest we walk along the river so that he could tell me more of what was going on with him and his friends. I knew early on that nothing of a sensitive nature should be discussed inside my apartment. He always implied that he was on the sidelines and I never learned exactly what his friends were up to, nor, in truth, did I ever want to know. Why did he tell me the things he told me? Most probably, it was all talk, but even talk could be incriminating if he and his friends were outed. Eventually, it occurred to me that he told me things because he needed a friend. I was happy to be that for him.

CHAPTER 18

THE HOLIDAY INN: INTRIGUE, ROMANCE, AND SHENANIGANS

"A hotel should be a gateway to new adventures. In a hotel, you're not just a guest; you're part of the story."
—Unknown

With the coming of the opening up of Tibet to tourists in the mid-1980s, many people who never considered visiting Lhasa were, like refugees seeking exit visas in the classic film *Casablanca*, scurrying about trying to get the necessary permit, which could only be obtained in Chengdu, Sichuan, China—the gateway to Tibet.

Not everyone who wanted to make the trip would be able to get the travel document. It was not an easy trip to Lhasa, whose small airport was about an hour away from the city. First, one had to travel to British Hong Kong, then onto Chengdu. Then, the fortunate ones—through sheer luck, timing, and, of course (as in that same classic film), money—were able to obtain their entry documents. At this time, there were unscrupulous people who demanded extra money under the table. (The Peter Lorres and the Sydney Greenstreets.) But others had to wait in Chengdu. *And wait...and wait... and wait...*

The lucky ones eventually found their way to the Holiday Inn, run by several ex-pats and the only international hotel in Tibet. The hotel was part of Chinese leader Deng Xiaoping's "Open Door Policy." Deng was trying to bring tourism into China. In Beijing, Holiday

Inn opened the first-ever international hotel in China in 1984. This was followed by the Holiday Inn Lhasa in 1986.

The latter had actually opened the year before as simply the Lhasa Hotel, and it was no small enterprise. It was five stories, had 468 rooms, and boasted a staff of 450. But the Chinese, with zero experience in running large hotels, struggled with even the most basic of innkeeping skills. Alec Le Sueur, in his wonderful account of his time working as the hotel's sales and marketing manager in *The Hotel on the Roof of the World*, writes of rooms being given away to the friends of staff members; long stretches of time when the front desk would remain vacant, despite lines of people either looking to check in or check out; overflowing toilets; and room bills going uncollected due to shoddy record-keeping. After six months or so, the Chinese finally decided their experiment in hotel management wasn't working and brought in the Holiday Inn folks. Even still, they kept their own people involved. Holiday Inn staffers had Chinese counterparts whose watchful authority they were ultimately under, adding a sort of Big Brother feel to their work.

When I'd arrived in Lhasa, I knew only what I'd read in travel books at the library and Books-A-Million. I assumed I'd be more or less isolated from fellow Westerners. But then the Lhasa Holiday Inn jumped out at me from a page of the *Lonely Planet*. Here was a place that Westerners gravitated to. Lhasa was not the crossroads to anywhere. Tibet was the final stop, unless one wanted to fly from Lhasa to Kathmandu, but that twice-weekly flight was suspended during the winter months.

Little did I know after my initial visit to the hotel, soon after my arrival in Lhasa in August of 1990, that it would play such a significant role during my three years in Tibet. We newly arrived ex-pats met a few of the permanent staff at the hotel the first week of our arrival. All good so far. It was all suits and ties except for the German chef of the Hard Yak Café. The general manager, another German, left his posting a month after we arrived, so I had no feelings about him one way or another and didn't miss his presence. This would change when the replacement, an Italian named Ernesto Barba, arrived a month later.

The Hard Yak Café had opened at the Holiday Inn a few months before I arrived. The main attraction for some of us were the yak burgers, served with American-style french fries. Yak meat has little fat, so the burgers were somewhat dry. Ketchup saved the day. The rest of the menu I cannot remember because I never ate anything else but the yak burger. In fact, the Hard Yak Café was above my pay grade; there was no more fat in my teacher pay than in the burgers, so most times I ordered only the fries.

Carol, the café manager, was Han Chinese and ran an efficient establishment, except that she wasn't able to nab the scoundrels who snatched the spoons, one of several unsolved café capers. One could buy small spoons in the marketplace, but they were inferior to those at the hotel.

My favorite waiter was David, another Han Chinese, who was in his late twenties. He had a dry sense of humor and never, ever smiled to indicate that he was trying to be funny. Maybe he was oblivious to how he came across to customers. On one occasion, when Mina and I ordered the hotel-made ice cream, David practically came unglued as he gushed, "Don't order that. No good!" Then he explained that it had turned sour, but the kitchen hadn't wanted it to go to waste. He looked out for us. Four years later, I would meet David at the Chengdu Holiday Inn. He had become one of the restaurant's managers. Good for him. Same old David.

During those early days, there were scholars, researchers, educators, incognito journalists, and adventurers at the hotel. But not everyone who entered the hotel had honorable intentions. Plainclothes police who roamed around belied these paradisical qualities. The Holiday Inn actually teemed with political passion.

The Hard Yak Café and the companion Himalayan Bar were each an oasis in an intriguing and mysterious place, a paradise far removed from the hustle and bustle of the home countries of the visitors. Heinrich Harrer, the man who wrote *Seven Years in Tibet*, his famous memoir of the time he'd spent in Tibet in the 1940s, came back to visit at one point. Mount Everest explorers came to stay at the hotel one time, too. It was after their climb. I heard about the climbers later and wondered why I hadn't seen them myself until I learned that they'd spent most of their time celebrating their achievement by getting plastered in the Himalayan bar, reliving their conquest with stories that gained both momentum and volume as the drinks continued to flow. I heard from hotel staff that there was talk of fumigating the place as the climbers had apparently gone directly from the mountain to the bar, bypassing sorely needed showers.

The Holiday Inn would not have been a five-star hotel anywhere else in the world, but compared to the alternatives in Lhasa, it surely qualified. For those with high expectations of luxury in Shangri-La, there was disappointment. The first unpleasant experience was often altitude sickness. Acclimating to 12,000 feet was problematic. Some of the Holiday Inn employees would place bets on how long it would take for a newly arrived tourist to succumb. Rooms were equipped with an oxygen apparatus for the guests who needed it, and many did. Mina and I never bet on anyone to fall victim, but we were always thankful for a few of the guides we knew who would allow us to use the meal tickets of the poor souls who couldn't keep anything down. We tried not to show our eagerness when inquiring about the health of the tourists.

The high-ceilinged lobby was quite cool in the summer months, and turned into an icy freezer during the winter. The location of the front desk was in a terribly unfortunate place, just to the side of the large entrance, where piercing, gale-force winds would race through. The employees behind the desk wore parkas and fingerless gloves.

There would be no lolling about in any of the seating areas during the winter months but, then again, few people would stay in the hotel during the winter anyway. The few who came were usually those who were in Tibet doing research or, perhaps, on a photography venture.

A short distance from the lobby were the WCs. Guests were overjoyed to find Western toilets among a few Asian-style squatty potties. Even in the warmer months, this "necessary" room was quite cool. To add to the institutional grayness, the ladies might have welcomed the lovely Pepto-Bismol colored toilet paper that might or might not have been present in each stall. In truth, one could never be certain if there would be any in a crucial moment. For the hotel's staff, the toilet paper disappeared mysteriously too many times to be ignored. They hired a member from the landscaping crew, complete with an official-looking uniform, to stand guard. No doubt the impressive uniform came with a salary increase. I'm not sure if the plan ended the toilet paper caper, but it certainly signaled to every guest that the hotel intended to wipe out this particular petty potty crime.

You ended your visit to the WC by washing your hands in the icy cold water and then, due to an absence of paper towels, drying them with an electric, wall-mounted air dryer that blew forth—you guessed it—cold air. Even in the warmer months, using all the patience you could muster, the blast of cold air would take upwards of five minutes to render your hands suitably dry, or at least less wet than they were. On several occasions, I witnessed Tibetan women gliding their wet fingers through their long hair, which seemed to do the job.

As one might imagine, running the hotel in such a strange land was quite a challenge for the hotel management. Logistical problems were constant. Supplies came infrequently over the rugged and sometimes steep roads that led to the hotel. There were rock and mud slides. Simple things, like towels, for instance, might arrive weeks after being ordered.

Management of employees was another problem. The locals hired for staff positions didn't always understand the Western business mindset. It was not uncommon for everyone at the Hard Yak to take their lunch break at the same time. And the exact time that guests wanted to eat lunch! Meanwhile, the people at the front desk were notorious for losing room keys. Keys were put in a box with corresponding numbers, but it seemed that most times the keys were placed into the wrong boxes. The janitorial chores were always entertaining to watch. The lobby floor was washed by mop after large buckets of water were splashed indiscriminately about and with little regard for where a guest might be standing. Bedsheets were dried by the sun, despite the presence of commercial dryers, and you'd often see a mosaic of them stretched out on the grass on the west side of the building.

Hiring and firing were subject to governmental regulations. Management needed permission to dismiss someone and it didn't always come easy. In fact, a Tibetan official by the name of Mr. Jig Me was appointed to be deputy general manager of the hotel.

With the passing of months, the hotel would serve as my home away from home, my entertainment, and even a place of employment for two days. One day, one of the ex-pats at the hotel summoned me to see Mr. Barba, the hotel's new general manager. Ernesto Barba, probably in his sixties, was suave and always impeccably dressed. As it happened, I had met him before, quite by accident. We had been on the same plane traveling from Chengdu to Lhasa the previous September and he had invited me to share the Holiday Inn's Land Rover for the trip into the city.

The hotel's food and beverage manager had made Mr. Barba aware of my baking expertise. He and the sales and marketing manager had gone one evening to Mina's apartment for an Italian meal I had cooked. Also, on a few occasions, I had taken some baked sweets to the hotel for some of the ex-pats.

Mr. Barba's office was located in a building behind the hotel. I'd had little interaction with him since our trip from the airport and was bewildered by his request to see me. Mr. Barba was rather imperious and aloof, slightly intimidating. He had a well-known temper, too, and was by then being referred to around the hotel (behind his back) as "The Crazy Italian." Nevertheless, I determined that I owed him nothing and decided to go into the meeting loose and confident.

After some small talk, Mr. Barba revealed the purpose of his summons. He had had a long history of hotel management in various cultures in Europe and Asia. He'd been adept at marketing and publicity and had been looking for a way to bring tourists to the hotel in the middle of winter. As it was, the standard operational procedure was for the hotel to simply stop heating the empty rooms when the occupancy dropped below twenty percent, which was pretty much all winter long. Now, what lengths would a hotel located on the roof of the world go to in order to keep warm during a Tibetan winter? Mr. Barba had been thinking outside the box. He had come upon an idea he was sure would be a hit for the hotel: a Miss Tibet contest, a not-to-be-missed extravaganza.

It would turn out that Mr. Barba's brainstorm would not be without controversy, and on two fronts: cultural and political. A beauty pageant? We were in a conservative land, a conservative *communist* land. Now, it was well known throughout the hotel that Mr. Barba hated the commies and he intended to have some fun with the contest. What could possibly go wrong?

At any rate, as part of the extravaganza, held over several days, there would be a special dinner that Mr. Barba dubbed "Six Flags Over Jerry." Jerry was the chef and he was from Texas. Mr. Barba explained to me that the dinner would be Texas-themed and he wanted me to create some desserts for the occasion. Another Tibetan experience, I thought. How could I say no?

Mr. Barba offered to pay me for my effort. With little time for contemplating what I'd want for remuneration, I came up with the idea of him allowing my class of '92 a graduation party in the Hard Yak Café, complete with Yak burgers and fries, and dancing in the disco. He consented to my terms and I politely asked if maybe we should put the agreement in writing.

"*Siamo amici*," he smiled. "We are friends. What need have we for a contract?" And so I dropped the matter, choosing to maintain cautious optimism that Mr. Barba would hold up his side of the bargain.

In the meantime, I needed to hold up mine. When the day arrived for me to begin my short-term job as pastry chef, Chef Jerry showed me around the kitchen. Chef Jerry apparently had some faith in my abilities because later on, looking to entertain a gathering of the guests for the festivities, he decided he'd like to serve eggnog and came to me seeking a recipe. I remembered us making eggnog on the farm, where I'd be offered some before my father and older brother would spike it with whiskey. Like the pro that I pretended to be, I passed along a recipe to Chef Jerry, making sure to emphasize the one instruction I was certain about: do *not* use raw eggs, I warned him, especially the eggs around Lhasa.

Anyway, for my pastry chef assignment for "Six Flags Over Jerry," Chef Jerry introduced my two Tibetan helpers in the kitchen, a male and female pastry worker, and then gave me a tall hat and white jacket. In that moment, I fancied myself a Tibetan Julia Child. Then Jerry introduced me to the Tibetan chef, the only person in the pastry area who could speak any English. "Go to him if you need anything," Chef Jerry said, and then he left the kitchen and I was essentially on my own.

I proceeded to do the best I could with what I had to work with. First, I began to gather everything I needed to produce both apple and chocolate empanadas (or fried pies, as we referred to them down on the farm). This wasn't easy. The first thing I noticed missing was cinnamon. Cocoa powder was also absent. Fortunately, the few times I had traveled to Hong Kong, I'd brought back baking supplies. I lived to bake. From my personal stash, I was able to make up for the shortfall.

Working in a strange kitchen made progress slower than I would have liked, but the apples were, nonetheless, eventually peeled, cut up, and cooked slowly until done. The aroma wafted in the air to every crook and cranny, the delectable cinnamon mingling with the apples, a scent that might cause any chef to swoon, even the real Julia Child.

The thickened concoction had to be cooled and refrigerated until the next day when the three of us would continue this phase of production. In the meantime, I mixed up my own recipe for the pastry, to be ultimately fashioned into empanadas. The next day my aides and I met to finish the apple pies, each of us at different stations, rolling and cutting circles to be filled with the apple mixture. The aides worked like pros, which, I suppose, they were. A few trays were soon ready for baking and it was time to put them into the oven, a commercial version that I found myself unsure about. How accurate was the temperature setting? I stationed myself beside it and watched over it like a hen protecting her chicks.

With all the pastry baked without any catastrophe and a thin glaze of icing applied, it was mission accomplished. Then it was on to the chocolate. Ooh the chocolate! I was hesitant to use my own cocoa powder, my Hershey's container of veritable gold dust. It was a difficult decision: Hershey's, or the melted candy of the local Chinese wax-filled variety of chocolate? Part of me rejected the idea of donating my precious cocoa powder for a group of tourists I'd never see again. Another part of me wanted to protect my integrity as a (fairly) good baker. Oh, what a grave decision to be made! The latter won.

Hershey's could be replaced in time but integrity would be forever. If only all my decisions in Tibet could be this inconsequential.

An additional ingredient was needed: milk. Not locating any, I went to find the Tibetan chef but he was nowhere around. Neither was Chef Jerry and I had no choice but to try out my Chinese on one of my assistants. "*Nai fen*," I said with confidence, but all that was returned was a blank face. My assistant either couldn't understand Chinese or couldn't decipher my pronunciation. "*Nai fen*," I repeated, this time louder, as if volume had been the issue. Another blank face.

Then a lightbulb moment. The next attempt *had* to work. With the very best imitation of Daisy the cow, I loudly bawled out for all to hear, *Moo!,* all the while squeezing imaginary udders.

Success. Back on the farm, I would use the same action on a real cow and not get milk. This time, however, I got milk. We finished making the pudding and put it safely in the huge refrigerator, my work completed for the day.

Meanwhile, the guests for the Miss Tibet extravaganza were rolling in. A major part of Mr. Barba's plan had been to drum up publicity for the hotel by having the pageant covered by the media. This had presented a problem, however. Journalists at that time were not allowed into Tibet. Nevertheless, Alec Le Sueur had been dispatched to Hong Kong several weeks before to hold a press conference about the pageant at the Foreign Correspondents Club. There, he'd invited the journalists with the proviso that they could not declare they were journalists. Seventy-five "tourists" ended up making the trip to Lhasa—self-declared "housewives" and "teachers" and every other profession besides journalist.

The following night was the dinner, held in Chef Jerry's domain, the cavernous kitchen. A big, long table was set up. I'd been invited, not to dine with the guests, but to be recognized as the baker from Texas who produced the dessert. I was standing along a wall when

Mr. Barba introduced me and I gave a half-wave as the diners politely applauded, probably not giving a cow's udder as to who was responsible. Nevertheless, it was a good feeling. And all for a good cause.

As it turns out, that wasn't the only part of the deal I had made with Mr. Barba. He'd had one more request. He wanted me to supply a few of my female students to participate in an outdoor program by reading in unison some Tibetan poetry selected by Mr. Barba himself. This, too, was part of the Miss Tibet festivities. I had class the day of the reading, so I could not attend, but I coached the four young ladies many times both in my apartment and then out on a side street nearby. The street venue was to get them to practice their volume and enunciation and pace; I had no idea how far from the audience they'd be, but wanted to make sure they'd come across well.

The day of the reading I took some photos of the young ladies in their beautiful chupas and off they went. I tried to catch up after class, but, alas, arrived too late. Nevertheless, I was told they did very well and Mr. Barba was pleased. With my obligations out of the way, it was time for the main event—the pageant itself. In preparation, the hotel was a marvel of activity for such a quiet setting. The incongruous sounds of buzz saws and hammering took over as staff members constructed the stage, complete with an arched proscenium, and miscellaneous decorations for the ballroom where the pageant was to be held.

When the big night came, everyone was dressed in their best and there was excitement in the air. Or maybe it was apprehension. By this time, the government had become quite involved. They'd wanted to make sure the Miss Tibet pageant didn't make a mockery of Eastern culture. In fact, it was government officials who chose the contestants. The Tibet Cultural Bureau picked the girls and also selected the eventual winner, despite the seating of impartial "judges," who ended up pretty much doing nothing.

Nonetheless, the event was a fun-filled one. There were several warm-up acts including a Tibetan yak dance. And then came what I will always remember as the highlight of the evening's festivities, and perhaps the highlight of the whole week. Prior to the crowning of Miss Tibet was the awarding of Miss Foreigner. Chosen was a woman I had known named Mary-Ann Bishop, an American scientist who had been in Lhasa studying cranes. The prize? Mary-Ann's weight in yak cheese. Some of those buzz saws had evidently been employed to manufacture a huge set of scales, which were pulled into the ballroom via a horse-drawn carriage. Mary-Ann was made to sit on one scale while the yak cheese was piled onto the other. There was much applause and then the carriage started off, but not before the horse deposited a sizeable pile of what horses are known to deposit. Right there on the floor in front of the whole crowd. Now there was even more applause. And uncontrolled laughter. Mr. Barba was soon scurrying around frantically trying to find someone to clean up the mess, which elicited even more laughter. Finally, Mr. Barba located some poor soul who scooped it up to the raucous cheering of the crowd.

Miss Tibet was chosen soon afterward, but in light of the horse incident, the ceremony was a bit of an anti-climax. Nevertheless, we applauded as the contestants came out, all wearing different costumes from various parts of Tibet. One of the contestants was chosen as the winner, although exactly by whom and what means, I never did find out. Nor did it matter. A good time was had by all and the sight of Mr. Barba snapping into furious action to clean up the horse's contribution to the ceremony made the entire evening worthwhile.

It was even worth the fact that Mr. Barba ultimately reneged on his promise, conveniently forgetting what I had asked for. We had the graduation party, but I bore the cost.

Chapter 19

Never a Dull Moment

"A great hotel is like a great friend."
—Unknown

There was never a dull moment at the Holiday Inn. One day, Mr. Pinot, the hotel's food and beverage manager, approached Mina and me with his novel idea for feeding the next tourist crowd in the dining area. We agreed immediately with whatever wacky plan he had in mind when he agreed to our fee: a room for the night and hot showers. Thrown into the mix would be leftovers from the evening meal even though we knew we'd get the least desirable dishes. Chef Jerry, for instance, was known to disguise slices of Spam so they'd appear to be anything but Spam. Cover it with spicy red sauces and who would be the wiser? This didn't happen often, but there were times when supplies coming by truck from Chengdu didn't arrive on time. "On time" usually meant within a three-week window.

Our part in Pinot's scheme wasn't difficult, but perhaps somewhat demeaning, at least according to one feminist on the tour. But being in Lhasa for a long period of time sometimes called for a fun diversion from the day-to-day sameness of our living. We were given chef's hats and white coats to wear while sitting on stacked cushions under kidney-shaped tables that had holes cut out for our heads. Mina's table consisted of salads and my table was laden with desserts. We were coached to sit still with neutral facial expressions and unblinking eyes. Whenever a diner would come to the table to help themselves to a dessert or two, I'd say something such as, "Are you sure you need that extra dessert?" Or, perhaps, "Uh, uh, uh—isn't this your fourth time here?"

It turned out to be a fun time for all. Most of the diners were startled but would then have a good laugh. And demeaning or not, it was all worth it for the luxurious hot shower Mina and I cashed in on.

And then there was Mr. Barba's birthday party. It was low season at the Holiday Inn with only a smattering of guests. The ex-pats working there needed no better reason to entertain themselves; Mr. Barba's birthday was the perfect excuse.

I could only imagine the hilarious planning session, with each of them coming up with one over-the-top suggestion after the other, finally deciding on the *coup d'état.* The hotel's carpenters were given their instructions for constructing and painting the evening's surprise, and their completed object was kept under wraps until the appointed hour.

In the meantime, Mina and I were again offered a free room since the late hour of the party's anticipated end meant we wouldn't get back to campus before the gates closed. Another opportunity for a hot shower.

When the evening of the gala arrived, Mina and I rode up in our recently washed bicycles to the guard shack in the forecourt of the hotel. The "valet" on duty seemed not to have gotten the message that there was to be a gala, as he was wearing the same outfit he wore at all other times. We tipped him—actually a bribe—to make sure our "limousines" would make it through the night. Bicycle theft was rampant.

Then we entered the disco to find it adorned with revolving disco lights. Thankfully, it wasn't a black-tie event, so we were fine in our clean shirts, sweaters, and trousers. And for me, a full bath, as it was a Saturday! We chose our seats in one of many raised seating areas along the walls, positioning ourselves around a low table in order to get the best view of the festivities. Some of the invited guests were familiar to us, ex-pats from several NGOs and a few returning guests of the hotel. Notably absent were the local government officials who were barely tolerated on other occasions.

Then Mr. Barba entered with much applause. Let the party begin! The MC, who *was* wearing a black tie, welcomed everyone as corks were popped and champagne began to flow. Mr. Barba listened to several tributes, some serious, but some on the order of a celebrity roast. There were Tibetan songs sung by attractive young Tibetan women, and, with a seemingly unending supply of the bubbly, guests were in high spirits. Besides that barley beer, I'd never had an alcoholic drink—honestly—and I figured I'd be okay with my innocent flute of bubbles. Quite lovely, really. The waiter came by again and again and each time it was even better than the last.

Finally, the anticipated main event. Double doors opened with pre-recorded trumpets sounding a salute. In rolled a three-tiered, gaily painted birthday cake which made a lap around the dance floor before coming to a stop in the center. Within a few seconds, a hinged top opened and up popped Ellen from sales, clad in her two-piece bathing suit. This produced much whooping and hollering. I do believe that this was the only interruption in the delivery of rounds of champagne. Ellen saluted the birthday boy with an original song followed by her own version of "Happy Birthday" ala Marilyn Monroe.

Soon, the champagne was flowing again. I don't remember much about the ending of the party, but I imagine it was over somewhere around midnight. Mina and I claimed our promised room but first had to go through the check-in ritual at the front desk, handing over our passports. For some reason, I thought all of this was super funny and couldn't stop laughing. With this completed, Alec and Pinot led us upstairs to find an empty room that was guest-ready. They had to open several before finding one. Apparently, this, too, was hilarious and the guys had to keep shushing me in the hallway. Meanwhile, I tried to explain that the building was moving. Later, I realized I'd drunk too much of the bubbly. So *that* was what being "lit" felt like.

Monday came and everything was back to normal for me and, perhaps, a "crazy" normal for the hotel ex-pats. Just more fun times at the Holiday Inn.

CHAPTER 20

THE GENTLE GIANT

"You, sent out beyond your recall, go to the limits of your longing. Embody me."
—Rainer Maria Rilke

Sonam and I were at the middle of the snowy bridge that spanned the Lhasa River when a lone PLA soldier strode toward us from one of the two sentry posts located at either end of the bridge. We'd been taking pictures from the bridge of the newly fallen snow with the mountains and river as a backdrop. Contrary to what one might imagine, snow was a novelty in Lhasa.

We knew what the soldier's approach to us could mean. In China, there seemed to be a rule for everything. Sonam told me not to say anything. All I could do was to watch the scene play out before me. Sonam, his brow furrowed, his feet shifting one to the other, forced a nervous smile and greeted the soldier. Their eyes focused on my small camera. They talked back and forth as they moved away from me. Finally, Sonam turned and told me that I'd have to give up the film. It could have been worse; the guard had initially wanted the camera too. Had it not been for my friend's negotiating, it would have been taken. The Chinese law? No taking pictures of bridges.

As we left the bridge, I could tell Sonam was worried. He didn't talk much on the way back to the campus. I apologized for the unsettling incident, for it had been my idea. I imagined he was thinking of possible repercussions with his employment at the university as a Tibetan instructor. What one might imagine as a trifling incident could be brought to the attention of Sonam's employer and seen as an embarrassment—the losing of face, perhaps.

I'd met Sonam in the foreign language department after the start of the fall semester. Someone introduced us, but it was someone outside that department, for no one in the department could speak English. Sonam requested permission to come to my classes and would sit in the back of the room with a few other instructors. I was happy to have him. He joined the first-year class, the new students. Like most of them, Sonam was shy; even his slightly lopsided smile was shy. Some of the students referred to him as "fat uncle," but he wasn't fat by American standards.

Unlike the others, he rarely missed a class. I always wondered what he wrote in his notebook. He never spoke in class and would leave by the back side door before I could ever talk to him. How would I ever get to know him?

One day, I was determined to speak to Sonam before he had time to escape. With eyes looking downward, a nervous smile, and with a few students helping him, he did make an attempt to converse with me in English. Later, I suggested to the students sitting near him to speak with him in English, even though their level was low. Sometimes I wondered who was the most uncomfortable, for some of my students could have been Sonam's students.

Weeks turned into months and Sonam was still attending Speaking and Listening class. He communicated with me more than ever and I thought it would benefit him to practice English while biking with me around Lhasa. He accepted. It benefited me, as I'd gained another biking buddy and male companionship to boot. He enjoyed the outings as much as I did. Most of our trips were to the Barkhor where he would dicker with a merchant for an item I might want. After I indicated the item to Sonam, I acted the lone, disinterested "looker only," then walk away and let him bargain. He was my dealmaker, a typical Tibetan with learned skills. I never minded bargaining alone for small stuff, for it was fun. I dickered once with Sonam looking on. All involved were laughing as it was great entertainment.

All the while, Sonam's English was steadily improving and this promoted his self-confidence. The bike outings became less frequent, but there were other opportunities for his company. Occasionally, on a Saturday, I'd stop by for a short visit. There were no phones to announce my coming and one day I interrupted his reading of Buddhist scripture. This actually turned out to be an opportunity for me to tell him about the Holy Scripture. He didn't ask any questions outright, but maybe they were left unsaid.

One Saturday, visiting unannounced, I found Sonam about to eat Tibetan noodles and he invited me to join him. Of course I said yes, even though I felt I was intruding. Somewhere I'd heard that placing your feet under someone's table tended to go a long way toward becoming friends. Tibetans were an accommodating people, people who would never make a guest feel unwelcome.

Sonam's house was a one-room structure with his sleeping quarters separated by a curtain. His living area had two pieces of Tibetan furniture suitable for beds and a few straight-backed wooden chairs. A wok apparatus sat on a table near some cabinetry and was the only sign of a kitchen. Like most Tibetans, Sonam didn't own a refrigerator. Otherwise, the place was stocked with odds and ends and to any Westerner, Sonam might have looked like a hoarder. Someone with a minimalist decorating style could have well gone nuts with claustrophobia.

Being the gracious host, Sonam had already placed my steaming bowl of noodles on the small square table and shoved an extra chair over by the time I'd accepted his invitation. I gave Sonam an A+ for his finesse in elevating the common noodle into an extraordinary dish with yak meat and an unusual flourish of spices.

The chef ate with gusto, slurping every bite. No doubt, it would have been good manners to slurp in appreciation of the cook's effort, but I couldn't bring myself to betray the eating mores of my Western culture. Sonam noticed. "You no make noise when you eat," he said. I laughed and attempted to explain Western eating etiquette. Eating etiquette be damned, the meal ended and I couldn't have enjoyed it more had I been in the swankiest restaurant. Me, I'd have only added white table linens and a candelabra to set the scene.

Not long after that, I received an invitation to see Sonam's new TV. He was grinning from ear to ear when I arrived at the appointed time. I'm sure he made his purchase after having saved up for a long time. As with many items bought in Tibet, or anywhere in China for that matter, labels seemed to add a certain amount of prestige. And so it was with Sonam's TV. There it was, and there it would stay for the rest of my time in Lhasa: The Label, covering part of the screen.

There were labels on the sleeves of men's suitcoats, too, and there they would persist for, presumably, the life of the material. Sonam's did. I wondered if there was a law like the "this tag can't be removed" law in evidence on mattress labels in the US. Did anyone ever think of taking them off? Apparently, it wasn't a concern. Under Sonam's suit jacket, he wore a wine-colored vest every day except on the days he would wash and dry it. Like most Tibetan men, he wore something like long johns under his pants for most of the year. I know this for certain, for parts of them crept out from underneath. Tibetan men typically had money for one set of clothing, the two-piece suit that was their everyday wear. The only difference would be that in very cold weather, the suitcoat would be exchanged for a heavy jacket.

At any rate, he was proud of his TV. We watched a while, talked a little, and added to our growing friendship.

"Good morning, Merdis Laoshi." This was the polite and expected way of addressing any teacher. "Teacher Meredith." Tibetans had difficulty pronouncing the *th* sound. Sonam had rarely addressed me as *Laoshi*, so I was somewhat surprised to hear it.

We had bumped into each other that morning outside the teaching building. Sonam had finished teaching his early Saturday morning class and I was on my way to check for mail.

"Good morning, Sonam," I replied. "How are you this morning?"

"*Haoda*. Oh! Er...very good." A small slip-up that came with an embarrassed, apologetic grin.

The conversation went this way and that, but, in time, over the years, I would begin to imagine that it ultimately went in a direction that would lead me to a very special time in a very special place. A fantasy? Perhaps. But perhaps more an imagined manifestation of a secret longing. A fulfillment of an inner quest. A dream of a journey that I'd always yearned for.

And yet somehow more than a dream:

With his awkward greeting over, Sonam continued with something even more awkward. He wanted to know if I would go on a bike ride with him that afternoon. Was he asking me out on a date? I smiled to myself and later wondered what courage it must have taken to ask me even though we were becoming more comfortable in one another's company. He was looking me squarely in the eyes when he'd talk to me now. Still, I knew it didn't come easily for him. And I had no idea what the local customs were when it came to male/female relationships. Were the eyes important somehow? Did they signify a meaning that was lost on me? There were many things I was unaware of, except for one thing: there was a spark between us whenever we met.

As Sonam described his plans for the ride, it occurred to me that he must have been thinking about it for a while. Maybe our bumping into each other wasn't so accidental. He told me it would take an hour or more to arrive at our destination—a small community he'd visited when he was much younger. We would meet at one o'clock at the opening of the fence close to the bridge spanning the Lhasa River. And be sure to take something to drink, he advised. It was late June and it would be hot.

Back at my apartment, I assembled the required items for my backpack: Jinli Bao, lots of tissue of the WC variety, sunscreen, a small, damp hand towel enclosed in a large zip-lock bag (from the US), first-aid items, and a candy bar and packaged crackers. All these things seemed essential, even though we'd be gone for only a few hours. No need for a light jacket, for I'd be wearing a shirt with sleeves for protection from the high-altitude sun's rays. My usual outdoor attire consisted of jeans and athletic shoes, so I was all set.

Getting ready for our ride, I found myself feeling like a schoolgirl. In my school years (and even beyond my school years, for that matter), I'd actually had few dates. Dates I did have as a teen were sometimes without my parents' knowledge. I would stay a night with my best friend, whose parents were more lenient than mine, and my date would take place from there. So there I was, getting fidgety over a bike ride. But, really, the only distinction between this bike outing and others we'd taken around the Barkhor was the distance. So why should I be thinking of it differently?

Nevertheless, it didn't feel the same as our prior times together. In fact, I began thinking about how it might be perceived. My placement at the school signified to the administration that I had excellent character. The sending agency in the US had a reputation that was well-respected in this regard and I aimed to do my part to uphold it. My values were the values of my parents and grandparents, after all, and those were strong. But I knew it wasn't just a question of my values. It was the perceptions of others about my moral character through my actions. Was this bike ride appropriate? A single man and a single woman riding off together for such a long ways?

Appropriate or not, the time had come to meet Sonam. The broken fence wasn't far and I gave myself plenty of leeway to make sure I wouldn't be late. When I arrived, I assumed I was the first there. But I was wrong. On the other side of the fence and partially hidden by a bush, there he was, grinning as he spotted me. Evidently, Sonam didn't want to be late either, the first Tibetan I'd known who had a decent sense of time. I was touched that he apparently thought the bike trip special enough to warrant his punctuality.

We walked our bikes down a slight decline to reach the bridge that would take us across the river where our mystery trip would begin. A few moments later, I crossed my own personal Rubicon, though I wouldn't realize it until much later. We headed west on a familiar and narrow gravel road that hugged the river and mimicked its course curve by curve.

Before long, I felt as if I were being led down the road on a beguiling journey. The sun was warm on my face and the whisper of a breeze caressed my body as the wheels of our bikes created the slow rhythm of our movement. I wanted my spirit to feel everything of this enchanting valley on the roof of the world, surely one of the most stunning valleys in Tibet.

Looking to the north, we could see large birds floating effortlessly, having ascended upward, their stretched wings trapping the hot air from the sunbaked earth below, propelling the birds higher and higher as they rode the thermals. I thought about their freedom and it gave me a peaceful feeling. And I felt gratitude for my gentle, caring friend having suggested we go on this outing, providing me the chance to experience entrancing, undiscovered places where my mind and senses could become awakened and alive. Maybe it all served as a symbol of a pent-up passion for a life I'd never known.

In time, we turned south. Sonam never said how far we'd go in this direction, but I trusted that he knew how to get to the small community he'd set as our destination. This new road was much narrower than the other and would get narrower still as we proceeded. I felt as if we were in another realm when I noticed the trees planted along the way. With very few houses this far out, I hadn't expected to see any and it made me happy to know that someone had taken the trouble to plant them.

As the early afternoon sun began sapping my energy, we took a break and rested in the shade of one of those trees and I had some of my Jianli Bao. These were the days before bottled water. It wasn't unusual for Tibetans to drink hot drinks on the hottest of days, and so Sonam uncapped his thermos and chugged down some of his sweet tea. He offered me some, which I politely declined.

We made rest stops often, obviously for my benefit as Sonam always seemed more than willing to put many more kilometers behind us before taking a break. It wasn't lost on me that we had begun riding side-by-side. Sonam never let on that he was allowing me to set the pace. Whenever I slowed, he slowed, and I was aware that his frequent glances at me were made to determine whether I needed a rest. I was to see this innate quality in understanding for the remainder of the trip.

During our stops, he often attempted to make jokes, a difficult thing in another language, especially if your lack of fluency precludes your sense of comic timing and proper punchline delivery. But I would laugh as if the point of the joke was always clear, even when it was far from it. Then Sonam, with a jeweled twinkle in his eyes that I would start to notice more frequently, would laugh in turn. I found myself smiling at his ever-increasing smiling face. Did he notice?

As we continued on, the small mountains we'd observed in the distance began getting closer and looming larger. The valley was still spread out as far as we could see, and soon we could view what at first seemed like a man-made ditch leading farther south in a serpentine fashion. As our trail neared the ditch, we could see running water. It was impossible to tell where it had sprung from, possibly from an underground spring emanating from some mountain. Isaiah 35:6 came to mind: *Water will gush forth in the wilderness and streams in the desert.*

But I had also learned enough about Buddhism by then to have a passing thought about the Buddhist idea of the interconnectedness of all things. We were observing the same water that had at one time flowed perhaps thousands of miles from where we were. Most certainly it had its genesis in the Himalayan mountains, beginning as a trickle of melting snow, the trickle becoming a stream, a waterfall, a creek. Ultimately it would become a part of one of three mighty rivers in Southeast Asia. And where would it go from there? Even if it evaporated, it would return eventually, falling somewhere on the earth to become one with the flowing water of another stream or river or lake or ocean, all of which are connected. Lives are like that, it seemed to me in that moment. We flow through time and touch others and they touch us. Does it make sense to even speak of separation?

We continued and began seeing low-lying clouds creating halos around a few mountains. Soon we started seeing more trees, scrubby ones along with more slender trees, none of which were at all like the oaks and elms I was familiar with. Before long, we noticed animal poop, a certain sign that civilization was not too far ahead. Soon we could see planted fields, though we were still too far away to tell what was growing.

Then a small girl suddenly appeared from behind some trees, carrying a sling filled with dried, small limbs, apparently to be used as kindling. Sonam talked to her to find out where she lived. Then he helped her onto the seat of his bike to take her safely home. I walked my bike alongside and before too long, we came to her house and we found ourselves greeted by the family's huge mastiff, the home's formidable security system. Fortunately, with a loud shout from the child, the mastiff scampered away.

Until then, the entire valley we had biked through seemed to have a touch of loneliness about it, with the few houses we had come upon imbued with their own subtle melancholy. Around this house, it seemed peaceful. Other houses were nearby, families living harmoniously in a landscape that sustained them yet offered so little.

Away from the house, I saw newly molded bricks symmetrically placed on the ground drying in the sun, the same type of bricks that had built the houses. Not far from the bricks was a shed with a simple fence enclosing a small space that sheltered a few yaks. Later we learned there were pastures not far away where cows and yaks grazed, and dry grass was cut for fodder.

I thought of the pattern of the valley in which these people lived. The valley, dead and brown at times, then coming alive with greenness. The light of day making way for the darkness of night; the rains following droughts; sorrows and happiness intertwined—life's cycle, requiring patience, love, and gratitude from the inhabitants of this land.

The mother of the household, hearing strange voices, opened the door and greeted us with a smile as if she were expecting us. She was a beautiful young woman with long, shiny, raven hair in a plait encircling her head, and dressed in a traditional chupa. Sonam introduced us and the woman invited us to sit in the covered patio where she brought us sweet tea and biscuits. Entering the patio was like walking into a garden in full bloom. Flurries of blossoms scented the air. I noticed several potted geraniums perched on a ledge. This was an exhilarating surprise and a cheerful feeling came over me. A magical, secret garden of my dreams. My human emotions merged with nature and I felt transported, unlocking yet another layer of wonder. The few hours' time we would spend at that house felt to me like a symbol of my pent-up passion for a life I had never known.

The husband was away on business, the woman told us, but we were welcome to stay a while to rest. When she eventually went back inside her house to work, she allowed the child to remain to keep us company and to replenish our glasses of sweet tea. After we'd sat for too long, we rose to stretch our legs and allowed the little girl to guide us around. She took us to see the spring-fed ditch of water we'd seen from a distance. Pure, life-sustaining water, deep enough and moving fast enough to ensure it would remain cold. At one point, it cascaded down a great height, making for a beautiful waterfall. The girl and Sonam maintained an ongoing conversation, of which I was made a part through his spotty translation.

In the stream, I spied a beautifully rounded rock near the edge and reached my hand in to grab it. I could not have known it then, but that rock would be my metaphorical Sonam for years to come. I have it still: strong, hard edges softened by time.

The isolation of that part of the valley seemed to draw Sonam and me together in a way I would not have thought possible in Lhasa. Our eyes were not strangers anymore. In walking with the child and straying for a bit, we would eventually find our way back to each other's side, purposefully initiating a touch that was made to seem random. I think we both knew it wasn't.

In time, we began heading back to the house. When we reached the patio, we saw that the mother had replenished the container of sweet tea and the plate of biscuits. She insisted on filling Sonam's almost depleted thermos and then it was time to say goodbye—*ka li shu*, and thank you—*to duo chay*.

As was the custom with guests, our hostess walked us as far as the outer perimeter of the property and said goodbye. But the little girl strolled with us almost to where we had first met. I gave her a hug, which wasn't a custom, and bid her goodbye with a sadness I hadn't expected. There was sadness on her face too.

I'd always heard that the time spent on a return trip seems shorter than the outward journey, but I was hoping in this case, it would not be true. I wanted my time with Sonam to stretch out longer. As we made our way back, I noticed that our biking pace had certainly slowed down, as if we both were of the same mind.

When we reached a point about an hour's ride from when we'd begun, we spotted something ominous in the distance. A storm was brewing, with darkening clouds headed in our direction. We knew we couldn't outrun the storm. We were too far from Lhasa, yet too far along to make it back to the little girl's house. The electrical storm would soon be upon us. Sonam mentioned a cave he remembered from his youth when he and his brother had explored in the area and he believed it was worth trying to find.

We rode from one mountain base to another for a frantic half hour, all the while keeping our eyes on the approaching storm with its rolling black clouds and bolts of lightning. Lightning had always terrified me. With each flash, I was sure I'd be the target. Soon, rain began to fall, lightly at first. *Please, please, God, let us find the cave.* Meanwhile, I felt sorry for Sonam. His usual placid demeanor had turned into an anxious countenance. Then the rain increased in its intensity, the drops feeling like needles on my exposed skin. Soon it was a deluge. My small-brimmed, cloth hat and everything I had on was getting soaked, my shoes squishy.

Sonam soldiered on as I tried to keep up. Finally, he looked back in my direction and shouted something that I had trouble initially deciphering in the thunderous cacophony of the storm, but then determined to be good news. He thought he'd found the cave. The darkness from the storm made it difficult for him to be sure. We left our bikes at the base of the small mountain and began carefully to negotiate the now slippery rocks and boulders to reach the small opening about thirty feet upwards. Sonam yelled to me to hold on to the back of his vest so I might keep my balance but in doing so, I made it more difficult for him as he clambered up. Too, I didn't have "Tibetan lungs." It was difficult for me to climb without having a rest-stop every few feet. But with our refuge near, I forced myself to keep going.

Finally, we came upon it. Later, I would always refer to it as "our" cave. It would be much more than even this.

View of mountains from university building, Lhasa

Horse power—getting the job done

Gathering kindling, Bayi

Quite possibly a grain harvester

Shephardessses in the hills of Bayi

Sonam, wife and baby

CHAPTER 21

THE CAVE

"If I share with you my dream, you become part of my dream."
—Tibetan proverb

Gaining access to the cave proved dangerous. Loose rocks rested above the small opening and we dislodged a few of the smaller ones as we stooped to enter. Once inside this dank, musty, uncharted void, our eyes adjusted to the semi-darkness but we could not see far enough in to tell how deep the cave went. We moved forward a short distance so that I could stand. Sonam was too tall to straighten up but we didn't dare go forward any more for we didn't know what creepy, crawly things might have called the cave home.

Fumbling around, Sonam found a place where we could sit with a smooth wall for our backs to lean upon. Intermittent flashes of lightning were the only illumination. But regardless of whatever negative thoughts I might have initially had about the cave, it was to be our sanctuary, our refuge from the pounding, cold rain and the frightening bolts of lightning that terrified me with their deafening cracks of booming thunder.

Now we had our soaked clothing to deal with. The temperature would certainly drop as the night wore on. I'd been shivering since before we'd even reached the cave and now the thought of hypothermia was alarming me. Sonam, ever so delicately, suggested that it would be wise for me to take my outer shirt off. The time had come when we had to think of our safety instead of propriety. He opened his backpack and pulled out a small hand towel and asked permission to begin drying my hair, which was dripping water onto my shoulders and down my back. If I had not been so miserable in my cold, wet state, I would have regarded his offer as a most romantic gesture. Or I might have thought it to be a gesture of humility from one human being to another, a biblical gesture even.

With the hair drying sufficiently done, Sonam pulled out a lightweight zip-up jacket from his pack and told me to put it on. I protested at first, wondering how he would stay warm, but he would hear none of it. I put it on while Sonam removed his sleeveless vest and then his outer long-sleeve shirt, leaving him with a thin undershirt. Lastly, we took off our wet shoes and socks.

With this accomplished, Sonam took from his pack the hot tea that our lovely hostess had given him, offering it up to me first. No liquid ever tasted and felt so good as that initial cup of tea. It provided warmth with each re-fill. But then there was the inevitably long cold night to think about. How would we stay warm enough to stave off hypothermia?

My gentle giant agonized and apologized over our predicament, placing the blame wholly upon himself. Seated next to him, I tried to make him see that it was merely a normal occurrence of nature and that he could not have known beforehand. With this reassurance, he reached for my hand, declared it to be icy cold, then began warming it between his two hands. I felt in that moment an unexpected warmth, an electrical current flowing between us. Perhaps it had been there all along.

Sonam respected me with the same respect he would have had for a family member. I knew this intuitively. And I respected Sonam. I trusted him innately and I would find my feelings growing deeper for him as the hours passed. Was it romantic love I was feeling? Was it platonic love, or spiritual love? We each had our boundaries, whether acquired through culture or religion or both. As I had grown older, my boundaries had become less static and more fluid. "Flare up like a flame and make big shadows I can move in," the poet Rilke wrote as a directive from God. My shadow. Had I purposely kept it small and controllable? Out of fear and self-doubt? The armor I chose to wear for protection had perhaps become too heavy, too restrictive. And yet what would that mean in this cave, with this man, on this night?

The worst of the storm passed, leaving infrequent flashes to lighten our small area for a few seconds at a time. Soon we would exist in total darkness, but the onset of night would be a prelude to another kind of light. The temperature continued to drop and we both knew we had to decide how best to warm ourselves, but the deciding wasn't going to be easy. Sonam was the colder with his wet undershirt still on—the last vestige of decorum. I took the initiative and told him that it had to come off. Then we agreed on the best way for each of us to endure the night. At first, we sat half-leaning on the cold wall as close as we could get to each other. With Sonam leaning forward, he turned toward me and enveloped me in a bear hug. Shortly after that, I insisted that he wear the jacket and then his embrace resumed. Our bodies were the only warmth we could share with one another and trying to convince myself that this was normal took great imagination. For Sonam too, I'm sure.

It wasn't long before we knew, even in the velvety blackness of the cave, that we were looking into each other's eyes, as if our eyes had transcended the darkness. Sonam would occasionally reach for my hands to warm them in his. At one point, he unzipped his jacket and with a few words and hand motions directed me to position myself as closely as possible in front of him in an attempt to wrap a part of me in his jacket. We tried to move about a tad to get more comfortable but finally decided that in order to get any sleep at all, we needed to go back to sitting side by side with our legs scrunched up to our bodies as much as possible.

Meanwhile, the electrical storm was both calming and electrifying. I unconsciously wanted to experience it, but at the same time, I wanted to run in panic to the darkest corners of the cave to escape it. The storm raged deep inside me as well, growing deeper in intensity. I closed my eyes and imagined the beauty of the lightning, even as it struck at my soul. Then it calmed me and I was able to experience my two worlds and come to see that they could co-exist, sparking a release of the tension and conflict that represented my life before the cave.

Sonam offered his shoulder for a pillow, which was better than I could have hoped for. Falling asleep was not easy. I tried to project my mind into a wonderfully warm scenario, hoping the attempt would result in my falling into a glorious, blissful sleep. The scenario included my yearning desire for that which I knew I would not have. I wondered if Sonam, too, was agonizing over his boundaries as I was. I knew he would be protective of mine, and I would safeguard his, and we would remain safe from ourselves. This would be a gift we would give to each other. A huge part of me ached to expand my boundary into oblivion but what of Sonam? It would be unforgivable if I were to be the cause of regret. We remained resolute, with just enough wisdom to see us through the night.

I cannot say when sleep finally came. I have a clear recollection of Sonam's warm breath caressing my face and neck before I succumbed to a glorious dream. Morning came with grief for leaving the dream behind, a dream that had had all the intensity of the storm. I wondered if Sonam had dreamed the same. I was conscious of daybreak, but dared not move or open my eyes. At some point in my sleep, my head had slipped down and with a seemingly automatic reflex, Sonam's protective arms kept me pressed to his bare chest where I could hear the soft, regular rhythm of his heartbeat, a sign that all was well.

With my eyes soon open in the pre-dawn light, I looked upward to steal a glimpse of my protector, my gentle giant. The last person I thought of as I drifted into that blissful sleep was the same person who was gazing down at me that morning. Neither one of us attempted to move. Instead, we took in each other's faces as if in a trance. A sense of well-being enveloped me as I was certain it had Sonam.

Something wonderful and almost inexplicable happened to me during the night through my dream. Years later, I would interpret it through the power of myth, remembering King Tantalus from Greek mythology. The king was imprisoned and punished for a misdeed against the gods and thrown into a dark place. (A cave, perhaps?) He was made to stand in a pool of water beneath a fruit tree with low-hanging branches. Whenever he reached for the fruit, the branches rose, keeping the fruit beyond his grasp. Whenever he bent down to get a drink, the water receded before he could cup it in his hands.

With the dream—a dream within a dream—I came to see the cave as a place of purification, a place of redemption where I could be forgiven for all the misdeeds of my life, a place where the rain would wash them all away. I also saw it as a place of tantalizing temptation, a place where two longings were in conflict but ultimately found peaceful co-existence. The lightning was as threatening thunderbolts from Mount Olympus, frightening me in order to get my attention and to move me forward. In my dream I felt liberated, at peace with myself. I could awaken now and expect to hear that still, small voice that had been so easy to ignore: "Am I not enough?" Now I had an answer.

Sonam and I gathered our belongings and left the cave, a bittersweet moment for each of us. With our clothing spread out on boulders awaiting the sun to dry them, we walked around for a bit to stretch our legs. The cold of that early morning hadn't yet receded so we found a place to sit and attempted again to keep warm with our body heat until we could be warmed by the sun.

Each of us seemed to be lost in the quietude of that moment, each attempting to make sense of our cave experience. I can only speak for myself. My exit from the cave was as a delivery from a cocoon. I discovered a heavenly light that liberated me from the insidious darkness I had let in. I discovered a love that was to me as close to agape love as I could have imagined. I believed Sonam had come into my life to help me make the best version of myself. And my wish in that moment was for my dream to germinate into other dreams to warm me whenever I needed them through the rest of my life.

I trusted the deep silence in Sonam's eyes, the strength of his arms. And for those moments when his soul touched mine in that cave, I wanted to say to him, in terms of his own religion, that although we might not have been together in a past life, we had found each other in this one. And if he acknowledged the One True One, we could be assured of seeing one another in our next perfect life. But tears welled up in my eyes and words failed me. Sonam's words would fail him, too, so he spoke with his eyes. I listened with my heart and felt with my soul.

The rays of the sunrise were beginning to awaken the world to a new day, a beautiful sight with their soft glow growing in intensity behind the far eastern mountains until the grand moment when we could see the sun itself. We reveled in the warmth. With our clothes dried, we prepared to leave, descending carefully over and around rocks and boulders. Sonam hesitantly informed me that I'd have to return alone. Looking back, it's easy to imagine that he knew I'd have to return to my world by myself, that the path I was to take had to be mine alone.

It was hard to leave, but I knew that Sonam and I had already taken each other to a perfect and beautiful world. And now it was time to descend to the actual one. If we tried to live in that other world for good, it would only recede into the distance; it would have been as if we'd never been there at all. So we carefully made our way down to where we left our bikes. Sonam said that he would wait a short time after I left. Then he'd be along, following me at a distance in case I had a problem on my way.

We said our goodbyes, *ka li shu* and *ka li pei*, and then embraced. Sonam held my head in his hand and gently pressed it to his neck. His other hand was wrapped around my waist and we held each other tightly for quite some time, neither of us wanting the embrace to end, both of us knowing it would be our last.

Then we separated with an immediate longing that I would carry with me forever. I looked into Sonam's eyes once more, seeing that jeweled twinkle again, and I felt an uncanny sense of familiarity, as if I now knew this man soul to soul. It was a pull too pure to understand. I got on my bike and began to ride away. Not having gone far, with aching heart, I looked back to see my gentle giant for the last time. He waved and I waved back and I felt my eyes welling up again.

The return trip to Lhasa was a long one, as I didn't want it to end. After making a turn onto the main gravel road, I found myself nearing something I had not wanted to approach—the bridge. The tension was palpable as I slowly made my way across, this time a different crossing of the Rubicon. On the other side would be my self-reparation, my metanoia. Years later, I would read a quote by Nietzsche that would resonate when I thought of this moment: "No one can build you the bridge on which you, and only you, must cross the river of life. There may be countless trails and bridges and demigods who would gladly carry you across; but only at the price of pawning and forgoing yourself. There is one path in the world that none can walk but you. Where does it lead?"

As I crossed, I could not know whether Sonam was behind me, watching from a distance. But I felt his presence just the same, and, by extension, I felt an exquisite emptiness that filled my hours and days for some time to come, an emptiness that revisits me on occasion even to this day, haunting me on certain nights with its lonely sadness and its ineffable beauty.

CHAPTER 22

KA LI SHU

"You have been my friend. That in itself is a tremendous thing."
—E.B. White

The note was on my door when I arrived at my apartment after class. "You come to my old house this afternoon please. With my family. Have lunch. Be round at 11:30. Sonam." There was no time to RSVP as Sonam apparently believed I had no reason *not* to go. Just one more thing I had come to accept as part of the local culture. One's own plans must be put aside for the sake of the guest who comes to your door with a request.

Sonam came by at 11:30 as promised and off we went to his family's home. I had no idea what to expect for I had no idea what his family expected, nor what Sonam had told them about me. I did know that by then Sonam had a lady friend, a fiancée, whom I'd seen once not knowing who she was. She was at his house cleaning when I'd stopped by one day and after asking who she was, Sonam had smiled and said, "She is maid." A joke was implied, telling me that his English comprehension had more fully developed, but I didn't think very much about it at the time, leaving without really knowing the woman's role.

I wondered on the way to meet Sonam's family if they had said anything to him about our biking and picture-taking outings. I believed our age difference would be acceptable, almost fifty to thirty-five, but they would not have known my age anyway. Perhaps it was our teacher/student relationship that warranted the invite. At least that's what I hoped.

Sonam's family lived in a two-story structure of apartments built in a U-shape. The building housed somewhere around eight to ten families and the property was surrounded by a wall, accessible through a gate of large, double, wooden doors. A large courtyard served as a workspace for washing clothes, washing fruits and vegetables, and washing a passel of kids. The courtyard also served as a place of respite, albeit a noisy one at times. The elderly men passed time there playing mahjong and a Tibetan game using stones. I imagined women doing some gossiping there as they did their chores. There were several solar contraptions about for heating water, where kettles were hung until the boiling point had been reached.

In the courtyard for this little family get-together, there were more people than I had expected, all looking upon this foreign woman with kindness, but I nevertheless felt as if I were a panda in an American zoo, thinking me exotic in their narrow worldview. They looked me over. And over and over. In some fashion I was introduced, but I had no idea what was said. Murmurs were swirling all around me.

Then came the dreaded time for the meal when I might be forced to eat something I'd rather not. Thankfully, Sonam had informed the cook that I didn't eat meat or anything spicy, but that I'd eat vegetables and fruit. I had taught my students the word "vegetarian" early on, so as not to embarrass myself or any possible host. My students already knew that my favorite vegetable was potatoes, so I imagined Sonam also knew this for there were several potato dishes.

Much later, after I'd left Tibet, I would read on the internet that when a Tibetan man was serious about a foreign woman, he'd take her to the family home to meet his family, especially a brother if he had one. And I had, indeed, met a brother! Oh, my goodness, what had I done? But the visit ended uneventfully and I hoped I'd made a good impression as an American friend.

After I had become aware of Sonam's fiancée, I asked him frequently if he was married yet. He would always give a shy shake of his head. That went on until I would leave Tibet for what I thought to be forever. Later, I would find myself in eastern Tibet for another teaching assignment. "All roads lead to Lhasa."

Many of my former students would have scattered by then, some back to their hometowns where many would become English teachers, but some of them would remain in Lhasa. By word of mouth, some of them would visit with me.

Of course, Sonam was another one I wanted to see. Surely, he would have married by this time. I made my way to his little cottage through the open gate and up the path to his door. Sonam was overjoyed to see me. He invited me in and I discovered quickly that indeed he was very much married, for there was a baby in its mother's arms. Sonam introduced me to his wife and two-month-old son. Also present was the brother I had met. Everyone was in a celebratory spirit. I couldn't have come at a better time. As is the Tibetan custom, mother and baby do not go out until the second month, neither do they bathe, nor does anyone visit.

Sonam gathered the baby from his mother and cradled him in his arms for a while before asking if I'd like to hold him. Of course, I said I'd be delighted. While holding the little one in the crook of my arm, Sonam made a request of me. Would I give the baby an English name? I thought for a moment, then decided to name him "David." A Tibetan David. Along with the name, I offered a silent prayer that he would grow up to know God as the biblical David had.

A few years would pass after that and I would be back in Lhasa, having gone there from Chengdu where I was working. A young German man I met in a Western restaurant asked if I'd go to Lhasa to supervise the kitchen while his wife took their ill child back to

Germany. This couple were co-owners of a guest house, the Pentoc. He was willing to pay half my airfare, so I jumped at the opportunity to go back.

When I wasn't needed in the little restaurant kitchen, I'd wander around. The university wasn't far and I walked there one day to look up Sonam. No one lived in the small house anymore, so I had to ask around to find him. As it turned out, his little family had moved into a small apartment on campus. I found him at home with his small son, his wife being at work. We visited for a bit and before I left, Sonam went into another room and shortly came out with a hastily wrapped gift. It seemed to be a custom to offer a small gift to a friend who'd been away for some time, even if the person's presence was unexpected, thus entailing the wrapping up of a personal possession. Sonam chose a blank notebook to present to me.

As fate or fortune would have it, I would return again to Lhasa a few years after that. Not remembering where Sonam lived, I went to the Tibetan language department to see if he might be there. I asked a teacher where I could find him, saying his name and turning my palms up as indicating a question. He didn't speak English, but asked a passing teacher if she could help.

The passing teacher knew about Sonam.

"Oh, he died," she said simply.

I stood there for some time waiting for my brain to catch up to the blood-draining emotion that was coursing through my mind.

No one was there to console me, of course, so I left the building and walked as fast as I could, almost running back to the Yak Hotel where I was staying, trying to stifle what I knew would be coming. Alone in my room, I sobbed for my friend until there were no tears left.

Years later, on yet one more trip to Lhasa I would become determined to find someone who could tell me what had happened to Sonam. Then, and only then, could I let go of the weighty, unresolved, gnawing feeling of not knowing. Wei Hong, a woman from the university whom I'd known way back when, filled me in on Sonam's demise while visiting with me in the small lobby of the House of Shambhala, a boutique hotel located on one of the many alleyways leading to the Barkhor. Sonam, she told me, had died in a minibus accident. He and a few friends were off on a trip to celebrate his promotion to an administrative position. The bus went off the road down an embankment and rolled over, the driver and Sonam the only fatalities.

A young boy with no father. A wife with no husband. And me without my dear friend.

Ka li shu, au revoir, and goodbye Sonam Chimpei.

Chapter 23

Acclimating

"Everyone you meet is a part of your journey, but not all of them are meant to stay in your life. Some people are just passing through to bring you gifts, either blessings or lessons."
—Unknown

My two years' time teaching in Lhasa came to its ineluctable end. The final days were busy, what with student parties, including a very special graduation party for the Class of 1992. These days passed with me in a sad daze, saying goodbye not only to students, but also to some of my town friends. With many gifts from students and friends, packing became a monumental task.

The day before I was to leave, there was a knock on my door. To my pleasant surprise, it was the poet. We had kept in touch and I assumed he was there to say goodbye. Quickly, however, I saw that he was in distress. Before me was a frightened young man in a hurry. As it happened, the police had picked up his two friends and thrown them in jail. Now the poet was worried that he might be next. What he wanted from me was for me to write down my US address. I wrote it down and he slipped the small, folded paper into a slit in his trouser hem. What he intended to do with my address, I did not know. By then, I was becoming frightened myself, frightened that the police might come to my door at any time. I told the poet to get back to his apartment and tear out pages of books that I'd given to him with my name written on them. With that, he quickly left. *Ka li shu,* my friend. Go safely on your way.

I continued my packing, spent some more time in tearful goodbyes with students and friends, and left Lhasa the next day not anticipating that I'd ever be back. This caused me an almost unbearable sadness. In the two years I had spent living in that little city, I had advanced from merely being in Lhasa to becoming a small part of Lhasa's pulse. My senses had become heightened by the ordinary daily comings and goings of her people; the sights, sounds, and tastes becoming more common for me than anything foreign.

The poet's predicament alone would have added to my heavy heart. I tried my best to compartmentalize the whirl of those last days, to give equal weight to the final goodbyes. The poet had given me a small black and white photo of himself a few weeks before I left, which I eventually taped to my dresser mirror and which would remind me to say a daily prayer for his safety. That was the best I could do for him.

Back in the US, I found the going tough. If I had experienced culture shock when I had arrived in Tibet, I experienced it again upon returning to Texas. I had become surprisingly used to the way things worked in Lhasa and happy with my life there. Now it felt as if I were starting over in a place that seemed ironically foreign to me. It wasn't long before I realized I had come back to the US only to rediscover my old depression.

To make matters worse, I'd come back in mid-summer to find teaching positions mostly filled. When I did find a position, it was too far from the family home to commute. I ended up finding a room in a house nearby. But my classroom had bare walls and there was little money to purchase materials or time to plan. The job was teaching a high school senior English class and I hated it. Some of the kids were unruly and I felt anxious a lot of the time, even developing heart palpitations. I stuck it out for a while, then resigned, moving to

Longview where I rented a room from a friend of mine who owned a duplex. I began substitute teaching, which I liked more than teaching English to high school seniors. It gave me a reason to get up and get dressed every morning, even on days when I wouldn't get a phone call requesting my services.

At one point, I attempted to get information about the poet through an American friend in Lhasa, being careful to not name him in my letter. She asked a few Holiday Inn employees if they knew of his whereabouts and I soon learned that he'd been put in charge of the new leather factory outlet at the hotel soon after I'd left. But recently, he had not been seen.

In the meantime, I kept trying to fit back into life in the States. Six months came and went. In all that time, I was never able to shake the idea that my heart was back in Tibet.

That was my place, and I was not there.

So began the process of returning to China, this time through the International Mission Board (IMB) of the Southern Baptist Convention. By then, divorced individuals were considered for volunteer positions. The only problem was that it wouldn't necessarily be Tibet where they would send me. At the time, the political situation between China and the US meant no American teachers in Tibet. Instead, they offered me a position in Chengdu, which, of course, I had become familiar with as a stopping place between Hong Kong and Lhasa. It was close enough, as far as I was concerned, and sufficient to hopefully negate the terribly unsettled feeling I had had since my return.

Truthfully, there was nothing keeping me in the States. My sons were out on their own. Mike had finished his MBA, had passed his CPA, and was working for a bank in downtown Chicago. Joel was married and was facing his first deployment to Iraq. My mother was struggling with Alzheimer's. Within her general vicinity were three of my sisters, and I knew I couldn't have made a difference by being there. Not to my mother who, by then, no longer recognized me and was soon headed to a nursing facility.

After the requisite training and psychological profiling, I was off to Chengdu where my position awaited me at Chengdu University of Science and Technology (CUST). Naturally, the first stop was Hong Kong, where I would spend a week. There were a few odds and ends that needed to be attended to, including meeting my supervisor. I stayed at a place called the Louisiana Flats, a mission house at the Hong Kong-Macao Baptist Mission presumably funded by Louisiana Baptist. I had a room to myself with a double bed. From the window, I had a close-up view of the "Kai Tek Heart Attack" plane landings, the infamous forty-five degree turns that the pilots would have to pull off to land on the Hong Kong airport's notorious Runway 13. I could practically see the consternation in the pilots' faces.

I met my supervisor for lunch one day and he filled me in on my school, apartment, and coworkers. I visited the office of Global Partners, which was my division, and learned that I would be sent to Tibet in the fall. I met with my former personnel rep, too, who told me I had left a legacy behind in Lhasa, which was very gratifying. And I also attended an annual meeting of Christian workers assigned to Hong Kong, Macao, and China. There, I met two young men who were also on their way to CUST. They were returning Chinese language students and I was the newbie assigned as ESL instructor for two graduate classes.

The two young men accompanied me to Chengdu. Our first stop: Guangzhou, the passport/visa checkpoint, a three-hour boat trip from Hong Kong up the Pearl River. At Guangzhou, the first question out of the luggage inspector's mouth was, "You carry Bibles?" Without thinking, I said, "Yes." I actually had two for myself and a few extras for giveaways. The two young men gave me an incredulous look. Printed religious material was not allowed. The inspector indicated that I was to open my suitcase, but after a minute of trying to locate the key, she became annoyed with me for holding up the queue and waved me on.

From the checkpoint, it was on to the airport for Chengdu. Once there, we were met by Mr. Wong, the chairman of the English section of the foreign language department at the university. It was late when we arrived in Chengdu. Besides meeting Mr. Wong, we were met with the familiar smell of coal dust, coupled with the polluted hazy atmosphere of the city. In time, I would come to notice that whenever I'd be out for a while, I'd blow my nose and find black stuff on the tissue. One noticeable change was the elimination of the armed military guards near the planes. Instead, there were unarmed young men in blue uniforms.

It was dusk by the time we reached the university. Our van delivered me to my new home, a guesthouse familiarly called the Panda House, while the young men walked to their five-story residence building. I asked someone the reason for the name of the guesthouse and they told me, "Everybody comes to China to see the pandas. But as far as the Chinese are concerned, you're the oddity. They come by, they look at you. *You're* the Panda."

One of the first things I noticed upon entering the building was the dimness of the lightbulbs. They could not have been more than twenty watts. It made for a dreary, cheerless introduction to the place, adding to the sense of angst I felt arriving in this foreign city and new situation.

There were forty some foreigners in the Panda House, either teachers or students. I was on the third floor and my apartment had been vacated two weeks prior and it was dirty. The bed was made up and it wasn't until I had slept on it for two nights that I decided to see if I could put a blanket on the lumpy mattress for padding. What I discovered under my sheet was disgusting—a filthy mattress pad that had been peed on and bled on and no telling what all else. I stripped it off and shopped for another one later that day.

But this was just the beginning of the good times at the Panda House. The next night I was awakened by a mouse helping himself to a loaf of bread on a little table in the kitchen area. When I got up the nerve to cross the room and turn on the light, I discovered the mouse had managed to take four pieces of bread to the floor. When daylight came, I could see what the mouse's main objective was. Besides the bread, he had torn into a package of cheddar cheese I'd brought with me from Hong Kong. Obviously, the little fellow was trying to fix himself a cheese sandwich.

I would encounter this mouse again the very next night when he decided to expand his wanderings from the kitchen into the bedroom. In the middle of the night, I felt something fall on my hair. I reached over and switched on the table lamp next to the bed to see the mouse now sitting on the table. Upon his discovery, he jumped down and where he went I didn't see. I sat on the edge of the bed, legs folded under me, determined to stay awake the rest of the night. I was going to wait for that mouse to come out and watch him, hopefully, exit through the open door to the balcony. Toward morning I had to repeatedly pry my eyes open to keep my lookout, but finally I saw the mouse come out and make his escape. I closed the door behind him and managed to get a little sleep before the sun came up.

There were other problems with my little apartment. I had to boil my water for drinking and brushing my teeth. The toilet routinely overflowed and the bathroom floor was typically covered with water, despite the presence of a drain. I was fortunate to have a TV, but all I could get was a Hong Kong sports station.

Outside the apartment, there were cultural adjustments I needed to make. Walking about our part of the city one day, I ran into two Chinese friends I had met previously in Tibet who worked for a travel agency. One of them, Xiao Fen, asked me if I had eaten. Now, what I didn't realize at the time was that this was a Chinese form of greeting and a purely rhetorical question. It was their way of saying, "How are you?" In the States, you don't expect anyone to answer with a litany of complaints, even if they'd be justified in doing so. You expect, "I'm doing well, thanks." In Chengdu, my friend expected, "Yes, I've eaten." But, in truth, it was near lunchtime and I *hadn't* eaten, which is what I duly reported. Xiao Fen jumped into action, taking me to the dining area of a hotel and ordering me food, much of which I would never have ordered myself, or have any interest in eating. But what was I to do? Lesson learned. Have I eaten? You bet I have.

Of course, I discovered other interesting differences in culture. One evening I was introduced to someone who remarked that I "dressed young" and did not look to be my age of fifty-one. Naturally, I thanked her for what I assumed was a compliment. It was not. The Chinese revere older people. They are respected for their life experience and wisdom. You say "thank you" when a person tells you that you look older, not younger.

One particular aspect of Chengdu I never got used to was its bleakness. Seasonal Affective Disorder—SAD—had been recognized by 1994 but was a relatively recent discovery and rarely talked about outside of psychiatric circles. I didn't know of it. But I felt its symptoms—the depression, the anxiety. The city was as gray and muted as the skies. All the old buildings on campus were painted a dark gray, with contrasting deep red trim. Colorful clothing was apparently taboo, for most of what I saw were dark colors—brown, black, navy blue. Many older men still wore the dark blue Mao jackets, perhaps to stand in solidarity with the "Great Helmsman."

Eventually, I came to believe that the absence of colorful clothing was a way to deal with the dirt and grime from everyday living. If one desired a gray shirt and had a snow-white one, wait a few months and your wish would be granted. No Maytags here—hand washing was it. This is when I became acquainted with the concierge service at the

Panda House. Besides normal housekeeping, they would take care of your wash for a fee, even hanging it outside on the upper floor's "sun deck." But the constant humidity required a lengthy drying time, meaning my washed clothing was exposed to the dreadful pollution all over again, causing me to wonder about the futility of it all. "Ring around the collar" was a given here and no amount of detergent could get rid of the black grime.

Apocalyptic skies were the norm. The dense haze hung from the sky like an immovable lead curtain, so bad at times that it would blur the sight of tall buildings not even half a block away. There were bits of coal dust pinging at my face. It was no wonder that scores of the population were forever coughing and bringing up something repugnant from out of the depths of their throats. And depositing it wherever they happened to be.

The people of the city spent their lives tolerating the deterioration of their environment. No doubt the toxic pollution was responsible for thousands of deaths—a veritable death shroud. Somewhere I'd read that particulate matter was most harmful as it was able to penetrate the respiratory system and could cause cardiovascular disease, lung diseases, and lung cancer. The scary part of living in that environment was thinking that my life span could be shortened by years, depending on how long I lived there. Who knew how many? Five years? Much later, I would think about all this whenever I'd get a bout of coughing for some unknown reason and find myself wondering at exactly from what point those five years were going to be subtracted.

CHAPTER 24

STEAL, STOLE, STOLEN

"Moral excellence comes about as a result of habit. We become just by doing just acts, temperate by doing temperate acts, brave by doing brave acts." —Aristotle

SAD or not, I knew that deep down, Chengdu is where I was meant to be. But that didn't mean I couldn't do something to cheer things up. Starting with my apartment. Mind over matter is what it took to get me over the "I cannot cook in that dirty, rat-infested, measly, outdoor, poor-excuse-for-a-kitchen, kitchen." Instead of cursing the darkness, I was able to get it enclosed and painted within a few weeks. The painting included the bedroom/sitting room, too. And all of this done without paying a thing. I'd been contemplating painting it myself and one day, near the university's main entrance, I spotted a paint store. Imagine how surprised the female owner was when I began to look around. Painting and hardware were part of the male domain in China. I was equally surprised when I discovered the woman spoke English.

My shopping didn't take long because the extent of available colors included white, gray, blue, and a pea green that was ubiquitous around the city and campus. The bottom third of every building I saw was painted this particular pea green. I chose white. After explaining to the woman why I was in Chengdu, I could practically see the wheels turning in her head. Soon came her idea of bartering.

She had a niece who would soon be in her last year of high school and would be preparing for the university entrance exam. English was an important component, and the auntie knew her niece might need some help from a native English speaker. There on the spot, we bartered: tutoring for painting.

I met Shazia, the niece, and her auntie, Ayi, at my apartment the next day to iron out the details. The carpentry was included in this trade, so I was highly motivated to see that this girl did well on the English part of the exam. Shazia took me to meet her parents, non-English speakers, who lived at the dental training hospital, AKA dental school. They lived at the work unit, where her mother worked as a technician. Work units in China were where people within the same general field were gathered together into their own little communities and housed for free.

The bartering arrangement came with an unplanned perk when a crown of mine broke after chewing something hard. Shazia reported it to her mother, and her mother arranged for me to go to the dental hospital. After my arrival, I was taken to a huge room with numerous dental chairs and equipment arranged for instruction. Here, the perk suddenly seemed less valuable. It all looked somewhat archaic, a dental facility out of the late 1940s.

The scene brought back a memory of being in a dental office in the small town of Vivian, Louisiana, a short drive from where I was from. The dentist, Dr. Caldwell, could have been a mad dentist from a horror picture show, as far as I was concerned. His drill could have done horrible things to me. I yelled and jerked around at the sight of the needle so much that he couldn't proceed. I kept crying, "Put me to sleep! Put me to sleep!" At this, the bewildered man declared, "I'll put you to sleep with a hammer!" I even fought the gas apparatus at first, but then I settled down. We all settled down.

Here at the dental school, the chief instructor prepared me for the exam. Or did he? I only remember opening my mouth wide on command and having an instrument probing the inside. He must have been thinking, *don't let a teaching minute pass you by*, for three or four students approached the chair in turns, taking a look at my American dental history up close and personal, wearing no masks and breathing in my face.

The instructor kept busy explaining to everyone the mechanics of my dental work. *It can't last much longer*, I kept repeating to myself, and it didn't. I left with a temporary crown, probably produced by Shazia's mother. I'd wait until I was back in the US for a permanent one. In the end, the experience didn't cost me anything and I was grateful. Most importantly, I had a painted, enclosed, clean kitchen. Not quite home, but closer than it had been before.

Also helping to cheer me in those early days in Chengdu was the help I received from my students. I taught reading to one graduate class and writing to another, both three times a week. The students enjoyed helping me get acclimated for it gave them a chance to practice their English. And I needed their help. Lhasa had helped prepare me for life in a foreign land, but Chengdu had its own unique ways and means.

Another way for students, or anyone in Chengdu, to practice their English was English Corner. ECs were common throughout China—gathering places at set times where people met to converse in English. There was an English Corner in Chengdu that took place every Tuesday and Friday evening. Typically, I'd be the only foreigner there and be swarmed by mostly young people who wanted to practice their speaking and listening skills. One man who came around was Mr. Liu (pronounced "Leo"), a talkative sort, maybe a bit too talkative. Another regular was an older man with silver hair who would often strike up conversations with me. He was a retired engineer and I suspected he went to English Corner out of boredom. To myself, I referred to him as the "Silver Fox" but the English name he had given himself was "Tarzan." When I'd later think of him, I'd always laugh, imagining him swinging from the trees with Jane.

One of the more overwhelming things for me at first was the simple act of getting around. Chengdu was a city of around eleven million at the time over an area of about 5,000 square miles. With the help of my students, I learned the names of the major streets, but soon discovered that I also had to learn the various sections of the city, or at least my part of it. The streets went on and on and it wasn't enough to tell a taxi driver the name of the street you wanted. You needed to let him know the section of the street that you wanted to be taken to or you could end up miles away from your destination.

For the most part, I never went far and before I'd spent too much time in Chengdu, my students helped me purchase a bike. We bought it at a shop they knew of and, afterward, they volunteered to get it registered for me, offering to drop it by my place later. Then they walked me to the bus stop with instructions that Bus 17 would take me back to the campus.

When Bus 17 came by, a long, tandem bus, I got on with an armload of things I'd picked up after I had bought the bike, including a bouquet of flowers, which were very inexpensive in Chengdu, and a loaf of bread. I made my way to the back part of the bus, trying to ignore how filthy and crowded it was. The bus took off, making several stops along the way. A young man in a suit, noticing the people jostling me as they came onto and got off of the bus, motioned for me to keep my purse close to my side.

Finally, my stop came and I exited the bus and crossed the street where I heard some yelling from behind me. I turned back toward the bus stop and the man in the suit was standing there waving at me with one hand, with his other hand gripping the arm of a young woman he'd apparently just put in handcuffs. Bus 17, it turned out, was infamous for pickpockets. The man in the suit was an undercover cop. The woman, to my shock, had evidently lifted my money right out of my purse.

I crossed back over the street while the cop hailed a taxi. He motioned for me to get in the back seat with the alleged thief, which I had no intention of doing. Finally, he slid into the back seat with her himself and I took the passenger seat up front. We swung by the police station where the perpetrator was handed off to other officials and then to a small shop that I recognized as a photo shop. There, the plainclothes policeman spread out the contents of my purse and commenced to take pictures, for the record, I assumed. There were a good many 100-yuan bills in my purse (about $14 US each) and even one US hundred-dollar bill. After the picture-taking, it was back to the police station where the officer once again spread out the contents of the purse, this time bringing the pickpocket into the room to get a good look, so I surmised, of what she was prevented from getting away with.

All the official proceedings over, the purse was returned to me and the officer took a police car from the station and dutifully drove me back to the university. Of course, I had him drop me off before we reached the campus. I was new at the school and the last thing I needed was for everybody to see the new teacher getting out of a police car.

Back in my apartment, I counted the money again, only to discover that I was a 100-yuan bill short. This, too, represented a discovery about Chinese culture. Police officers, I would be informed, are expected to be tipped. With no offer from me forthcoming, the officer had taken it upon himself to see to it that he received the proper gratuity.

My next experience with petty theft would come within a week. My new bike? Sure enough, someone stole it. Bicycle theft, in fact, was commonplace. I now knew this firsthand, having given up my brand-new bike to the bike mafia. With this in mind, Xiao Ma, a Chinese friend whom I'd met in Lhasa, volunteered to take me shopping for a used bike.

Xiao Ma worked as an interpreter for Japanese tour groups, mainly in Tibet. I had met him in Lhasa and he was the kind of person I probably would not have become friends with back home. He talked endlessly and, frankly, could be a bit obnoxious at times. But when you're in a foreign land, your standards for friendship sometimes slide a little. Xiao Ma was friendly, spoke English fairly well, and liked to hang around the people I hung around with. Hence, a friendship was established.

At any rate, Xiao Ma agreed to take me bike shopping and his long-time lady friend Xiao Li accompanied us. We went by bus and then foot until we arrived at a well-known used bicycle business. And a busy place it was. There were bicycles of every description imaginable, every shape and color, a Chinese Santa's workshop of bicycles. Indeed, Santa would be envious.

Xiao Ma began educating me on the finer points of purchasing a used bike. For starters, you turn the bike over to look for any identifying numbers that could link the bike to a previous owner. But this would be rare, for after taking the bike apart, a bicycle elf would use a sanding device to strip it of all paint and any hint of identifiable clues. It was then that I noticed the odor of paint in the air and understood. Learning about culture, even bicycle culture, takes time. I was wandering amidst stolen bicycles, a veritable chop shop, and I was left to wonder if I'd be buying back my own recently purchased and recently stolen new bike.

I also wondered whether the people of this city took a shop like this in stride. Just another fact of life accepted with stoicism. If so, was stoicism just another word for defeatism? The country was a bicycle nation, but the government treated bicycle theft as relatively minor, even though it was, in fact, a major criminal activity. Many people were poor and could barely afford a new bicycle. The fee to register a bike could be prohibitive in and of itself. Chinese people looked to the government for most everything but legal protections, for bicycle ownership and everything else, were poorly managed, poorly enforced, and subject to corruption.

An example of this was brought to my attention by a male student who told me of buying new shoes from an independent shoe shop. After wearing them a single time, they began coming apart. I advised him to take them back, but he slumped his shoulders and uttered, "What's the use?" He knew that the shop owner would have no recourse with the wholesaler who sold him the shoes because the wholesaler would find no recourse with the manufacturer. My student was the one who would take the loss. It was buyer beware in those days and one had to be smart and cautious when purchasing goods with the meager resources one had.

That day, I left the bicycle place with the ugliest, oldest bike I could find. Even a Sichuan farmer wouldn't be caught dead on my bike. The chain kept slipping, jolting me as if to propel me over the handlebars. The upside? There was little risk of a thief thinking it was valuable enough to steal.

Xiao Li, my new friend now, was a shop owner herself. She had gone to university and studied business and operated a little street shop where Xiao Ma worked. Xiao Ma presented himself as a successful businessman and took a lot of credit for the shop's success, but that's not exactly the way I saw it. In fact, bedlam ensued one day when Xiao Li took the train to Canton to buy some clothing for the store and left Xiao Ma in charge. A male customer, much larger than Xiao Ma, entered and quickly took exception to his overbearing personality. Words were exchanged. One thing led to another and a little pushing escalated into a knockdown, drag out fight.

I heard it about the next day. Xiao Ma had been taken to the hospital. I went there expecting him to be on life support but found him in a six-person room looking pretty fit for someone who had supposedly just outwitted the death angel. As it turns out, Xiao Ma was looking for a payday, getting himself admitted to the hospital for a certain period of time to prove he'd been hurt so as to collect from the man who had fought him. The truth, Xiao Ma confided to me, was that the fight had been a victory for him. The unfortunate customer had blood all over him. I knew better. If there was blood on the customer, surely it was Xiao Ma's.

Xiao Ma hung around the hospital for a few days, sneaking out at times during the day for food, since hospitals in China didn't provide it. Friends and relatives of the patients had to take it upon themselves to bring meals to the hospital. Xiao Ma would leave, but always make sure to return at bed-check time so that his stay there was duly noted. I never did find out whether he collected anything from the customer. I imagine if he tried, the customer might have decided to put him in the hospital for real.

Feeling small in front of 999-room Potala Palace

Tea time at construction site with invited passerby

End of line for author. Going home, 1992.

Barkhor market, Lhasa

View of Lhasa from Potala Palace

Golden yak statue in the middle of
one of main intersections in Lhasa

CHAPTER 25

STUDENT LIFE

"There are two educations. One should teach us how to make a living and the other how to live."
—John Adams

In my classes of wall-to-wall students, typically forty-plus, there were noticeable differences from what I had become accustomed to in Tibet. The age of the students was the first difference, of course. The CUST students were post-graduate. But another significant difference was their backgrounds. The Tibetan students either came from small towns or the countryside, with some coming from the very small city of Lhasa. Many of them had scant knowledge of the world at large. They loved their families and communities and were taught to love their country, China at large, through their school's indoctrination with no thought of harboring a differing opinion. At least not an open one.

The post-grads were different in that most of them had robust opinions. The majority of them had grown up in cities. In their younger school days, they had been required to wear a knotted, red neck scarf to indicate they were "Young Pioneers." Now they were required to attend a class espousing socialist ideas and communist ideals.

After passing the university entrance exam, out from under the thumb of their parents and teachers, they now had just a taste of freedom. They could breathe. Some students even told me that their very restrictive educational experience prior to the university was like being in prison. They were slaves to the goal of passing the dreaded, two-days' long university entrance exam. They had little free time for playing as children, and later, as teens, little free time to do whatever teens like to do.

I learned a bit of Chinese and university culture by walking around the campus. For one thing, I noticed no handholding between the sexes. When I later made a comment about this to a student, he said it was a rule, and that if caught, the "perpetrators" would be fined. Harnessing the hormones on campus after the post-Mao years was an experience in denial. Did the authorities really believe this edict would keep these young people apart and put the fear of Mao in them? In fact, there *was* handholding. I never quite got over my astonishment at seeing young men holding hands. It wasn't really strange to see the young women walking hand-in-hand, but when I'd see one finger encircling another's finger, female *and* male, that's what confused me. My own prudish background, I suppose. And as far as the hormones, with my small-town sensibilities I had no idea what a hormone was capable of doing. But the Maoists did, apparently.

I also learned something about communal living at CUST. The student dormitories were an excellent example of it. The standard room was small and crowded with three bunk beds and three small desks. The WC was down the hall. As in the Panda House, I wondered if there was a moratorium on normal wattage lightbulbs for I never saw a well-lit dorm room or hallway. Classrooms had at least sixty-watt bulbs so most of the students would study in a classroom at night, until the bewitching hour when a timer would turn the lights off.

The student bathing routines were interesting. There were two central bathhouses and there was a specific time twice a week when students could take advantage of the showers. Whenever I was out and about on campus, I'd see students with their wash pan of toiletries heading for the bathhouse. Large hand towels took the place of bath towels.

Punishments for rules infractions were meted out in various ways, but an especially noteworthy one was to handcuff the perpetrator to a tree. For how long, I didn't know. Maybe hours. The tree had to be small enough in circumference for the person's arms to reach around. It was, I suppose, an ingenious method of punishment in its way for the shame and degradation it created.

There had been foreigners in or near Chinese universities for decades, so it wouldn't seem that strangers would be the objects of attention. But there were incidents with the local campus citizens, mainly involving women, that had me stymied. Whenever I would pass a woman on a sidewalk with no one else around, the woman would invariably cast her eyes downward and toward my feet. It gave me pause wondering whether these women all had foot or shoe fetishes. I finally asked a female student what this could mean and she replied with two possible explanations, each most likely concocted at the moment of my asking. Chinese women might feel shy or self-conscious in coming face-to-face with a foreigner, according to the first explanation. Or, according to the second explanation, they could be assessing my wealth by the condition of my shoes. I had to hand it to my student for her feasible, or perhaps feeble, explanations, as she had clearly been thinking on her feet—in English, no less.

Indeed, the capacity for truth was another issue on campus. It brought me no pleasure to suspect that I was being lied to over and over again. Invariably, whether I was asking an important question or a frivolous one, the answer would be "yes." Over time, I came to understand the Chinese way of thinking, much of it held over from previous times. The ingrained belief was that one should never cause another to feel disappointment or shame, to "lose face." So, the other person was told what he wanted to hear. It was difficult for me to discern if "yes" really meant "yes." It could have meant "no." A cultural practice or not, I didn't find that being unsure of another's meaning was a particularly easy way to effectively communicate.

CHAPTER 26

BAYI OR BUST

"I don't know where I'm going, but I'm on my way."
—Carl Sandburg

The secretary of the Hong Kong office handed me an old section of a map to show me the location of my new assignment. Someone had circled "Linzhi" to make it easier to locate since all the place names were mostly unpronounceable. Not being able to be of any more help, she gave me an apologetic smile. This office was not the one of the main sending agency, but the one seconding me to the Chinese-approved one.

At the main sending agency office, recognized as the premier teacher placement group for China, I received more information about the small agricultural college. Linzhi, I learned, was the name of the prefecture, an administrative jurisdiction made up of a number of counties. Nyingchi was the county, and "Bayi" was the town. I would fly to Lhasa and from there, it would be an eight-hour trip on mostly narrow, gravel roads and over a high mountain pass, gradually descending into the eastern area of Tibet.

My teaching partners, a couple just older than me from Connecticut, would meet me in Lhasa and our trip by Land Cruiser to our school would begin the following day. Ray and Myra were ideal placements for an agriculture school. They had a farm where they grew Christmas trees and Myra had worked with 4-H. Once I met them, it didn't take long before I determined their personalities—Myra the extrovert and Ray the introvert. It seemed to work for them. Essentially, we were three middle-aged farmers on our way to learning about how it was done in this faraway place, much of it without the benefit of modernity. Learning how to adapt would become a necessary skill for us. It would be adapt or be miserable.

In Lhasa, we did some last-minute shopping for essentials. Who knew what would be available in Bayi? I bought some Beijing butter, the real deal. It was good to be back in Lhasa, even for a short stopover. I had a chance to visit with some people and it felt like a homecoming of sorts. Too bad it couldn't be for longer.

Our driver from the agricultural college met us at our hotel early the next morning. His expression didn't belie what he was probably thinking when he saw our luggage, at least eight pieces plus our bags of purchased supplies. What we hadn't known was that the driver had taken on a male passenger who'd needed a ride back to Bayi. The space we thought we'd have was not to be. Instead of a rather tall Ray riding comfortably in the front seat, he was now squeezed in the backseat with us two women. With a bit of engineering luck, wedging our take-ons under and between our legs, we all managed to fit in. It definitely would not have been a good trip for a claustrophobic.

There were two routes to Bayi. We took the northernmost route, which would shave off some time. Both roads were winding with dangerous blind curves, but our route would climb steadily until the highest point, the Mila Mountain Pass with an elevation of close to 16,500 feet.

The start of the trip was somewhat dull for we were not in the area of the higher snow-capped mountains, but it didn't take long before the "oohs" and "aahs" began. Would I ever tire of these beautiful mountains? Rounding curve after curve, we observed more of the same, but something inside us saw each mountain scene as more beautiful in its snowy grandeur than the last. And then there it was:

the perfect mountainscape. Myra asked if we could stop to get out and take it all in. Being as there was not much of a shoulder, the driver stopped on the road, a steep grade at that point. It took some doing for Ray and Myra to extricate themselves from the take-ons and leave the Land Cruiser. I decided it wasn't feasible for me to get out, so I stayed put.

While the others were out stretching their legs and enjoying the landscape, I suddenly detected movement. Indeed, the car was moving—backward! I couldn't crawl over the bags quickly enough to get out, so I screamed frantically while banging on the window to get the driver's attention. He ran to open the door and set the brake, bringing the car to a halt. Tragedy was averted, but my confidence in the driver waned a bit at that point.

On the road again, we navigated switchback after switchback, gradually climbing higher and higher. I wondered if we were approaching "nosebleed" altitude to accompany my ear-popping. In fact, we were approaching the mountain pass. The altitude must have affected the Tibetan men in the front seat for it appeared as if they experienced something otherworldly at that moment, something from the Buddhist spiritual realm. *"Kiki soso lha gyal lo!"* they shouted with exuberance as the Land Cruiser crested the high point. "Victory to the gods!" After the near calamity with the rolling car miles before, I would have shouted with them, had I'd known at the time what they were shouting.

They weren't the only ones moved by the summit. Prayer flags festooned the immediate area along with bits of colorful paper with mantras written on them, flung by the faithful from car windows or by those who stopped to experience the moment. Mountain passes are sacred spaces for Tibetans. More than marking the point where an arduous climb gives way to a dramatic descent, they are also regarded as battlegrounds where good and bad gods are locked in an endless struggle against each other.

Our driver's god must have been a good one, for we were soon successfully descending the high, windswept, barren pass, a natural doorway into the eastern side of Tibet. It wasn't the best road, narrow and bumpy, but was at least much improved from what earlier travelers must have experienced, a practically impassable mountain range with a single precipitous trail.

This road to Bayi left an unforgettable impression on me. I had seen the real "Roof of the World," the highest I'd ever be.

Miles after having descended the pass, we reached the foothills, where the climate was warmer and more moist. There was richer vegetation and we saw Yunnan pine, birch, and fir trees. On both sides of the road there were occasional hills covered with large bushes. It was at one of these spots that the Land Cruiser stopped for a "nature calling" and leg-stretching event, men on one side, ladies on the other. All one had to do was to scoot up the hillside, choose one's very own privacy bush, and feel relieved. Except—wouldn't you know—a young shepherd boy was in the immediate area looking after his sheep. He didn't seem surprised at all to find a strange-looking woman hiding behind a bush and skirted by as if this scene played out for him every day. Never underestimate your perceived aloneness.

Reaching Bayi could not come soon enough. I had no preconceived ideas of what the little town would look like, so I willed myself not to make quick judgements. What I was really interested in was getting out of the body-numbing sardine can. We crossed the long bridge spanning the Yarlung-Tsangpo River and turned left before arriving at the front gate of the Agriculture and Animal Husbandry College.

We had made it.

CHAPTER 27

HOME SWEET HOME (SORT OF)

"Only those who risk going too far can possibly find out how far they can go."
—T.S. Eliot

At the front gate, a few of the school's administrators, including the school's Tibetan president, came out to greet us, and there were welcoming smiles and handshakes all around, along with intermingled Chinese and English chatter. Translating the jumble of words was Mr. Zhang, head of the English Department and our new "Mama Hen." He would be our caretaker and intermediary between the administration and us for the duration.

The first stop was to my ground floor apartment. Seeing my Panda House apartment in Chengdu for the first time came to mind, and I decided that if I could make that relatively clean and homey, I could do the same here as well.

Mr. Zhang was all smiles as he led us three pandas first to my apartment, then down the narrow street to Ray and Myra's second floor abode. Mr. Zhang told us we were to be feted with a welcome dinner in the dining room in the administration building. After dumping off our luggage, we made it there and were promptly served tea, then ushered into the small dining room where the table, following the norm, was being filled with many dishes of cold food.

This would be my foray into politely refusing food I didn't care to eat, such as what I saw swimming in spicy-hot red sauce. I announced respectfully that I was a vegetarian, but my explanation apparently didn't get through the Chinese filter, Mr. Zhang, for my plate would stay full even if I didn't put the food there. And from my banqueting experiences in Lhasa, I knew the arrival of an entire fish swimming around in a sea of blood-red spicy sauce indicated to me we were only halfway through this gastronomical experience. It amazed me to see multiple pairs of chopsticks (*khotse*) attacking the glassy-eyed fish until its mutilated flesh floated around in the sauce waiting for still-hungry mouths. I vowed I would never eat anything that was staring at me.

I much preferred to cook for myself. In my apartment I found what I needed to boil water and a suitable pan for cooking on the electric tripod cooker. Hot tea, bread, peanut butter, and butter was enough to satisfy me until I worked up the courage to shop at a small nearby street market. At first, I was an anomaly to the people there and they had to get accustomed to me and my broken Chinese. I would point to what I wanted and ask, "*Yi jin, duo shao quian?*" One pound, how much? In time, I would become an expected visitor and my questions would be anticipated before I could ask them. And with the assortment of vegetables and fruit at the market, I knew I'd be eating healthier.

The school offered the best it had, and I appreciated it, but I'd be lying to say that I landed into problem-free circumstances. The truth of the matter was that after arriving in Bayi, it took me a week or so to acclimate. Before classes began, I needed to make some improvements, mainly to the kitchen. It was disgustingly dirty. There was a two-wok cookery station embedded in a cement "cabinet" with two holes beneath for wood fuel. I knew immediately I would not be using it. The black soot from burning wood had covered much of the surfaces.

Hard to miss was the screened window in front of the cookery. It was so embedded with brownish-orange fat that no air could possibly pass through. I took it down but of course this created an opening for mice and rats. At the time, I had other things on my mind and determined that later I'd get a workman to fashion me a replacement screen. Besides, there would be few times that I'd need to open the window.

The most important room/cubicle was the WC—water closet—and closet is an accurate description. You couldn't exactly say it was commodious. The customary urinal was centered in the middle of the cement floor, and a cold-water shower head reigned (and rained) from above.

Bathing was different here, in that I didn't heat water for dumping in a small kiddie pool as I had in Lhasa. Here, I used a five-gallon plastic bucket for the tempered water. Positioning myself on a narrow board spanning the urinal, I used a small plastic bowl to pour water over myself in preparation for lathering up. The remaining water was for rinsing. So much for dreaming of soaking in a warm bubble bath with candles and soft music for ambiance. Bath time was speedy, for the WC was always cold.

If someone had asked me my least favorite color, I'd have told them "orange." Upon entering my bedroom for the first time, I was struck by the many ways orange paint was used on the spartan furnishings, mainly the bed. The wheels were already turning in my head as I began to visualize what magic I could perform to make satisfactory changes. To my surprise, the floor was covered with a room-size rug, and not an orange one. This, fortunately, was my favorite color, green. But I soon learned that the rug was like Velcro, trapping anything that landed on it. Walking on it with stocking feet created quite a sticky situation.

Then there was the room with the three-legged chair. The chair was new, as were the other few pieces that completed the furnishings.

The chair and matching sofa were covered in brown faux leather, probably the best Bayi had to offer. The floor was concrete, but polished, making it easy to mop. A wardrobe and small table were present, but I couldn't stop wondering about that lopsided chair. Someone had moved the furniture in; had it not occurred to them that something wasn't quite right? I was still learning the ways of the people, and I ultimately decided it was a matter of responsibility. The mover's job was to move. Nothing more. I eventually found a block of wood to stand in for the missing leg and took to warning anyone who sat in it to be careful lest he/she experience a moving moment.

A narrow, window-lined porch extended the length of the apartment. It was years' old dirty and a trash pile for the inhabitants. Something caught my eye outside one moveable window. There was a ladder positioned there. Maybe for a quick escape or an elopement? Or maybe it was considered the back door. One would have to walk a long way around the long line of connected apartments to reach the back, so this made some sense. I used it a few times myself before someone took it away, as well as the little fence that created a yard.

Of course, the circumstances of the apartments were normal for the locals. It was just the way things were. There were no thoughts of improving, and I'm sure most people didn't have the funds to make improvements anyway, especially to places they themselves did not own. Nor did most people have the skills.

For me, the kitchen set-up was the place where I'd spend a lot of time, so I knew I had to make some remarkable improvements. Rodents had surely made this their holiday escape, for there were all the usual signs. Armed with an old broom, I hoisted myself up to the top of the cabinet to brush away pellets from two of the three cement shelves located on an adjoining wall. There was no point in killing myself with irresponsible climbing, so I later managed to borrow a ladder from someone before I proceeded any further.

Mr. Zhang accompanied Ray, Myra, and me on our initial trip into Bayi, this on bicycles furnished by the school. We rode all over the small town, then shopped for housekeeping items. I found exactly what I needed for my kitchen: rolls of linoleum. Choosing my favorite color and pattern of green and cream, my mind was churning out myriad ways I would use it. I'd never laid linoleum, but how hard could it be? Shopping finished for the day, we hired two pedicabs to haul our purchases back to our rooms.

I couldn't wait to get started with the renovation and had the roll of linoleum on the kitchen floor in no time. I was a girl on a mission. The length of the roll was greater than my measurement so that I'd be sure to have plenty. The first cuts I made were for covering the two long shelves. What I was especially proud of was that the linoleum covered the cooking cabinet with the two holes. Not only that, but it covered the smell of old, rancid smoke left over from years of wood, coal, or yak dung patties used as fuel. A sharp knife made the few cuts required and everything else was seamless. The unpleasant odors were gone in no time and the kitchen was soon worthy of a *House Beautiful* spread.

Remembering something my mother told me years before, I next concentrated on the lone window. "Windows are the soul of a house," she'd say. I found a seamstress with a treadle sewing machine on a small campus street and presented her with pieces of measured white cloth for two window-length curtain panels, and long, narrow strips to be gathered for ruffles and tiebacks. I'd made the necessary pencil marks where she needed to stitch, which she did flawlessly. At last, my kitchen did, indeed, possess a soul. The ugly window was transformed.

With the kitchen reasonably clean, I was ready to cook. I say "cook" because I couldn't bake without an oven. Or could I? Never underestimate the ability of someone with a creative streak who likes to eat, even with only an electric-coiled, tripod apparatus. Biscuits?

No problem. With a few ingredients, a slender rolling pin, and a sharp-pointed knife to cut around an inverted glass, the biscuits were ready for my heavy, pre-heated, oiled iron skillet. When brown on bottom, flip them, and cover with the iron lid. The build-up of steam and heat allowed them to rise and brown perfectly. Bring on the jam and butter.

The apartment was starting to feel like home.

CHAPTER 28

OLD MAO TSE DENG HAD A FARM. E-I-E-I-O

*"No race can prosper until it learns there is as much dignity in tilling
a field as in writing a poem."*
—Booker T. Washington

Cows: *check.*
Pigs: *check.*
Chickens: *check.*
Goats: *check.*
Roosters: *check, check, check.*
Orchard: *check.*
Vegetable garden: *check.*

By all appearances, I, again, lived on a farm. No need to call in a veterinarian, land management expert, or botanist to this college of animal husbandry and agriculture, for it appeared to have everything a farm would have and more: blacksmith, carpentry shop, slaughterhouse, supermarket, EMS, barber, post office, dance hall, five & dime (*wu & jiao*), linguist instructors, off-campus swimming facility (Brahmaputra River), massage therapist, and various extracurricular activities.

Unfortunately, I was an unwilling participant in "hog-killing time," as we referred to it back on the farm in McLeod. Early every morning, before I rolled out of bed, I'd hear the sound of a dying pig, dying from being stuck in such a way so as to preserve the blood. It wasn't a good start to my day. I cringed, having to endure for too many minutes the moans, weakening as the seconds passed. "Squealed like a stuck pig" was not just an expression anymore.

Later, from my sparkling clean kitchen window, I'd see that pig being hauled away in a wooden handcart, with its short, porky legs hanging off. Somewhere along the way, it would be cut up and taken to the market. If I happened to pass the market in the early morning, I'd see all of it arranged in a sporadic order on tarps, and if I'd had time, I'd imagine myself rearranging all the pieces like a jigsaw puzzle, for all the parts were there and I do mean all the parts, including pans of blood. For the span of ten months, I was never tempted to eat pork.

A more pleasant part of the farm was the apple orchard—multitudes of trees with drooping limbs full of golden fruit that glowed in the soft autumn sunshine. My first trip to gather apples was with a few of my students, and only after getting permission. We didn't have to pick any for the ground was covered with them in various stages, from rotten to perfection. We could afford to be choosy. With the mix of rotting fruit and the sweet, grassy vegetal aroma of those crispy orbs of gold, I left the orchard with pleasant memories of the fun that came from gathering apples back home.

If my companion apple-pickers gave a thought to what I'd do with that pail of apples, they never let on. They didn't seem to be interested in me at all. That went on for months. Their English wasn't good, which might have made them hesitant to even try to talk to me. Oh well, I'd have to deal with that later; now I had apples to peel.

What *would* I do with all those apples? An old-fashioned Chinese forty-watt lightbulb flashed on in my head, and after weighing the pros and cons, I saw dried apples in my future. The sunporch was reasonably clean and I told myself, "I can do this!" My mother had done it years before, about the time when she came to trust me with a paring knife. Seated around a number 2 washtub, my sisters and I peeled and peeled until our fingers were red and hurting. When there were enough apples for our mother to deal with, she cored and sliced without the benefit of a mandolin.

In our side yard rested a tall oil tank, the kind one would see in the oilfield. It was iron and twelve feet in diameter and had been hauled there by a neighbor who owned a pipe yard. Thinking the top would be a perfect spot for drying apples, my mother climbed a ladder, spread the cloths on which to lay the apple slices, then carried them up. After spreading them out, she left it to the sun to finish the job. Later, on one of her inspections, she noticed that some of the apples were missing. Naughty brother!

Now that I was becoming more and more acquainted with the shops in Bayi, I brought back to my apartment some screening which I scrubbed and arranged so that the apple rings would get the full impact of the sun through my south-facing windows. A benefit of the enclosed sunporch was the natural room freshener the apples became, and the drier they became, the stronger the aroma. The apple drying was a success.

I continued learning about my new environment, knowing that soon, classes would start. But I had much to learn. That there was an agricultural school in the east of Tibet was pretty much all I knew before I'd arrived. Months before I left for Bayi, one of my Tibetan students who took a class in my apartment in Chengdu attempted to educate me about the area. The first thing she wanted to know was if I knew the meaning of "Bayi." I had no clue. Her explanation: The population consisted of one Tibetan to eight Chinese. In the Chinese language, "ba" is eight, and "yi" is one. That small military town was named for the August 1st military action years before, a grudge against the government taking control of Tibet's land.

Being the vocal one of the class of three, this student went on to exhort me to be aware and vigilant of the old animistic Bon religion, which may have had its reputation expanded with increasingly fantastic "facts" as the years had passed. Urban legends? Maybe. But the thought of poisonings, especially of strangers, and other "witchy" deeds gave me pause. "Be careful," she warned. In the end, I refused to imagine boogeymen behind every tree. Besides, Bon was an old religion, pre-Buddhism, and had become a small sect that had stopped sacrificing living beings long ago. (Hadn't it?)

The area of Tibet where Bayi was located was beautiful in all seasons. We arrived there near the end of the summer months and were greeted by a plethora of flora and fauna. Chinese are known for their posy prowess and it was in evidence all over the school grounds. I recognized the cosmos immediately. The trees lining our narrow apartment street were still green and provided shade for the length of it. Many evergreen trees dotted the campus, along with some large deciduous ones.

The campus was spread out, belying the small number of students it served, which was approximately 1,200. One of the two large buildings was the administration building where everyone who was anyone had an office, but we three foreign teachers did not merit any space. The other one was the auditorium with connecting small rooms.

All the classrooms were contained in what looked like portable buildings lined up in rows. Each had one door and a few windows. And, of course, there was no heating system. In the winter months during break time, students stood outside to get warmed by solar heat. Believe me, I was outside, too.

At least one building housed a listening lab whereby students donned headphones and followed instructions from the teacher. Mr. Jiang invited me to observe his class in action in the lab. Or I believe "inaction" would be more appropriate, for the students acted as if that was their first time there. It brought back memories of Tibet University's new classroom building and the computer lab. Before anyone could sneak a peek at the new computer-age sensation, one had to take off his shoes. By the time I got around to seeing it, the corners of some linoleum tiles were curling upwards. To my knowledge, the lab was never used. The building aged considerably in just one year.

Come second semester there would be a new classroom building on the Bayi campus complete with a disco. I guess one could consider it Tibetan innovation and ingenuity. Imagine yourself as a student who was studying in one of the classrooms in the evening with the bass perpetually pounding in your ears. Needing a break, you go down to the first floor to the disco at the end of the hall. There, you loosen up the neurons in the brain and then go back to studying assured you can go full tilt until the lights go out at ten. Such innovation!

Presumably, it didn't take long for the news to spread to the outside world of the Tibetan president's ingenuity in appropriating (or maybe "misappropriating") a few classrooms from the architect's plans to house the disco. Before I could get to know the gentleman, he was out the door and replaced by a stern-looking Han Chinese who meant business. I didn't even have time to thank the expelled president for my pretty green Velcro bedroom rug. Rumor was that he'd given himself a parting bonus. In any event, the disco ended up a memory of what could have been.

When it came time to meet our fellow English teachers, Mr. Zhang accompanied us to the administration building to the foreign language office, which meant English only. There, they seemed to be giddy with excitement. There were three other new teachers, all Han Chinese from adjoining provinces. A huge surprise for me was to meet my former student from Tibet University who had been placed there, as she was from the Linzhi area. This would be Jane's second year.

Another big surprise was to be introduced to Mr. Liu, the man I'd met briefly at the close of English Corner at CUST in Chengdu weeks before. What were the odds? In the months that followed, I found him to be good natured, with a hefty sense of humor, dependable, and devoted to his students. But the main thing I'll always remember is that it would be Mr. Liu who would teach me to waltz.

Miss Jia, as I always called her, was a young, first-year teacher. She had a sparkling, witty personality and smiles and laughter were an integral part of who she was. She came from northwest China and was the only person I knew who called one of the multitude of caves in her province "home." In her mountainous area, land resources were scarce. And temperature control was great in the caves, she reported.

The last of the teachers were new to teaching, a young couple recently married. It seemed to me that they could have passed for high schoolers. And I was struck by how poor they were. For many months they walked to town and back, unable to afford a bicycle. When they were finally able to buy one, the wife rode on the bar. Most of the time, I'd only see them at departmental meetings, and always felt compassion for them.

I had two classes—one reading and the other speaking and listening. My students were all Han Chinese—not a Tibetan in the bunch. I never knew why.

It wasn't unusual for students to be shy in the beginning, but what I faced on the first day was more than shyness. They sat in their seats as rigid as statues with me thinking I'd need the jaws of life to pry open their mouths. There was improvement as the weeks went by, and they loosened up more after an outing by the river. Sad to say, to this day, I cannot remember a single name. Well, maybe one name: a student by the name of Rong Wei. How could I ever forget that one?

In any event, I'd done the best I knew to do, always willing my attitude to make the difference. And in the end, there would be a lot more enjoyable times than not-so-enjoyable times.

Spice market

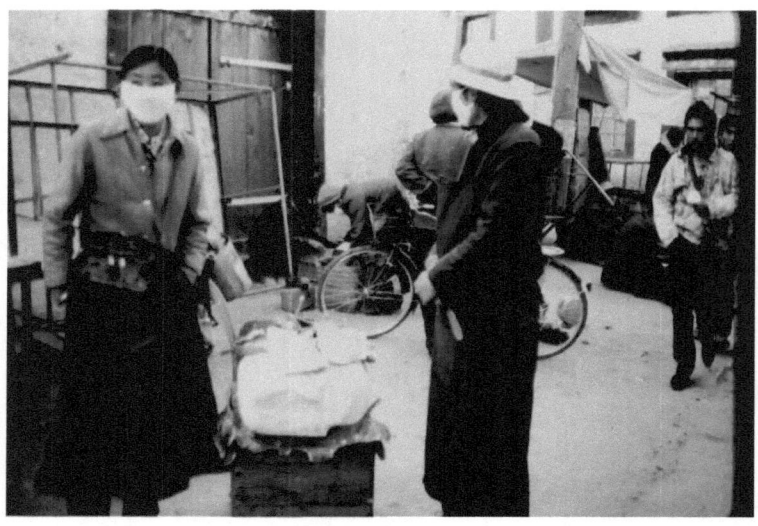

Butter sellers on street

Teahouse "grandpa" and author, Lhasa

Prayer wheels

Welcoming committee of one

Himalayan mountains viewed from plane

CHAPTER 29

FRIGHTS AND LOSS

"Disappointments are natural life occurrences. Their lifespan depends on how long they dominate your thoughts. The shorter, the better your life will be."
—Dodinsky

Another Saturday, another trip into Bayi. Some days I'd bike and other times I'd walk, each providing a different perspective on the passing scenery, both requiring some degree of evasive maneuvering to skirt the potholes and sometimes muddy streets. The long bridge I'd have to cross acted like a wind tunnel, and I'd have to brace myself for the gusts that would whip through the narrow valley and try to steal my hat.

After crossing the bridge and making a right turn, I was in Dodge City again. The shops along the street were built with lumber that had never been painted. Some had false fronts as one would see in pictures and movies of Wild West towns.

There was always a feeling of seeing everything as if for the first time. Where, for instance, did that small food shack come from? Curious, I debated stepping inside but quickly decided it wasn't a place I'd want to dine. The interior was dark and foreboding. At least there were no dogs—none that were waiting for scraps to be thrown on the floor as in Lhasa. Maybe the dogs were in the kitchen, and not scrounging for food, Heaven help them. I tried to put the thought out of my head, but from that point on, I thought of the food canteen as "Ptomaine Tavern."

A little farther down the street, I noticed a family of three coming my way. As we drew nearer I could see that they were definitely not townsfolk. With their worn, outback-type clothing, and matted hair, they looked out of place. My eyes zeroed in on the small child, whether a male or female, I could not tell. The child, too, wore a dirty looking, raggedy article of clothing, and with a mop of hair as matted as an old sheep dog. At the moment when our eyes locked, the child let out a whimpering cry and hid behind the parents.

I'd never had that reaction from anyone before. My instinct caused me to stop in my tracks and then move as far away from the family as I could. What must that child have been thinking? A white spirit from an unknown religion?

I would learn more about the people, like this small family, who would sometimes come into town. There were Tibetans who lived far away from Bayi who called the mountainous, glacial area home. The men were allowed to own firearms because they were hunters and gatherers. A sword hanging from their waist was a necessary part of their attire. When a son was old enough, the father would teach him the art of hunting. As far as food, there was little ground on which to plant. Their diet was heavy on meat and dairy. In the early winter, the entire family would go into town to trade furs, yak butter, and perhaps other things. With the money, they'd take back barley, tools, and new clothing. And in this case, the visions of a strange, out-of-place white woman.

With my light shopping done, I walked back to campus carrying my weekly supply of fruit, not giving a thought to what my next town encounter might be.

The poor child I had inadvertently scared in town would not be the only person I would frighten. Soon Halloween was upon us, the season of frights.

To refer to the lives in Tibet as spirit-filled would not be wrong. The Buddhist world is filled with powers of darkness—multi-armed beings, demons lurking about, and evil spirits of the worst kind. To what extent they controlled the lives of my Tibetan friends or those who lived in isolation, I never knew. This I did know: superstition was everywhere. At festivals, all manner of frightening beings were celebrated. It was in eastern Tibet that my belief in evil spirits was heightened to the point that I never wanted to celebrate Halloween anymore. If only I'd had this epiphany *before* I suggested it for an English department party.

My partners and I wanted to share some of our culture—our food and holidays—with our new friends and colleagues. At an October department meeting, we suggested an activity that on the face of it, would resonate with their familiarity with the spirit world. Now, how to explain Halloween to them and the concept of trick-or-treating and scary masks? We lightened it up some by describing the amusement of bobbing for apples, and other fun and games, traditionally ending with a bonfire, although we'd never suggest we could actually have the bonfire. Wood was a precious commodity. We talked about the masks, deemphasizing the creation of masks of a satanic nature. The idea for a Halloween party was welcomed and a date was set for the following Saturday evening.

Until then, my teammates and I spent our free time collecting and buying items from the town's markets to create a party atmosphere: a few gourds, crepe paper for making streamers for the ceiling of my apartment, a tub for apple-dunking, and a load of fruit. I bought a few yards of white sheeting. Later, we scoured the grounds of the campus for dead grasses (taking what I hoped were dead grasses, and not purposefully planted ornamental ones).

By the time Saturday evening arrived, Ray, Myra, and I had everything arranged. We hadn't disclosed to one another what our masks would be, but when I answered the knock at the door, Ray and Myra came in wearing rather benign face coverings. Me? I was Casper the Friendly Ghost. With black markings circling my cut-out eyes and plenty of cloth to cover me, I was prepared to go *Boo!*

Ready to greet the partygoers, I stationed myself on the fourth step of the stairway to the second floor. With each arrival, I gave my best shot at "*woooooo*"-ing and flapping my arms. The guests had not expected this and reacted with nervous chuckles. Finally, one person appeared who I had not anticipated, an elderly Tibetan man who only wanted to go upstairs. Of course, I didn't know this at first. I only noticed a person coming up the stairs, prompting me to greet him with my best performance yet. "*Wooooooo*" I moaned, flapping my sheet covered arms.

The poor man never did make it upstairs. He turned tail and ran as fast as his elderly legs could carry him. Naturally, I regretted mistaking him for a party guest. What must he have thought? Would he have imagined the stairway to be haunted? My hope was that he didn't actually live upstairs, but that he was merely visiting a friend, though future visits would surely be few and far between.

At any rate, everyone arrived with their homemade masks of everything you'd expect living on a "farm"—pigs, cows, chickens. Nothing too scary. It was clear they had taken great pains with their creativity and art. Let the party begin! Nobody was enthusiastic about bobbing for apples, which should not have been surprising, given it's a game meant for children. The food seemed to be the most appreciated aspect of the party. But in my memory of that night, I can only see a poor old man racing back down the steps and into the night.

When I considered distance and isolation in Bayi, I soon thought in terms of time: how long would it take a letter to reach the US or even Lhasa? How much time could I expect to spend in the telecommunication office in town in order to reach the outside world? For an international call, I could forget it. All calls, even a call to Lhasa, had to be routed through an operator in Beijing. This would be after having to wait in line for the phone booth, which was not without its own hazards. One day, I checked in with the all-powerful queuing monitor, waited my turn, and then entered the booth. At that moment, a man decided to jump the queue, squeezing into the single-person booth and forcing me up against the glass panel, assuming, I suppose, that I'd surrender the booth to him. I reacted spontaneously with the same "I'll schlap the debil out of you" spirit that had infused my five-year-old self on that train so many years before, and gave the man a hefty shove. He fell backward out of the booth, almost losing his balance, with an expression on his face that told me he had *not* expected that. Then he lost his place in line and ended up at the very back of it. Don't mess with Texas.

At any rate, sending letters was much less of a hassle, though not completely hassle-free. There was a hole-in-the-wall post office on campus where one could buy stamps and mail letters. Anything related to packages I could not trust. A few packages from friends in the US never arrived. Because all packages were opened at the post office to inspect for anything deemed questionable, it would not have been unlikely that someone took the contents for themselves.

My letters were always weighed, and even though I had the same number of pages—two front and back written on onion-skinned stationery—the postage was usually different. A few times, my letters were returned to me for insufficient postage. Two or more days delayed. Eventually, I smartened up by gluing on more than enough postage. A glue pot with a small bristled brush was on the table for the convenience of patrons. Envelopes required that same glue for the flaps to seal.

I didn't know for certain, but outgoing mail from the main post office probably went by way of a daily bus headed for Lhasa. In the year 1994, this was seen as the height of modernity. By contrast, in 1949, acclaimed US journalist Lowell Thomas, and his son, Lowell Jr., made an almost unheard-of trip halfway across Tibet to Lhasa. In the classic, *Out of This World: Across the Himalayas to Forbidden Tibet*, Thomas Jr. writes of how one day, on horseback, they overtook a man who was loping along with a sack on his back and a spear in his hand. Turns out he was one of the Tibetan mail carriers. The carriers traveled on foot, running most of the way. Less sophisticated than our Pony Express. The spear was the carrier's badge of office. After five or six miles, another man would seize the mail bag and the relay race against time would proceed.

A few months before my departure from Bayi, an escorted group of ex-pat Tibetan language students from Tibet University came to Bayi on their way to other sites and visited the college for a few hours. I'd met several of them previously in Lhasa, so I thought I'd send out several rolls of film with them to be developed in Lhasa where I knew the quality was greatly superior to what I could find in Bayi. The plan was to have them send the developed pictures back to me. I wanted to distribute them to many people—shopkeepers, fruit sellers, and especially the children I'd come to know.

In fact, I had taken some wonderful photos of the neighbor children. It was near Easter, and I had invited them to my apartment one afternoon to dye eggs in preparation for the first-ever Easter egg hunt in Tibet. The day before, I went into town to find baskets and anything green I could turn into grass. The English department helped in scouring around for anything that could color an egg, such as tea. We told the children to bring old shirts to wear for dying. They arrived at the appointed time, eager to see what was going to happen. If only I'd had a movie camera. Because they'd never done this before, each step was exciting. Before long, they were dying their eggs as if they had done it many times. While the eggs were drying on old newspaper, we treated the kids to refreshments. Later they put a few eggs in their baskets to get a look and feel of the new experience.

The following Sunday afternoon, Ray and a few of the male English teachers took the dyed eggs up the hill behind the school and hid them near the rushing stream where bushes and large rocks made good hiding places. When we assumed enough time had elapsed for hiding the eggs, Myra and I led the children, all holding onto their basket handles, over the back stile and up the hill. They were so excited we had to corral them to keep them from running on ahead of each other. Once there, we told them where in the general area to search. Such a fun afternoon!

That was only one reason I'd wanted quality pictures. I had rolls of wonderful photos. I handed them over to one person in the Tibet group with express instructions *not* to send the negatives back with the prints, just in case they got "lost" on their way to Bayi. I waited and waited to get those prints back, but nothing ever came. Once I was back in Lhasa a few months later, I was told that, counter to my careful instructions, the photos and negatives had been sent together. No one could ever have understood the grief I experienced for the loss of those negatives, representing as they had, a significant part of my life.

It took a long time before I could express it out loud, for I was afraid grief over something as benign or "trivial" as rolls of film would make me seem foolish. Much later, I would come across a quote by author Martin Prechtel: "Grief is praise, because it is the natural way love honors what it misses."

CHAPTER 30

TIBETAN MEDICAL SCIENCE AND INTERESTING TEMPLES

"Do you not know that you are God's temple and that God's spirit dwells in you?"
—1 Cor. 3:16

It made sense that the Agriculture and Animal Husbandry College, not unlike all work units in China, would have access to medical personnel. For us, it was Dr. Stickum, or so I called him. No matter the affliction, the treatment seemed to be injections and the hooking of one up to an IV. The residents didn't seem to have a problem with his services. In fact, he was highly touted. Cold, flu, bronchitis, Hepatitis A, having fallen off a ladder, or general feelings of being unwell, someone would make sure the good doctor was called.

My initial contact with Dr. Stickum came a few weeks after my arrival. After finishing some shopping downtown, I flagged down a pedicab to take me back. We settled on a price and were on our way, me with a few plastic bags filled with fruit and assorted items. Time was money for the driver, so it didn't take long to get near to my building's entry. While I had both my hands holding onto the bags, the driver veered off the narrow street, putting us on a decline toward my entry without having the good sense to slow up. He misjudged the space between the trees he was heading for, not taking into account the fact that the carriage was wider than his tricycle.

With a loud bang and jolt, I was thrown out. I hit the ground and promptly rolled into a tree.

The driver, clearly disturbed by what he had caused, tried to lift me by grabbing me under my arms. I yelled at him to stop. I didn't want him to touch me, for I didn't know if I could even walk. I pointed to an entrance down from mine and yelled Mr. Zhang's name. The driver ran toward the door, yelling as he did so. Thankfully, Mr. Zhang appeared, quickly ascertained the situation and insisted that the poor driver be punished. I suggested the driver be allowed to go on his way. After all, I had wanted him to take me directly to my entry, and with my flight out of the pedicab and my rolling on the ground, I would have made it had it not been for the tree.

Mr. Zhang, wanting to do something, helped me inside, and then called for Dr. Stickum who speedily arrived with his medical bag of miracles. This was my first close-up view of Dr. Stickum and I was surprised to see how young he was, twenty-four, I would learn, and no more than a first-aid person, really. He had been a "doctor" for two years, and his leather-clad body and cocky youthfulness did nothing to set my mind at ease. He examined my back, which had several abrasions, and, in spite of my clothing, managed to dab them with some sort of medicine. I suspect he was disappointed that he had no reason to give me a jab. Either way, I was grateful for his presence. My body didn't want to move for days, but before long, I was well again and thanking God for watching over me.

There were other things I learned about Tibetan medical science. One day, while walking along a street lined with shops, I stopped long enough to observe a man proudly showing the contents of his bucket to a shopkeeper. His demeanor suggested that he might have been carrying around a bucket of gold. I sidled up close enough to see what looked like a bucket full of knobby roots instead. Some kind of food delicacy, perhaps? Later, I mentioned what I'd seen to Mr. Zhang, who smiled and explained that the bucket must have held a rare fungus found in the hills of Bayi. In fact, it was rare enough that there was a law in place stating that only Tibetans could harvest the fungus.

I didn't bother to ask Mr. Zhang what the use of the fungus was, assuming it was something medicinal. It wouldn't be until I returned to the States that I would come across an article that explained this mysterious fungus. As it happens, for the price, the man may as well have been selling gold. This fungus (scientific name: *Cordyceps Sinensis*) is a parasite that feeds off of caterpillars. It's more commonly referred to as "caterpillar fungus," and people like the man with the bucket make a living searching high and low for the fungus-infested dead caterpillar bodies. A pound of them can bring thousands of dollars.

But why? Why such demand for a fungus? Well, as I learned, the caterpillar fungus has another name: the Viagra of the Himalayas. It's an aphrodisiac! Supposedly. There don't appear to be any legitimate laboratory studies that can confirm its effectiveness in this regard, but try telling that to the men who eagerly put up real money to, shall we say, get a little extra jump in their step? Of course, for the price, you could buy a ton of Viagra, but the use of the caterpillar fungus has become something of a status symbol. Instead of, say, wearing a really expensive watch, you can just pull out your *Cordyceps Sinensis* to show the people around you how well you're doing.

Now, it must be said that there are other, less risqué, reasons for using the fungus. It's been used as a traditional Chinese medicine for everything, including cancer. (Again, with no supporting studies.)

Nevertheless, I have to believe that the value comes from the supposed potency characteristics.

Learning about the caterpillar fungus had me regretting the lost opportunity to become wealthy. Had Mr. Zhang fully explained the perceived value of the fungus, I could have put those kids to better use than hunting Easter eggs that day. We could have been searching for *golden* eggs. A fungus hunt! Fun, educational, and profitable, something that would have put a bounce in *my* step.

Perhaps there would be no need for the above-mentioned fungus if the people who feel they need it for, well, the purpose they need it for, would simply visit a temple such as the one I visited one day with a close friend of Mr. Zhang's.

I'd been introduced to Mr. Gongbo Tashi soon after my arrival at the college, and I'd often come in contact with him. Probably in his early thirties, Gongbo was an affable young man born into a farming family in western Tibet. At some point, his family had relocated to eastern Tibet. After finishing the equivalent of high school, he became the only Tibetan student to be enrolled in China's Northwest Agriculture College in the late 1970s. At some point between his years at that college and the time I became acquainted with him, he was an instructor and later a professor at the Agriculture and Animal Husbandry College in Bayi.

Gongbo was married to Wangmu, also an instructor at the college. During the spring semester, she attended my Speaking and Listening classes while sitting in the back of the room. Her sister, English name, Debbie, was a student of mine at Tibet University, class of 1993, who taught at the local middle school. Wangmu and Gongbo were the parents of an adorable four-year-old son who went by the name of Mo-Mo.

One day, Gongbo invited Ray and Myra and me to his family home up in the hills behind the college. He and his young family lived there with his elderly parents. His mother greeted us at the door and, with typical Tibetan hospitality, indicated our seats and immediately offered the traditional milky sweet tea. (I was thankful it wasn't yak butter tea.) After being offered our re-fill, we were ushered out to view their small apple orchard where Gongbo told us of the grafting of various varieties. He was truly a man of the earth. As we wandered about, he hoisted Mo-Mo onto his shoulders so he could stay with us big folks step for step. I could feel the love Gongbo had for Mo-Mo.

There was much to discover about Gongbo Tashi. I would learn over time that he was instrumental in introducing quinoa, a super grain, a complete protein grain, to Tibet. This came after reading a report about it in an English newspaper in 1987. Quinoa was said to flourish in several South American high-altitude countries. Gongbo believed the grain could be quite adaptable to areas in eastern Tibet, with altitudes of between 3,000 and 4,000 meters above sea level. He knew that if he could get it started, with many trials that would be sure to come, he'd be able to help improve the health of the local population. Meat and barley were the core foods eaten by Tibetans, with local fruits and vegetables available only in season to round out their diets. In the highlands, meat, dairy, and barley were the main diet, with fruits and vegetables mostly unavailable. Quinoa would be a great addition, and Gongbo became a man with a mission. After traveling to the United States and Mexico, he studied at the International Maize and Wheat Improvement Center in Mexico in 1988. He brought seeds back to Tibet, and in the early 1990s, the Tibetan government approved his quinoa cultivation project.

It wasn't long after I learned about Gongbo's quinoa quest that he invited Ray and Myra and me to accompany him to an area, miles from Bayi, to where he had a trial crop growing. He reserved a car and driver and soon we arrived at a surprising sight—the quinoa, growing on an island, sort of. I don't remember Gongbo's explanation of how machinery could manage the water, which was actually a narrow tributary of the Yarlung Tsangpo River. At the time of the planting, the water level was low to non-existent, and the same again at harvest time. The process seemed rather creative to me for making land suitable in which to grow something.

We three stayed on dry land while Gongbo went in a small boat out to the island to inspect his crop. It seemed wherever we'd travel to, there were children appearing out of nowhere, and so it was here. We tried to teach them a few English phrases after asking them simple questions in Chinese, and there was laughter all around.

The crop inspection finished, we were off on another amazing leg of the trip. Gongbo took us to a place that was as alien to me as anywhere I'd ever been. It was a temple, but not just any temple. It wasn't until we'd begun to ascend the steep stairs leading to the entrance that we realized just what kind of temple we'd come to. We were at the foot of the Fertility Temple. How did we determine this? Well, let's just say the subject matter of the carvings on each side of the steps left us without any doubts whatsoever.

That was not the only temple I would visit around that time (although it was the only fertility temple, for which I was grateful). Mr. Liu arranged an outing to a monastery/temple about thirty-five kilometers from Bayi. Every group needs a Mr. Liu. He was our English department's volunteer activities arranger, as I saw him. A shrinking violet he was not, for he seemed to be involved in every activity at the college, so it came as no surprise that he created interest in a Saturday outing, a bicycle trip, no less. According to Mr. Liu, it would be an enjoyable way to bond with each other and to possibly expand us *laowei's* (foreign visitor's) understanding of the ways of that part of Tibet.

Not everyone was on board with the promised fun time. I later came to realize that some in the department knew exactly of the "fun" that we bikers had in store for us. There was wisdom in their years at the school, *and* with time spent on Mr. Liu's activities. When early Saturday morning arrived, there were eight of us at the staging area, but no Mr. Liu. He sent his regrets by one of the bikers. Should that have been a red flag?

Mr. Zhang took on the responsibility for the trip. Thankfully, he at least knew the way, the only one who did. Laden with thermoses and snacks, we were off, pedaling down the yellow brick road. Actually, almost all the stretches of the road were unpaved, with pebbles and sand to contend with. Adding to that difficulty were some muscle-stretching hills that seemed to get higher and higher as we went.

We three Americans began the trip hale and hearty but throwing the hot sun and our ages into the equation, one of us came to the point where turning back was the only option. Ray, the oldest, eight years older than Myra, began to feel ill and knew he couldn't go on. Two others in the group went back with him. I couldn't imagine Myra not accompanying Ray, but she seemed determined to complete the trip and stuck with us.

Soon, two others gave up. We were dropping like flies. Now there were only three of us left to soldier on. For me, it wasn't merely to visit yet another temple; it was an adventure I wanted to complete. I didn't see myself as a quitter, even though I was nearing fifty-three years of age. Maybe Myra, probably around fifty-seven, saw it that way too.

Finally, we turned off our main road onto a path that led to the temple. As we neared, Mr. Zhang suggested we hide our bikes in the tall weeds off the trail so we didn't have to walk them up the steep incline. I'm not certain that I'd describe what I was doing as "walking"—it was more like trudging at that point, and hoping my wobbly legs would keep me upright.

And then, there it was—Lamaling temple. I couldn't have been any happier if I'd been a Buddhist, prostrating all the way from Bayi, continuing on to circumambulate the two holy sites. I was that tired.

Before climbing the high stairs to the entrance, we walked through a grassy courtyard in front of the main temple that a few doleful mountain goats called home. Looking upward, we saw a decorative element one couldn't miss: draped cannonball-sized, brightly colored wooden beads all across the front.

At the entrance, we took off our shoes, as was the custom. (Oh, what a relief it was!) All throughout were statues and puppet-like images. From the outside, the temple resembled a four-tiered wedding cake. At the top was a small chapel containing yet another statue which doubtless meant something to somebody.

There was another building nearby, but time and distance kept us from staying longer. After a filling meal of ramen noodles (boiled water provided), we walked down the long path to where our bikes were hidden. We hadn't gone far down the main road when Mr. Zhang noticed that a wheel on his bike was going flat. The road we were on was not really a main road to anywhere. We hadn't seen another vehicle on our way to the temple, and we had reason to be worried.

Mr. Zhang took one of our bikes to go look for an abode where there might be someone to render aid. We contributed all the money we had on us, which wasn't much, to entice someone to come and help us. One hour turned into two. Waiting was difficult. And scary. Here we were, two white women sitting beside a road, neither of us capable of carrying on a dialogue in Chinese, let alone Tibetan.

Finally, in the distance, we heard what sounded like an engine making popping noises. And it was coming right toward us. Shortly, along came a motorized two-handled machine with a small cart behind it, Mr. Zhang leading the way. He'd bargained with the driver to take us to Bayi and pay him more money when we'd arrive.

The cart had its downside. If we had not held on tightly to the side, we would have been lofted upward several inches every time we hit very rough spots, which was most of the time. Along the way, the driver made a stop to pick up a man walking beside the road, a hitch hiker, who couldn't believe his luck in getting a ride into Bayi. More money for the driver. We were like sardines in a can, what with the three bicycles and four bodies, becoming a close-knit group by necessity.

Eastern Tibet was home to many military garrisons, so it wasn't unexpected to see soldiers in the area. Before long, I noticed two young PLA men walking alongside the road just ahead of us. They looked to be young and benign, what with their sloppy camouflage clothes and cloth shoes. Our Tibetan driver made it clear what he thought of the Chinese in his home, veering off the road and aiming directly for the soldiers, forcing them into the ditch. We continued on, fortunately without the soldiers taking any action.

Not long after that, things became more uncomfortable. It began to rain—a cold rain. The darkened skies fooled me into believing it was later than it actually was. Finally, about a mile from campus, we met our rescuers with Ray leading the way. Somehow a large truck was found to go look for us. Everyone was worried that something had happened to us.

Oh, yes, Mr. Liu had joined the posse. In fact, he was the one who'd found the truck. Did he have an idea in his head for the next great adventure? I wasn't about to ask.

CHAPTER 31

MORE ADVENTURES IN BICYCLE THIEVERY

"Opportunity makes a thief."
—Francis Bacon

Just another lazy Saturday in the sleepy confines of a nondescript college in a secluded valley of a faux Shangri-La. To assuage my boredom, I biked into town looking for anything that might pass for amusement or excitement.

There was always the shop owned by a minority woman—not Han, not true Tibetan—whose goods helped the shop resemble a mercantile establishment and whose supply of hats always struck my fancy. The owner, whose name unfortunately I never knew, seemed keen for me to try on the latest imports, without any expectation that I might actually buy one. I suspect my presence alone was good for business. I was considered an oddity in town and my appearance at the shop usually brought in a lot of lookers. Some would come in to check out the merchandise I was checking out, while others were less bold and content to stand outside and observe the "panda." There were no cultural rules of decorum that would prohibit people from staring, and some would keep it up until they were either bored or had somewhere else they needed to be.

From the shop, once again without having made a purchase, I paid a visit to the fruit sellers. These were usually five or six women standing near the department store with their wooden carts filled with apples, peaches, or whatever fruit had been shipped in. As soon as they'd spot me, the chattering would begin and they'd vie for my business. They all offered the same fruit so the successful purchase hinged on the bargaining. My heart wasn't in the haggling, but I knew it would be considered rude not to play along. The negotiating always began with *yi jian, duoshao qian?* One pound, how much? I'd accept the offer after a few rounds of back and forth. After visiting them a few times, they came to see that I was buying from each of them in turns. Taking pictures of them at their carts and giving them the photos made them happy and made me a forever friend. Knowing that they couldn't have made much money after standing around all day by their carts and settling for a meager profit, it was my hope that I could at least put a little levity into their days.

It wouldn't be a trip to Bayi unless I made an appearance at the two-story department store. It was fronted with huge blue glass, and I had noticed that blue glass was showing up in some of the other newer buildings, as if it were the latest decorating trend. It did add a little something to the otherwise colorless cityscape. Two Han Chinese women, no older than teenagers, it seemed to me, were in control of the second floor. For my first few visits there, we'd smile at one another and I'd try to look for something I might need. Someone must have instructed them on the fine art of salesmanship, for they'd pick up anything and everything and offer it to me for a hopeful sale. Later on, after becoming more familiar with one another, and assuming no other customers were around, I'd go waltzing down the aisle to the music playing on the floor, with the two young women laughing and clapping along. It was a welcome diversion for us all. The child within was alive and well.

On this particular day, having tried on hats, haggled for some fruit, danced around the second floor of the department store, and wandered around the city sufficiently, I hopped on my bike and headed "over the river and through the woods" for the campus. I always enjoyed biking down the tree-lined narrow street, especially in the autumn when the slanted sunrays would create trees of gold. Others were enjoying that laid-back Saturday afternoon, as evidenced by a small group of men visiting outside the first entry to the apartments. They looked up as I approached, but I didn't hear the childish "hellos" I'd sometimes hear. I arrived at my entryway, parked my bike inside it, then went in for a short while, figuring that I'd bike to the post office to check for my mail a little later.

Soon, while getting a drink in my kitchen, I thought I heard a sound coming from outside my door. Hearing nothing further, I dismissed it, but then happened to glance out of the kitchen window to see one of the aforementioned men riding slowly away from my entry on *my* bike. Something inside me spurred me into action. I raced out of my door, flip-flops smacking the ground as I gave chase. The thief was pedaling nonchalantly down the street on his ill-gotten new ride, and I could have caught up with him if I hadn't committed one huge strategical error. I yelled to anyone who might hear, "Stop, thief!" At that, the rider sped up, quickly putting distance between us.

I watched as he turned left into the little street where the kindergarten was located. In the meantime, Mr. Zhang, who'd heard me yelling, came out of his apartment to see what the hullabaloo was all about. Wasting no time, he formed a posse, Tibetan style, and directed some students to rush to the entrances of the school to head the thief off in case he was attempting to leave the campus. But the posse turned up nothing. I knew it would be difficult to ever retrieve the bike, as it looked like every other bike you'd see on campus. In hindsight, I should have put something on it to identify it for such a heist as this.

A month or so later, as I was walking to the administration building for an English department meeting, I stopped by the fence of the kindergarten to watch some of the children at play. Just as I turned to continue on my way, I noticed a man coming out of a side path carrying a child on the back of his bike. He was at least fifty yards away, but when our eyes met, he immediately turned back the way he'd come.

I ran up the street in hopes of seeing him on the side path, but he was nowhere in sight. I hid behind a tall bush in hopes he would come by. I was sure he'd been on his way to drop off his child at the kindergarten when he'd spotted me. In the end, no man, no bike. And I was late for the meeting.

CHAPTER 32

LOSSES

"Death is a distant rumor to the young."
—Andy Rooney

It was a sunny Saturday afternoon, and I was out strolling on campus, enjoying the cool breeze of early spring. I felt a sense of peace. More importantly, I felt as if I were right where I was supposed to be. God was in His heaven and all was right with the world.

Then I happened to glance up from my reverie and noticed, a short distance away, students coming from the front gate, trudging toward their dorms. They walked with their heads down and their shoulders hunched, as if carrying a great weight. They came in small groups, twos or threes, or in some cases alone. Nobody was talking. My sense of peace was suddenly replaced with a sense of unease.

A few days later, I came upon the chance to learn about the occasion that had brought about the solemn procession of students that Saturday afternoon; I ran into Mr. Liu, the town crier of the campus. But Mr. Liu, for all his verbosity, was tight-lipped that day. I kept pressing and finally prevailed. The students, a somber Mr. Liu informed me, had been made to witness a particularly gruesome sight. Yet a sight not altogether uncommon in communist China.

In fact, China has a long history of public executions. It's estimated that during Chairman Mao's time, millions of "enemies of the people" were executed. The rate has slowed considerably since those days, but China still has the highest rate of executions in the world. And those are the ones we know about. According to Amnesty International, only a fraction of executions is reported. The annual toll is treated as a state secret. We know, however, that most are not only public, but mandatory to attend, especially by students. Executions are warnings, summed up by an old Chinese saying, "Killing a chicken to scare the monkeys." Even children are encouraged to watch. I saw other, less deadly, forms of punishment, too, mostly based on the idea of humiliation. While living in Lhasa, I watched as prisoners on the backs of flatbed trucks were paraded around the streets.

What the students were made to witness that otherwise beautiful Saturday afternoon was a fellow student being put to death. Mr. Liu wouldn't divulge specifics, saying only that the young man was pronounced "guilty of a heinous crime." That's all he'd tell me, and I decided not to press the matter any further. In time, I would come to learn more about these executions. Typically, the condemned is made to kneel. Then, either a military person or a local police officer, depending on the classification of the crime in question, puts a bullet through the base of the skull. To add insult to injury, the executed person's family is forced to pay for the bullet.

In this case, knowing the distance between Bayi and Beijing, or even Lhasa for that matter, I imagined the execution was probably meted out by local authorities, perhaps increasing the likelihood of a more arbitrary, less official, punishment.

I also wondered, knowing the long distances from their hometowns that most of the students were, and knowing of the scarcity of telephone communications, how long it would take for the family of the poor student to learn of his fate. They may not have received word until days or even weeks after his death.

I thought a lot about the other students, as well. They were classmates. Some perhaps strangers to him; some perhaps close friends. What would being exposed to such a ghoulish scene of violence do to them? Were the students left alone to have to mentally sort it all out? Would they talk about it, even amongst themselves? I imagined some would suffer a delayed reaction, maybe even post-traumatic stress. What would they do with their feelings of helplessness, their powerlessness in the face of such a macabre incident? And what would those feelings do to them?

I knew that talking about death was a taboo subject in China, even considered disrespectful. There's an irony in this because all the major religions that shape Chinese beliefs and customs—Confucianism, Taoism, Buddhism—regard death as a natural part of life. Buddhism in particular, with its belief in reincarnation, sees life and death as parts of a continuous cycle of rebirth. Nevertheless, thoughts of death were kept to oneself. Most likely, each student was alone in his or her grief and confusion.

The grief would get worse that spring.

The Yarlong Tsampo river serpentined lazily through the valley of Bayi like a blue satin ribbon. It added more beauty to an already stunning part of the world. Evergreens were everywhere, making me feel like I was in a valley cocooned by emeralds. Tibet has been described by various monikers: The Roof of the World, The Land of Snows, The Land of White Clouds. Bayi reflected it all.

For much of the year, the river—fifteenth-longest in the world, originating in the northern Himalayas, and flowing almost 2,900 kilometers before meeting its destiny in the Bay of Bengal in India—seemed to move along as a result of the constant wind tunnel effect of the valley. While it had its calmer moments, everyone knew to beware the spring and summer months when the river became so much more powerful. It moved with speed and passion, earning respect and even fear.

The Yarlong Tsampo is often regarded as the most isolated, dangerous river on the planet. There are stretches of rapids in the lower gorge that some say God himself would have to portage. After it enters India, it's known as the mighty Brahmaputra. There it provides life to the people who depend on it. It *is* life, they say. It is never death. The Brahmaputra has flowed for hundreds of thousands of years. If death occurs because man has encroached its plain, the death, the people will tell you, is a suicide. The river does not kill. Nature cannot be corralled by man-made boundaries or beholden to man-made errors of judgement. Or acts of naïve bravado.

In late spring the year I was there, just weeks after the execution of the student, when the river began to get rowdy and restive with its warmer waters from the thawing mountain snow from upstream, the young men of the campus were also getting rowdy and restive. One day, they headed out for a day of fun and relaxation. Somewhere downriver they found the perfect spot to wade into the water. I do not know if all could swim, but knowing how to swim doesn't mean you should. Why would anyone choose to wade into a raging mountain river? To young people, life without the occasional adrenaline rush is too tame to conceive of.

And so it happened. One of the group lost his footing at the hands of the strong current and was unable to recover. His friends tried to grab him, but the angry river had him in its grasp. All they could do was watch as he was swept away until he went out of sight.

Once again, I'd heard by the grapevine about this second tragedy. Once again, I approached Mr. Liu for information. He told me the drowned student would probably not be seen until the body would reach India. I could see anguish etched on his face. The young man had been his student.

Again, I was made to wonder at what was going through the young minds of the student's classmates, now having to internalize two deaths in such a short period of time, having to contemplate the years of potential life violently taken away, having to bear the losses, losses each would have to carry with them for the rest of their lives, in their own ways, in their own hearts.

It was a beautiful spring in a beautiful part of the world. That year, the beauty was juxtaposed with death, two unexpected losses that, like the students, I carry with me still, in my own way, in my own heart.

Nuns on steps of Nunnery

Frequent visitors to my apartment, Bayi

Mother with baby in middle of street hoping for alms

Beauties of Bayi

Stupas on mountain

March Madness at Tibet University, 1991

CHAPTER 33

CHRYSALIS

"Every man's life ends the same way. It is only the details of how he lived and how he died that distinguishes one man from another."
—Ernest Hemingway

The community in which I grew up could easily have been the buckle in the Bible Belt. It seemed in my teen years as if the buckle was tightened a few notches. There was no slack for waywardness. And waywardness included dancing, even ballroom dancing. The waltz? The closest I ever got to the waltz was listening to my older sister's recording of "The Blue Danube."

Then came Tibet. In October of my year in Bayi, it seemed there was a dance contest. It was none other than Mr. Liu who made me aware of this. He was in the market for a dance partner. I was intrigued. I was not in the Bible Belt anymore and feeling somewhat liberated. Dancing? Why not? I explained to Mr. Liu that I had never danced, but he was undeterred. He would teach me, he said. But where? When? These problems were solved after I told Ray and Myra. They agreed to chaperone the dance lessons in my apartment. All that was needed was to push the few pieces of furniture against the walls (taking extra care to handle the three-legged chair). Mr. Liu would provide the music.

The lessons went well. My steps were tentative at first, but soon I found myself being taken to surprising heights of joy by the music and the movement. Dancing: who could ever find fault in something so expressive, so freeing? Why had it taken me decades to discover this jewel of human activity?

Nevertheless, after several lessons, I did not share Mr. Liu's confidence that we were ready for any contest. I wasn't sure why he'd asked me to be his partner in the first place. Ray and Myra suggested that it might have been a feather in his cap to dance with the foreigner, since there had never been a foreigner at the school before.

Whatever his reason, the annual dance contest was approaching and there was no turning back. Among other things, that meant deciding what to wear. Formal attire was something I'd never thought about needing at "the farm." Formal wear for me would have been wearing my newest pair of jeans (or the clean pair). Enter the local sew lady and her treadle sewing machine, located on one of the narrow lanes on campus. A trip to downtown Bayi yielded a few *ji* (yards) of red cloth. Neither of us came close to being a fashion designer, but we got the job done. My mid-length full skirt was paired with a long-sleeved, white, silk blouse (okay, polyester).

On the day of the contest, I decided to go to the beauty salon located on Bayi square. I knew it probably wasn't wise to try something for the first time before an important occasion, but heck, everything that happened to me in Bayi was a first. Why not continue crawling out on that shaky limb and hope for the best?

Mr. Liu must have been worried that I'd be negotiating a hairdo from a weakened position, and mostly with hand motions and pantomiming. Taking no chances, he went to where I was being coifed and made sure I didn't come away with a horrible "do." Probably, his efforts had more to do with his ego and reputation than the state of my hair. In his mind, the physical appearance of his dance partner was a reflection on him. We left the salon and headed back to campus. I couldn't have felt more protected if I'd had the US Secret Service at my beck and call. Actually, I was beginning to feel suffocated by all of Mr. Liu's attention. Clearly, nothing was going to keep us from taking the stage that evening.

In fact, he arrived at my apartment to escort me to the auditorium before the agreed upon time, taking no last-minute chances that we might not make it or that I might somehow change my mind. I had no such thoughts, although I did feel a slight sense of uncertainty, a nagging fear that I may commit some terrible dancing *faux pas* and embarrass my partner. It was Mr. Liu's reputation that was on the line. He saw himself as capable and supremely self-confident. Me? Nobody knew me. I was just the foreign panda.

The back room of the auditorium was all abuzz. The dancers waited with nervous excitement, each with a designated number pinned to his or her back. Groups of five were announced; the winners of each group would vie at the end to determine the overall winners. I had no expectations. I limited my ambitions to making sure my feet would be in sync with Mr. Liu's leading. I knew we were up against seasoned dancers.

We were the third group. I peeked out from the side of the stage to see how other couples performed. Some were better than others, but all clearly had more than three lessons under their belts. Mr. Liu was going to have to over-perform to cover for my inexperience. Still, I held out hope that I could leave the stage with my head held high and Mr. Liu's feet still intact.

At last, it was our group's turn. Mr. Liu and I walked out onto the stage hand in hand. *Just four minutes. You can do this!* We began to dance near the front of the stage, the exact place I didn't want to be. I tried to follow Mr. Liu's lead, but something was wrong. Something was off. Way off. And it wasn't me. Mr. Liu's movements were more walking and pushing than actual dancing. He had clearly forgotten the steps. With all my own jitters, it had not occurred to me that Mr. Liu might be experiencing nerves of his own. In fact, he was in full-blown panic mode. While the other couples swirled gracefully around the stage, we stumbled toward the rear. Mercifully, the music stopped, the audience clapped, and we retreated from the stage with Mr. Liu not saying a word.

Needless to say, we didn't make the cut and our evening came to an inglorious end. Mr. Liu never spoke of it again, no doubt wishing to scrub the experience from his memory for good. For me, I took it as a lesson learned: Never, ever, enter another dance contest.

But it was not the end of my nascent love affair with dancing. Wednesday and Friday nights, the campus dance hall was the place to be. Really a large room with colorful streamers festooning the ceiling and a sparkly ball hanging from the center. Chairs were situated around the walls for those not dancing. Some of the non-dancers were women who only went to socialize, some carrying along their knitting. Because I couldn't conjure up anything more exciting, I began an extended relationship with that room. On both nights, the doors opened and closed with me. I mostly learned to make peace with the boredom that usually arrived with the setting sun, but it wasn't always easy. The dance hall saved me.

Most of the attendees were younger adults, except for Mr. Liu and me. Oh, yes, Mr. Liu didn't miss a night. During the first semester he went alone, for his wife had earned her half-year sabbatical and was in Chengdu. After she returned for the second semester, she would sometimes go to the dance hall even though she never danced.

It was Mr. Liu who suggested that we resume my dance lessons. In no time at all, I was ready to move on to the fast waltz. Most of the time, there were fewer couples when the music played fast. That made for more room for us as we covered the floor, swirling to the music, with our steps in perfect synchrony, acting as if we owned the room.

Sometimes, exhausted, I thought I'd never make it to the end of the music, but I was determined not to give in. The exhilaration I felt in my soul as I swept around the room was my miracle, a transformative moment. It was as if I were unleashing and celebrating my inner child, scarcely even aware of my partner. The music and movement provided an explosion of freedom. I was released from the chrysalis that had encased me my whole life, a chrysalis of culture, religion, generations of family values, and personal naiveté.

I made a decision somewhere on that dance floor on one of those nights: I would, every day from that time forward, attempt to celebrate the unleashing of my inner child, to laugh and dance and sing....into the Mystery.

CHAPTER 34

THANKSGIVING

"Gratitude can transform common days into Thanksgiving, turn routine jobs into joy, and change ordinary opportunities into blessings."
—William Arthur Ward

My oven arrived!

November 8, or thereabouts, was a day of celebration in ole Bayitown, at least on the tree-lined campus street where I lived. It was pure joy to know the boxes I'd entrusted to a stranger, a truck driver in Chengdu recommended to me by a Chinese friend, had arrived safely after a three-week journey over rough roads and up and around many mountains. When I parted with my almost-new oven, some clothing, and myriad teaching supplies in late August, I wasn't sure if I'd ever lay eyes on them again. In this part of the world at this time, trust and prayers were all one had to rely on for peace of mind and heart.

One might wonder why an approximately 28-inch by 14-inch electric oven would bring me such happiness. Baking/cooking had always been a part of my life, ever since my mom allowed me to bake my first cake, unsupervised, at the age of ten. That didn't go so well but I persevered until more than just my father would dare eat any of my slowly evolving repertoire of treats.

266

There would be other ovens I'd buy during the following thirteen years I lived in Chengdu, but this particular one was special. I came to realize it was the beginning of God's plan for me, a means of introducing my future students and friends to His Son. Sharing my baked goods with friends in this place was a way to show love and goodwill. God uses a myriad of ways and willing servants to further His Kingdom. Why not food?

I began baking soon after the oven arrived. The first significant baking was for a surprise birthday party for Mr. Zhang. For that, I made an orange date cake and a carrot cake decorated with carrots made of icing. Later came various breads: cinnamon rolls, Italian yeast rolls, apple-spice, sweet potato. My apartment was soon dubbed "The Bakery." Various aromas wafted through the kitchen window.

It was nearing the American Thanksgiving holiday when I thought of inviting six officials of the Foreign Language Department to experience some typical holiday foods, as much as I could offer with a combination of local ingredients and mixes sent in a "Care" package from the States.

It took me all day to cook with only the aid of a small, tripod, electric-coil burner, plus the oven. The day before, I'd gone to the small city market to buy the chicken for baking, and some eggs. I was fortunate in acquiring the latter because they were rare in this town. Why all the roosters and not a hoard of chickens? I was left to wonder. Some items for baking I'd brought in with me in August, including real butter bought in Lhasa. I'd planned for a day such as this before leaving Hong Kong. A little bit of home always helps. I have to admit that I was quite impressed with myself for what I was able to put together in my kitchen. The menu consisted of Asian white sweet potato fluff flavored with tangerine juice with marshmallows on top, mashed potatoes, Stove Top cornbread stuffing, chicken gravy, glazed orange and honey carrots, Spanish rice, green olives, cranberry-orange relish, and homemade yeast rolls.

The guests arrived and I offered them a small taste of hot apple cider as a welcoming drink. I had to know that they liked it before I'd give them more. Only two did. One of the guests made a horrible face, letting me know his opinion in a way that needed no further translation.

To say that my Chinese guests were under impressed with the meal is putting it mildly. It wasn't that I believed they would gobble everything up with gusto, but I wasn't quite prepared for the additional facial expressions that came along, belying good manners in any culture. Would it occur to them that I might not look upon *their* banquets with lip-smacking, drooling anticipation while looking at the beady eyes of the ubiquitous large fish swimming in the requisite ocean of red, mouth-numbing liquid?

At the time, I didn't know of the complexities of Chinese dining that involved guests. One thing I did know was that the honored guest was seated facing the door. The guest would be further honored by the person sitting to their right. It would be this person's duty to see that the guest ate some of everything by placing food on their plate whether they wanted it or not. As a guest myself, I would always employ all my skills to prevent this from happening, but the food would begin to pile up, with my right-seated "helper" continually prodding me to "Eat. Eat." What I *did* look forward to was the arrival of the huge bowl of rice, thus indicating that there would be no more dishes to be brought to the table. Rice was served last because it was considered "common" food and not worthy of the Chinese banquet table that featured varied meat and fish dishes. I was usually the only one who ate any of the rice, which would guarantee that at least I wouldn't leave hungry.

At any rate, my guests thanked me for the meal regardless of their true opinion of it, and a few days later, on our true Thanksgiving Day, Ray, Myra, and I invited all the English department people and their spouses to gather in my apartment for a potluck celebration.

We three provided our Western food to augment the Chinese food, or maybe it was the other way around. This time I made cornbread dressing from scratch. For the *pièce de résistance*, I made a walnut pie, which few wanted. Too sweet. Before we ate, Ray read from the Book of Psalms and led a prayer of thanksgiving. For my part, I was especially thankful that in working around the availability of electricity, I was able to get the meal prepared.

A couple of weeks later, I spent more time in my kitchen and made a pot of vegetable soup with chicken, homemade rolls, scrambled eggs, and apple crisp for seven of my first-year students, each of whom had received the highest marks on their mid-term exam. I scrambled the eggs because one student told me earlier that they all missed eating eggs, for they didn't get them at the school because of the scarcity. Now, *they* ate with gusto, making only pleased expressions and leaving nothing on their plates.

This scarcity of eggs, incidentally, was something of a head-scratcher. The campus had an overabundance of roosters, but where were the hens? The roosters had few members of the fairer sex to charm with their strutting and crowing. They weren't used for food, either. The only time I found them useful was in the morning as an alarm clock. But they started early. Too early. One rooster, at some distance away from my apartment, crowed every morning at precisely 3 a.m. A closer one joined in later. By five o'clock, there was a cacophony when all of these "alarm clocks" would begin in earnest. Ray and Myra endured five roosters and some caged chickens below their second-floor apartment. I was fortunate to have just one penned up outside my building. Irritants such as this had to be tolerated as something we couldn't control. A good night's sleep would have to be put on hold.

The best I could do while lying in my bed listening to all the crowing was to formulate a poem, written to the rhythm of "Down in the Valley." To wit:

Requiem for the "Three O'clock Cock"

Across Linzhi Valley, the valley so low,
Three in the morning, hear the cocks crow.
Hear the cocks crow, dear. Hear the cocks crow.
Across all Linzhi Valley, hear the cocks crow.

(Ray) "Sleep will not come dear, sleep will not come.
Get cotton for my ears, dear, or they'll ruin my eardrum."
(Myra) "What did you say, dear? You sound far away.
The cocks are so deafening, I can't hear a word you say."

(Ray) "I see your mouth moving, but I don't hear a sound.
Are the cocks all conspiring, soon as their feet hit the ground?"
(Together) "Let's plan a cocknapping. Let's plan it for three.
If more than one's crowing, we'll make it a spree."

(Ray) "Make ready the pot, dear. We'll have 'rooster stew.'
Twenty cocks are all crowing? It's stew for a crew!"
Across Linzhi Valley, the valley so low,
It's three in the morning—no cocks left to crow!

CHAPTER 35

LONG DECEMBER

"It was the best of times, it was the worst of times...it was the season of light, it was the season of darkness."
—Charles Dickens, *A Tale of Two Cities*

December had always been a magical month for me, and I expected the same in Bayi. In my younger years, there was Santa Clause, and the traditional last-minute trip to Atlanta, Texas, fourteen miles away, for my parents to buy tree lights to replace the burned-out ones, a box of icicles for the tree, last minute gifts, ribbon candy, and bags of apples, oranges, and nuts in the shell. Back home, we kids, as young tree-decorating engineers, kept moving lights around to various spots on the tree to meet our particular specifications.

In Bayi, I found a few Christmas cards, though I wondered how they made their way to that distant place. Some were even in English. I also found miniature colored string lights, but no other tree decorations. I was confident the tinsmith in town could fashion a star for my tree, which I hoped to acquire later. The school gave us permission to go out to the wooded area of the low mountains behind the campus to cut our own Christmas trees. I also planned to cut some green boughs of cedar and holly, and also some greenery with small red berries. With my handmade decorations, I couldn't wait to see how the tree would evolve from my imagination.

The child in each of us makes us long for a little of the wonder and awe we experienced years before. Like a white Christmas. One morning, I looked out my kitchen window to see a dusting of snow on the ground. I would expect to see snow on the mountain tops, but it was unusual to see it on the ground in the valley. Winter had its special beauty, more so at Christmas time, even on the other side of the world. Little did I know, however, that events would conspire to derail my Christmas plans. There would be no tree, no handmade decorations, no tin star.

It all started with the usual winter challenges. My feet were always cold. Teaching was arduous in the freezing classroom. During the break, I'd step out into the sunshine along with my students to try to warm up. This could have been a contributing factor to my waking up one day in bed with chills and then sweats. My aching torso felt weak for days, and if this wasn't enough misery, I began to experience a bad toothache that lasted three weeks. Sometimes Tylenol helped; sometimes it didn't. The night to beat all nights was the night I had the bad toothache, spastic colon, hot flashes, and a headache. How I even noticed the headache in all of that remains a puzzle.

Nevertheless, I soldiered on. I enjoyed my Monday mornings in December because I didn't have classes on Mondays. I stayed in bed with the comforters pulled up around my neck. After I had made my coffee, of course. I found this to be a good time to write letters.

Electricity was always an issue at that time of year. It was usually off between 8:30 a.m. and 7:00 p.m. I had a slim, upright, oscillating, dual-tube heater, but it was useful to me only when there was power. Bath-time had to be scheduled when I could heat water, but the water was usually too cold to even think about it. If I did heat it, enough of it to fill a five-gallon bucket, I'd have to step into the icy shower room/WC. Most of the time, I didn't find it to be worth the trouble.

One December day, Ray and Myra and I were told about an up-coming school-wide performance extravaganza in which we were expected to participate. A Chinese female teacher who knew a few songs in English requested we join with her to sing as a quartet. She chose "Oh, Susanna" and, remarkably, "Down in the Valley." I thought about offering my creative rendition but decided to keep that one to myself.

Our newly formed group met only once to practice, which turned out to be sufficient, for all the practicing in the world would not have helped. No one would ever mistake us for the Maguire Sisters, partly because of "sister" Ray's inclusion. At least it can be said that he tried.

Me, I had my own issues. The days leading up to the program were miserable for me health-wise. Besides the lingering discomforts, I felt that something new was coming. I struggled to keep going to class, feeling worse by the hour and unable to stay warm. I needed rest, or a leave of absence. Instead, on the night of the program, I trudged to the auditorium even though I knew I was seriously ill.

There was a small anteroom just off the stage where an electric coil heater was failing to warm anyone who wasn't sitting right next to it. I sat on a small stool nearby, slumping more and more until my body was at a ninety-degree angle. On stage, the acts that preceded ours were taking forever. And now I was feeling nauseous. Could I go out there? How much applause would we get if I threw up in front of a full auditorium?

From my memory of that inglorious occasion, I only mouthed the words of our songs, leaning on Myra the whole time for support. After leaving the stage, a female student of mine happened to be in the little room, and I asked her if she'd be kind enough to see me back to my apartment. She did so, holding me up the whole way back. Seeing me safely inside, she left, and I dropped into bed where I would remain for the next week, leaving it only for trips to the WC.

My first trip to the WC the next day was revelatory. Coca-Cola-colored urine and a white stool. Just what manner of death was I experiencing? Myra came over to see about me and seemed just as worried as I was. She returned later with soup that I was unable to swallow. Soon, it was even difficult to swallow any liquids. Just raising my head was a chore. Myra alerted Mr. Zhang, who came into my room, took one look at me, and promptly secured a vehicle and driver to take me to the military hospital for an exam and tests. Two days later, I went back for more tests. Both times I was told to be prepared to stay for a few days, but, to my relief, each time I was sent back home. I knew it was only because conditions at the hospital weren't good and there was an overriding need for the doctors to save face. But that was okay with me. The last thing I wanted was an icy cold room in the hospital and a replay of my Lhasa hospital stay. Instead, on the second visit, the doctor wrote out an order for IVs and penicillin for Dr. Stickum to administer in my own warm room. Penicillin seemed to be the standard medical response for any malady, prescribed even for the common cold.

Back in my apartment, Mr. Zhang summoned Dr. Stickum, who set about connecting me to an IV with another one at the ready hanging from the pole. I asked if he would be back to connect the spare, but Dr. Stickum said I could either change it myself, or anyone who happened to be with me could change it. This would require pulling the needle out and reinserting it. I winced just thinking about it. The lucky person would turn out to be Miss Jia, who came by later for a visit, the timing of which put her in the unfortunate position of having to do the deed. She was scared stiff at the thought, but after she calmed down, I pointed out the alcohol-soaked cotton the doc left behind and gave her the step-by-step instructions. With the mission accomplished, Miss Jia left my room probably thinking of changing her profession, so proud was she of herself.

For days, I rested in my bed under my downy comforters with the small heater running every moment that the electricity would let it. If I weren't so good at bouncing back from illness and sorrow, I would have found myself in a very sorry state. Not that I was doing much bouncing. At first, it was all I could do to go to the WC without my legs buckling. One night, my upstairs neighbor, whom I didn't even know, came down to my room to give me a back massage, one of several she would give me over the next few days. And she was good at it. I hurt all over, my body screamed, but I endured it. Pain never felt so good.

In the meantime, Ray and Myra went to the telecommunication office in Bayi to let a colleague know of my illness, who, in turn, consulted a book entitled *When There Is No Doctor*. Based on my symptoms, the diagnosis was clear: I had hepatitis A. The book advised no medication. Only broth and water until such time as I felt ready to eat solid food.

A week went by, and I began to get my appetite back, able to consume small quantities of vegetable soup. I'd remain weak for some time, but there was no time to be weak. I was due in Hong Kong during the holiday break for, once again, our placement organization's annual conference. In fact, there were two organizations who were having conferences and I had planned to attend both. The trip would take me to Lhasa, Chengdu, and then Hong Kong.

Mr. Zhang worked on the arrangements for me, making sure there would be a room for me at the Holiday Inn in Lhasa. That would not be difficult because there would be very few people who'd want to book a room at that time. Fortunately for me, there was a steep winter discount. That was the good news. The bad news was that the low occupancy meant the hotel's heat would be turned off.

Meanwhile, Ray and Myra had been contacted by someone in Lhasa to let them know that one of my placement organization's insurance carriers for those serving outside the US was considering sending a helicopter to deliver me to Lhasa. This must have been the Cadillac of insurance carriers. I had my doubts that the government would allow it. Either way, I turned the offer down. Instead, Mr. Zhang came to tell me that we would be leaving for Lhasa on the

24th, Christmas Eve, in a Landcruiser he'd secured, along with a driver. Mr. Zhang would accompany me all the way to Chengdu. For him, it was a paid vacation away from school. By the time of departure, I was up and around and ready for my extended absence. In fact, I would not be returning until sometime after the Tibetan New Year, which was in March that year.

On Christmas Eve, the frosty air hit me hard as I stepped outside in the pre-dawn. Once on the road in the Landcruiser, we began to climb higher and higher, the narrow gravel road becoming icier and icier. We sometimes slid our way up and sometimes slid our way down. The driver and Mr. Zhang never appeared worried about slipping and sliding, but my body was constantly tied in knots anticipating a major calamity. An hour outside of Bayi, we suffered a flat tire, but were soon on our way again.

Our first non-tire-related rest stop was for a potty break. It was easy enough for the men, but I knew I was too weak to climb up and around the roadside berms to find some privacy, so I stayed in the car. By lunchtime I was about to explode as we stopped at a small village called Gongbo'gyamda. Not much there except for a crudely built building where one could get boiled water and a dish of noodles and vegetables for cheap. I carried with me some bakery bread and a thermos of tea, so I was set for breakfast. What I needed to know was the location of the WC. Someone pointed out a small, shed-like building a good distance from the "restaurant."

I walked there gingerly over a bumpy, snow-covered expanse, to discover a foul odor emanating from the structure that even the freezing temperature could not cover up. No way was I going in. Instead, I went around back, out of view, and did what I went back there to do. Much later, when I would eventually return to Bayi, we'd stop at this same village and I would visit this same WC. Only it would be March, the snow would be gone, and I would see, disturbingly, why the ground was bumpy months before, and just exactly what the bumps were. Not everyone bothered to make it all the way to the WC, and the bumps—the very bumps I had walked upon!—were no longer frozen.

While the men took their time eating, drinking, and smoking (there was no smoking in the car in deference to me), I walked around the little village. I had a lot of Hong Kong small coins in my bag, so I began giving them out to the children who surrounded me. This was a restricted area, and these people had rarely seen foreigners—if at all.

Back on the road, we eventually reached Mila Pass, the highest point before descending toward Lhasa. There were several long switchbacks, and the road was icy and narrow with a shear drop in many places. Several times the car slid sideways and fishtailed. Once, we stopped near the edge to allow a truck to pass by and once, on an incline, the motor died and all I could think about was the drop-off and the sudden wish that I had agreed to the helicopter rescue after all. Fortunately, the driver got us started again and we continued on.

We arrived in Lhasa by mid-afternoon. It was good to be back, and even better to be visiting the Holiday Inn once again. Chef Jerry and Mr. Barba were gone by then, but others had come to take their place. After checking in, I was keen on staying in my room lying down without the sensation of sliding. Later, a few people I knew in Lhasa from my organization came to see me and check on my condition. After they left, an international call came through from the insurance company in Houston to check on my condition and to ask if I wanted them to send a nurse to accompany me back to the US. I thanked them, and said I'd be fine as Mr. Zhang was traveling with me.

To celebrate Christmas Eve, the hotel chef planned a dinner for the few guests of the hotel and anyone else around who wanted to celebrate the holiday. There wasn't anywhere to go outside of the Holiday Inn. I'd reserved my space earlier, not knowing if I'd be able to eat anything, but I was greatly surprised and my spirits lifted as I entered the Hard Yak Café. It was lit by individual upright heaters dispersed around the tables that gave off a candle-like glow. There was beautiful Christmas music of German origin playing softly. The menu gave options: rabbit with brown mushrooms, venison with port, roast duck with orange pepper sauce, or grilled wild boar. It was all too rich and exotic for my sensitive stomach at the time. I had some tea and a little dessert, and enjoyed conversing with the people at my table—a Dutch couple, a man from Switzerland, and three Americans, one of whom I had previously met in Chengdu.

Santa came around to all the tables presenting *hadas* (ceremonial white scarves), and a red Holiday Inn shopping bag with the same stuff guests tend to add to their belongings when they leave their room. But no towels! Santa's beard was fashioned with *hadas*. (One does have to be creative.) A large British woman who was interning there was Santa. The chef even created a huge gingerbread house that went on display along with a bûche de noël. It was more than I would have thought possible at this time in this place, so far from the traditions of home in the US. The miracle of Christmas, I realized, can travel with us anywhere we happen to be in the world, as long we keep Christmas in our hearts.

On Christmas morning, I awoke to bright sunshine in a room warmed by one of those upright heaters. Not much happened that day, except for putting in several phone calls to family members. They were all relieved to know that I was getting better. Then later in the afternoon, several teachers from the university came to take hot showers. The hot shower was an absolute treat, a far cry from having to fill a five-gallon bucket with heated water. Life was very good.

The next morning was another early departure, but this time it was to go to the airport, about forty-five minutes from Lhasa. Mr. Zhang and I were soon on our way to Chengdu.

CHAPTER 36

CONFERENCING

"A strong friendship doesn't need daily conversation, doesn't always need togetherness, as long as the relationship lives in the heart, true friends will never part."
—Oscar Auliq-Ice

It was 5 a.m. and *deja vu* all over again. The same numbing cold and the all-too-familiar bumpy ride to the airport. Except this time I rode in a Landcruiser from the hotel. And the driver was not quite the speedster as the driver from the university's airport run in the past.

As expected, two of my male Chinese friends met Mr. Zhang and me upon our arrival in Chengdu. They'd let me know previously they would be there to take me to Sichuan University where I would convalesce for an undetermined time. Also there to meet me at the airport were one of my former Tibetan students from the minority college, and two young men from my organization who were teachers in the College of Education.

After I introduced Mr. Zhang to my Chengdu friends, he remarked that he felt as if he were traveling with a queen. (Not a queen, I thought to myself, but the original "Dalai Mama.") Where Mr. Zhang went after our arrival, I cannot say. I wouldn't see him again until I'd return to Bayi in March.

Leave it to Harry, my dependable student from graduate school, to arrange for me a place to stay. It was in a building at the university's back gate and was called the Reception Hotel. The room was large with an adjoining WC (with a bathtub!). I learned there'd be hot water for fifteen to twenty minutes in the mornings, and again at about 7:30 p.m. Same tune, same dance. There was a wall heater to keep me cozy, for which, with my illness, I was exceedingly grateful; I could never seem to stay warm.

It didn't take me long, however, to discover that the room's exterior door wouldn't close properly. Yes, this hotel room had two doors. With the memory of rats running rampant at night, there was no way I could stay in a room with a faulty door. I talked to the staff, and by nighttime, they had repaired the door with a brand-new lock.

This hotel was a good place to be, especially since I knew some people in the building from when I lived at the Panda House. Across the hall was a couple from Denmark with three children. Their cook and babysitter was a sweet, little Chinese woman who had done my laundry when I was there before. She agreed to cook for me, enough food for three days, which I was able to warm on a borrowed cooking element. Then I met a young Chinese woman whom I had met the summer before I'd left for Bayi. She helped by washing some of my clothes. My Heavenly Father was looking after me.

It wasn't long before my former students found out that I was back on campus and many of them visited me often, even though it was a busy time with coming exams. Harry made time to bring a campus doctor to my room for a visual examination. The doctor examined my eyes for signs of jaundice, finding none, fortunately. The next day was tiring as I had a steady stream of visitors from noon until 9:30. One visitor overstayed his visit that evening: the Silver Fox, AKA Tarzan, the older gentleman I had met at English Corner. He had heard I was ill and it was kind of him to come, but I grew more leery as time passed. I appreciated his concern for my well-being, but it struck me that he was paying *too* much attention to my well-being.

Eventually, too tired to converse, I pulled my comforter up around my face and shut down. Tarzan got the message and took his leave.

My students and friends seemed shocked by my appearance—pale, thin, and very weak. My hair had gone almost totally gray. My eldest sister wrote to me, telling me to fear not: "Miss Clairol" would come to the rescue. She had sent hair coloring on ahead to Hong Kong for me. When I finally get there, I thought, I should gain back at least ten pounds and lose about ten years. (Sadly, the Clairol my sister sent would prove to be the wrong color, and the only color available in Hong Kong would, naturally, be black.)

For two and a half days, I stayed in bed feeling tired and weak. My stomach had shrunk and I had no appetite, managing to consume only crackers with a little bit of tea. Hepatitis A requires rest and good nutrition. I had the rest, but good nutrition was hard to come by. I wasn't hungry and the available Chinese food was oily and/or fried.

Outside, the winter conditions of this city of eleven million souls were typical and exactly as I remembered them to be: gray, cold, misty, and foggy. The sun was hiding far above the polluted sky, the smog so thick you'd never guess the sun was even up there. I imagined the snowflakes that fell one day to be poisoned, having come as they did through the clouds of industrial waste. Or maybe they served the purpose of cleaning the air a bit. Hopeful imagining.

After almost a week inside, the walls of my room started closing in on me, and I was more than ready to break out. Some friends had given me a soft wool scarf and warm gloves to add to the ones they'd given me three years before. Someone told me about a new joint-venture department store with a food section. Just wanting to get out, indifferent to destination, that seemed as good a place as any. I knew I'd enjoy sleuthing around for any Western food items I could find. Writing the address down for the taxi driver, I felt a momentary streak of energy. It didn't last long, but it was good to get out for a bit.

I continued to convalesce. If my hepatitis wasn't enough to deal with, it was compounded by bouts of painful gas in my abdomen and chest. I couldn't take anything for it lest my liver be harmed.

Finally, after two more weeks, it was time to leave Chengdu with a few other teachers from my organization. We'd been told that we'd attend a one-week Mandarin crash course in Guangzhou, once called Canton, before traveling on to Hong Kong. But after we landed in Guangzhou, it turned out that the course would not be for me. I was to go on ahead to get checked out by a doctor in Hong Kong, one I was familiar with from a previous stay. He did the usual blood tests and the first injection for hepatitis.

From there, it was on to a large apartment where we teachers were housed until the time came for our meetings. Then we moved to the site of the conference—a nice hotel. And it was there that I came down with something else: bronchitis. What next? Fortunately, a liver, gall bladder, and spleen scan were negative, so it was just a matter of time before I'd be completely recovered from hepatitis. I also had an ECG and stress test, which I passed. Evidently, I was ready to go back to Tibet in relatively good shape (the bronchitis would resolve itself in time), but the doctor armed me with a codeine painkiller just in case.

In the meantime, one of our sending agencies cautioned us that in March there would probably be a demonstration by Tibetans on the borders of Nepal and India to mark the fifty-ninth anniversary of the Dalai Lama's escape to India. If it happened, it could mean a lot of trouble, but probably not touch us in Bayi. Most likely, we wouldn't even hear about it there. Either way, we were told to feign ignorance and not make any comments. In other words, keep a low profile.

After the conference ended, it was back to the apartment until the next conference, at which time, it was on to another hotel. But I was tired out from attending meetings and decided not to attend any more. For the most part, I remained in my hotel room for that week.

Finally, conferencing was done. On February 26, I left Hong Kong for Chengdu where I stayed for a few days, then it was time to return to Bayi. I'd been away a long time.

Drunken Celestial Being Restaurant

Looking across to Barkhor Café.
Best french fries in Lhasa.

Lhasa's own "7-11"

Traffic control officer at Lhasa intersection and author

Studious '93 class

Cute neighbor kids

Chapter 37

Back in Bayi

"Simplicity is the ultimate sophistication."
—Leonardo da Vinci

Kiki soso Iha gyal lo! Victory to the gods!

After leaving Lhasa heading east, we arrived at Mila Pass, having climbed to an altitude of over 16,000 feet. Even if the front-seat occupants hadn't yelled the expected traditional praise to the gods, I think I would've screamed it out at a volume never heard before. And so I did. The volume of my *kiki soso* was commiserate with the gratitude I felt for the two near misses we'd had along the way on the narrow, graveled mountain road, one of them happening as our Land Rover approached a tight blind curve, still icy in its shadows.

Without a second to spare, the oncoming truck, clearly in our inside lane, managed to veer sharply to avoid a possible deadly crash. Our driver lost control as our car slid sideways on the ice, almost resulting in a sideswiping mere seconds after missing the head-on crash. The comfort station stop at Gombo'gyamba was welcomed and necessary.

It had been just another trip of being banged around, protecting our heads from hitting the roof, and hoping no fillings would pop out. When we arrived at our stop, we ate the obligatory noodles, refilled our thermoses, walked around to make sure our legs were free of kinks, and visited the thawed-out ground leading to the WC. And here was when I learned of the nature of the bumps on the previously frozen ground. The spring thaw was filled with surprises. The ground, hard and covered with snow three months before, was now a veritable above-ground sewer. I couldn't get back to my campus apartment soon enough.

In fact, the "farm" had never looked so good as we passed through the gates of the school after the final hours of driving. We backseat passengers extricated ourselves from the many packages wedged around us and I managed to get my belongings into my apartment.

It was good to be home. Within hours, I was experiencing the many familiar sights and sounds of the past semester, namely, the too-close-to-my-apartment, 6 a.m. sticking of the pig. And, of course, the rowdy roosters were as obnoxious as ever.

My stay in Hong Kong, a city that never sleeps, could have been a million miles away for all the ways it was different from the frontier town of Bayi. Always having electricity in H.K. was a given, and I never once had to plan my day around its availability. For a couple of days after arriving back on campus, the power was sporadic. Three days after my return was the first time I had anything hot to eat. Until then, it had been bread and peanut butter, bread and cheese, and bread and tuna.

A few days after returning, two of my male students dropped by for a visit. They, too, had been away, visiting their respective hometowns for the duration of the two New Year's celebrations. Before leaving, one of them said that he would bring over some nuts he'd brought back from his home especially for me. That evening, he came by with the bag of nuts and insisted right away that I eat one. They looked like miniature acorns, but who was I to question the advisability of sampling what he'd grown up eating?

Almost immediately after swallowing one, I experienced an allergic reaction that became severe within minutes. My throat constricted, making it difficult to talk or swallow. I needed help. Mr. Zhang's entryway was not far, and with my student following me, we headed there.

Fortunately for me, Mr. Zhang was outside talking with Gongbo Tashi. I grasped my throat with my hand and attempted to tell him what was wrong. Their reaction? One of them smiled and chuckled. "It's not funny!" I tried to say, learning later that this was a cultural reaction to unpleasantness.

Mr. Zhang hurried to find a driver to take me to the hospital. On the way I explained to him what I thought I needed to counteract the reaction, which I believed would be an injection for that purpose. My greatest concerns were if the doctor would know exactly what I needed, and would it be available? As before, in other health-related situations in Tibet, I was fearful in the beginning, but would later lean heavily on my faith in the Almighty that everything would turn out okay. It always had, and I'd gone on to live another day.

After arriving at the small, gray building, Mr. Zhang went in to find the doctor. Both eventually emerged and came to the car to tell me that we'd need to go to the two-story detached "emergency" room located behind the hospital. I envisioned myself being in Dodge City, climbing the stairs to visit Doc Adams. Fortunately for me, it was much better, but like Doc Adams's office, there was no electricity. We went into the dark building lit only by the doctor's flashlight. When we stepped into a medical room, the doctor found a few candles to create enough light to work by.

I watched him with some trepidation as he fumbled around to locate the correct medicine and syringe. Before he administered it, I asked Mr. Zhang to write down the name and dosage of the injection in case someone down the line might need it to determine how I'd died.

Mr. Zhang dropped me off at my apartment entryway about 10:30 p.m. Sleep wasn't on my agenda that night for I was afraid to drift off lest something unforeseen happen as a result of the injection. But it was the correct medicine and I began getting better. The three o'clock "alarm" sounded, courtesy of the always reliable "three o'clock cock," but I was still awake.

A few weeks into the semester I gave a cultural lecture in the newly opened classroom building's small auditorium. Because attendance wasn't mandatory, about twenty-five came, and as expected, only a few asked questions, which didn't surprise me, given their listening and speaking levels. The subject was "The US Government: Origin of Democracy and Structure." As one might imagine, it was an abbreviated presentation. I made posters of the Bill of Rights and of numerous quotations by Abraham Lincoln, but after looking into the students' blank faces, it occurred to me that I'd probably lost them somewhere between the definition of "democracy" and Point #1.

After I finished with the "lecture," in an attempt to make things more interesting, I gave out cancelled US postal stamps with pictures of the flag, thinking that the attendees would appreciate them, especially if they or someone they knew was a stamp collector. I also had door prizes I handed out after drawing numbers from a bowl. Prizes included an American flag key chain, a small US flag, a small Texas flag, and a "picture" of George Washington (in the form of a one-dollar bill). Then to add more interest, I told them I had another picture of Washington. They all assumed it would be another dollar bill, but when I gave the last winner the prize, everyone broke out laughing when it turned out to be a picture of the Washington Monument. Always leave them laughing, I figured, regardless of how much (or how little) they understood.

There was always something pleasurable to do in Bayi if one was a lover of nature's simplicity as I was. On a Sunday afternoon, my teammates, seven students, and I, walked far up the gradual slope of the mountain path in back of the college. We passed through a Tibetan village and came upon a group of about fifty villagers planting small fir trees furnished by the government.

We followed the mountain stream most of the way, even crossing through a yak pasture. As we gazed at the far-away higher mountains, we saw a waterfall that descended a long, long way, far enough to where we could not see where it eventually pooled. The higher mountaintops still sported their glistening snow. A more tranquil setting could not be found. Rhododendrons were in full bloom, and wild strawberries, along with miniature irises and more flowers I couldn't name in hues of purple, blue, and yellow bloomed over open areas as we wound our way back to campus. Who could say that God was not in His heaven and all was right with the world?

On a few Saturday or Sunday afternoons, when I needed to be alone, I'd climb up and over the stile to begin an outing without a planned destination. A person in love with nature will always have a path laid out before her and a song to sing along the way. Once I cleared the campus back wall, I could see the hill and path stretch out before me, and I felt as if I could walk on forever, never coming to the end of it.

Being alone with nature, I felt like some newborn creature opening its eyes to a world it had never known before. Without the chatter of others on the trail, I was acutely aware of my senses as never before. In that moment, I might have thought of myself as a transcendentalist.

The gentle breeze carried from a distance an almost imperceptible sound of cattle, sheep, or goats with tinkling bells. I discovered small wildflowers on the forest floor and took in the woodsy scent of the deep green firs and cedars. The mountains were magnificent with snow on the higher peaks, and some trees had started to bud in the warming springtime. It wouldn't be long before the rainy season would begin. As it was, the mornings were quite cloudy, with white ice pellets raining down a few times—a beautiful thing to watch.

On these walks, I was always aware of the danger of coming across a wild animal, like one of the big cats that inhabited this part of Tibet. With reluctance, I would begin my return to campus, but not without walking toward the sound of the gushing stream of water on its race down the hillside from the small power station. I'd stop long enough to allow this peaceful, albeit noisy, scene to make an impact on my being, feeling it might get lost in time if I did not drink it in. One afternoon, for insurance, I chose a beautiful, rounded stone from the water's edge, which I treasure till this day.

Well into the second semester, I had had no dealings with anyone in the administration. I could probably recognize the face of the new president, having met him at the fall sports meet, but I would not have been able to identify any administration members if I came face to face with them. Until after classes had moved into the new classroom building, that is.

One morning, a week or so after the move, there was an urgent knock on my apartment door. Upon opening the door, I was puzzled to see one of my male students standing there. It turned out he'd been sent to inform me that I was late for class. *Late?* It was forty-five minutes until class time.

I hurriedly gathered my teaching materials and made my way to class. In the meantime, Myra had also been informed. We walked together until we reached the front steps, then Myra went on as I stopped to wipe off my wet shoes. Later, she would tell me of her encounter with three officials who had been standing just inside the door. One of them, a smallish man, pointed to his watch and shook his finger at her. Myra, being Myra, shook her finger back at him and tried to explain why we were late and what she thought of his rudeness. The little man with the shaking finger indicated through his motions that Myra should zip her mouth and then made shooing motions as a way of dismissing her.

A minute later, I encountered the same trio of officials, and tried to explain that no one had informed us of the time change. My excuse fell on ears that did not comprehend English, and I was reminded of my five-year-old self and what *she* would have wanted to do, namely, "schlap the debil" out of someone. There are some things one never outgrows.

With that incident behind me, I could always find solace and joy by going to the newly opened teacher's dance hall three nights a week. This was a favorite place for many and got so crowded on some nights that it was almost impossible to not bump into others. The first night I attended, my Chinese friends and I stayed through the last song, which ended about midnight. It was a fast, four-step waltz and a long one at that, but I was determined to finish, even though I was exhausted. One Sunday night, when the crowd was even larger than normal, I was forced to leave early, the result of too much dancing on a bad bruise that circled the ball of my foot, causing me to hobble for a time and miss the following dance night. Too much of a good thing.

On another weekend of work and play, after taking pictures of my students planting trees near the river, and giving them a hand, I retreated to my apartment to spend some quality time baking. First, I baked a pecan pie to be served with *real* whipped cream, the "long life" variety I had purchased in Hong Kong. The pecans and Crisco I found at a wholesale market. I'd dreamed of this pecan pie for weeks and was determined to find all the ingredients I'd need. The end result was near perfection. As Bob, Myra, and I tried our best to eat our first piece(s) with modicums of gentility, I was sure I caught the sound of gentle purring. Only in Bayi could such a treat have given so much satisfaction. Let it never be said that pecan pie can't be a good oatmeal substitute for breakfast.

The following weekend, I made lemon bread using some of the butter I'd purchased in Chengdu. Then, to off-set the sweets I was baking, I bought vegetables from the market, including lots and lots of potatoes. Homemade bread and potato soup were two of my menu items. I still had enough of the quinoa that Tashi had given me earlier to add to soup and potato croquettes. A teacher in my department gave me some millet to use. Let the baking continue!

CHAPTER 38

THE LONG GOODBYE

"If you're brave enough to say goodbye, life will reward you with a new hello."
—Paulo Coelho

Spring arrived in earnest. It was late April and frozen precipitation would not be seen again in the valley before late autumn. But with the new promise of soft sunshine, budding flowers, and revived spirit, I had not moved on. Everything about me was frozen in the biting winds of the Bayi winter. If I had taken the time to assess my time there, maybe I would have noticed the nuances of my everyday life, its taken-for-granted pleasures, and its disappointments. At certain times I wanted to feel everything: the pleasures of dancing the waltz, the walks into town, baking, and, in general, the laid-back atmosphere of the place. But there had been some dark days that I had hidden away somewhere inside of me, unaware of until later.

A bright spot for most of the spring semester was the twice-weekly night classes with military doctors, nurses, and even a bus driver in attendance. At first, I greeted the news of these classes with dread, assuming they would prove to be a waste of time. How wrong I was! My class of beginner-level students was a delight. Miss Jia was young and funny and did a wonderful job of explaining the grammar and vocabulary for each evening's class. From what some other students told me, the intermediate class was apparently boring, not fun like ours. In fact, our class ended with a party that the students arranged in appreciation. For me, it was a lesson not to prejudge with a negative attitude.

Time, meanwhile, was winding toward the end of my teaching stint at the agriculture/animal husbandry college. At times, time itself could be either too tightly constricted or unmercifully expanded, all according to my feelings at the moment. Sometimes I felt as if my world—my time—expanded far above the tallest peak, floating blissfully on ever-changing cloud formations. Other times, I became aware of the months, weeks, and days until the moment I'd have to leave, and it would hit me that it would either never come soon enough, or it would come before I'd be able to make peace with it.

With a few weeks left, Ray, Myra, and I toured the local wool factory where yak and sheep donated their winter coats so that the privileged could have theirs. The fabric shop was what drew my interest with its fine wool offerings. I bought enough to have a pair of slacks and a blazer made. Packed away in one of my plastic tubs after all these years are the slacks, regrettably of no use after returning to the US, somehow mysteriously shrinking more than a few sizes.

One day, I walked the trail back into the mountains with a few students and my colleagues, aware it would be my last time. I suppose if I'd been by myself, it could have been a mind-clearing, spiritual hike. But it was peaceful, nonetheless, and that would be enough. We saw children, a lot of children, with their little pails gathering wild strawberries. What a wonderful scene it was, reminding me of berry and nut gathering back home.

On and off the trail I spotted bushes of wild spirea; at least it smelled and looked like the spirea I remembered from Texas. We came upon wild peach trees loaded with small unripe fruit. The peaches reminded me of the small Indian peaches my mom gathered from the last of the remaining fruit trees near the barnyard fence on our farm. Before returning to campus, and before reaching the noisy and fast-moving stream where we would have lunch, we came upon some of my Ag. II students harvesting some roots. Ooh—fungi, perhaps?

Of course, it wouldn't seem normal in my time there if I didn't succumb to some illness or other. This time, practically on my way out, I came down with chills and an ache-all-over condition, compounded by arthritis in one leg. Not wanting the medical attention of Dr. Stickum, I diagnosed my illness as a sinus infection that kept me in bed for a few days. I sent word that I wouldn't be able to give the culture lecture—"Mass Media in the US." Just as well, as I had nothing to give away that would properly compensate the students for having to attend.

As my days there dwindled down, I found myself noticing the night sky more. The night sky in Tibet was magical for me. It was all bright, vast, and beautiful, the stars seemingly within reach. It wasn't lost on me that although I might have been just a speck of dust, presumably insignificant in the vast realm of the universe, I was in fact attempting to live out as best I could my God-given significance, however small. And it wasn't meant to be lived out as other specks of dust lived out theirs. It had to be different somehow. But somewhere in those days and nights, without becoming aware of why or how, there was an undefinable darkness intruding into my life. Whatever it was I felt, and for whatever reason I felt it, gazing at the stars—satellites on their pre-ordained orbits—was reassuring for me. God was in control.

When did I see and feel that darkness for the first time? When did I really know that there was something amiss with the armor I had so steadfastly depended upon to protect me from this very thing? I'd forgotten about the dark feeling until I set about writing this book. Now I remember. Reading my written words on the page has helped me to see my imperfect self as I was, not as I had wished myself to be.

It was cumulative, the events that led to this mindset. Illnesses that I thought, looking back, I had breezed through, but hadn't. Frustrations from living in a vastly different culture, even while trying to accept and make the most of my circumstances. Then came the death of my mother and the deployment to Iraq of my son. I often felt isolated. There were mixed feelings about leaving Tibet. I wanted to go home, but what was home now? I had changed. I was not the same person who had arrived three years earlier. Where did I belong exactly? It all came together in a perfect storm of stress. And it didn't help that I was not sleeping well. Sometimes I'd lie awake most of the night, eventually falling asleep just in time to be awakened by the three o'clock cock. I knew, of course, that my problems were not much different in scale than what others go through during the course of their lives, but it was my misfortune to have hit the proverbial brick wall in a time and place that I would not have chosen. Years later, here in front of my keyboard, it has all come back to me.

Fortunately, however, so have the bright spots, like the times when a small group of children would stop by to visit, often with small bouquets of hand-picked flowers. Sometimes I regret not remembering their names, except for the boy who seemed to be the leader of the posse—Dawa, Tibetan for moon. They were good kids, all about ten years old. I'm sure their loving attention was because I was an oddity, the foreign panda in their midst. I trust I always exuded love toward them. Do they lovingly remember me? Do they remember me at all?

The children surely helped mitigate the stresses I was feeling from the job itself. A new college president had come on board in November, and since that time, our contracts had not been fully honored. Mr. Zhang explained part of the reason was that the president, Chinese, considered us "trouble." It was almost as if we didn't have a contract, for the school did whatever it wanted. For instance, they presented me with my hospital bill for December, even though the contract stated that the school would be responsible for health-related issues. Rent and electricity were deducted from our pay in February retroactive to the previous September even though our housing and utilities were to have been provided. At one point, I was presented with a bill for my stolen bike, and if I failed to reimburse the school, I would not be given my last salary. All this added to the pressure that I had been internalizing.

Meanwhile, through my Lhasa contacts, I learned that Tibet University had accepted me back for the next school year. But I also heard that the atmosphere was growing more tense in Lhasa with the thirtieth anniversary of the "peaceful liberation" of Tibet coming up that September. All foreigners, especially tourists, would be kept away for a month. I would have to decide whether or not to go on to Chengdu in July, knowing that I might not be able to get back into Tibet. But my residence permit would expire in September, so it was a must that I get to Chengdu where I could have it extended. Another reason that I'd need to go to Chengdu was that I'd been assigned to help out in a summer sports/English clinic in an outlying private high school with a group from East Texas Baptist University from Marshall, Texas. Maybe I'd serve as their gofer.

I did find one important means of stress relief. A person is fortunate when a hobby can become an invaluable comfort. But when one lives in an isolated place with rudimentary amenities, a beloved hobby might not be possible, or at least to the degree to which one may be accustomed. I'd never considered my interest in cooking/baking as a true hobby, but after being in Tibet for a short time, it became one. Unlike, for instance, woodworking, I could feed myself with my hobby, partly due to occasional food packages from the US. Most of the items were "add-ins," like vanilla extract, or sour cream powder. So when I retrieved a small package from one of my sisters a month or so before leaving Bayi, I was ecstatic. Now I could make my own maple-flavored syrup and butter-flavored *anything*. My bread baking kept improving: potato rolls, butter crescent rolls, and spring onion, everyone's favorite. Perhaps reiterating, but I was rolling in dough.

Beginning in early June, I began inquiring about the likelihood of securing a truck heading to Lhasa to take the majority of my possessions. From past experience, there hadn't been much furniture in my Tibet University apartment. The school agreed to let me buy the large wardrobe, my only storage unit, made in the woodshop shortly after I'd arrived, and a small corner unit that held the TV. Soon after, I visited the woodshop with a drawing of a dresser with mirror that I wanted to buy, the only mirror that would be in my apartment. Now if I could just find a truck.

A friend from the Public Security Bureau promised to be on the lookout for one. After a few false starts, he learned of a twenty-member tour group that had come to Bayi on a security stop to check papers. My friend asked the driver of the luggage truck if he'd take my things, to which he agreed. But I never heard anything more and the opportunity slipped away as the truck left the next day without anybody contacting me. Looking back, I should have planted myself at the point of departure and not let that truck leave without my belongings. The driver certainly hadn't cared about the agreement he'd made, and the incident ratcheted my stress level near to the boiling point.

"Do you know anything about delayed stress? I think it's catching up on me—and I've already been thinking to myself, 'If only I can make it X number of days.'" This was in a letter I wrote to a sister. Everything I set my mind to do had become a hassle, a mountain to climb over. Even buying stamps at the main post office had become difficult for me. Calling Lhasa and talking to friends from my organization about concerns was nearly an impossibility. I'd been to the telephone center twice in three days with no luck getting through. For the first time, I was beginning to feel closed off from the world.

The day of departure from Bayi was to be July 5. My mind vacillated from preparing to leave to what would be in store for me when I got back to Tibet University. I was told the three teachers there would not be returning. Meanwhile, I requested that I be given a second-floor apartment. Why second floor? I knew that the water pressure in the building prevented water from reaching the third floor. It was a relatively new building but designed by architects who'd probably flunked out of school.

My three-legged chair and five-gallon shower bucket now seemed like only minor annoyances, but I hadn't much time to make comparisons. A good thing, considering. I finally passed that particular day when time had been moving too slowly to when it speeded up, and I found myself struggling to take care of last-minute tasks. If only I'd been more aware that my Heavenly Father was in control, had *always* been in control.

To simplify things, I decided to give away most of the possessions I'd collected in Bayi, the ones I'd fretted over so needlessly weeks before. Miss Jia was aghast and happy to be the new owner of the daffodil yellow dresser, even more so since she was getting married in the summer. Mr. Da and his wife, Mei Mei, would get the wardrobe and TV stand (although it might be a long time until they could afford a TV).

After I'd told Mr. Da about the furniture, which was, no doubt, considered a windfall for him, I presented him with a key and instructed him to come with me to my apartment to find out what it would unlock. Once there, I led him around the three rooms to find something that needed a key. He wasn't focusing, so I had to point to the bike. What happened next is something I'll never forget. The look of bewilderment, the watery eyes, and his words, "You've done something noble." Seeing his reaction, I found myself feeling embarrassed; the bike had cost me practically nothing. Why had I been so concerned about a few possessions? Later, I would come to understand why my plans for these "important" things came to nothing.

The day before we left Bayi, as a way to say goodbye, I walked around the campus, prayed for the people there who had welcomed me into their community, and took photos. As I strolled, I met people I'd never seen before. Having pictures taken with them felt like a last-minute bonding. Later in the afternoon, Mr. Liu agreed to meet me at the dancing room, along with his wife, for a last waltz together. It was as bittersweet as I knew it would be. It would be twenty-eight years before I'd ever waltz again, on a Rhine River cruise with the activity director. And then, only for one dance.

That last evening some of my colleagues came by my apartment to bid me farewell. One by one they left, with Mr. Zhang and Mr. Liu remaining. When it was just Mr. Liu, I had the opportunity to give him some books, including one special book—the Bible. With Mr. Liu's departure, I closed the door on another unbelievable journey in my life. Sleep didn't come easily that night. And it wasn't because of the three-o'clock cock. It was the excitement and the uncertainties of the new, mostly uncharted, adventure that lay ahead.

By early morning, bags packed (with zippers straining to keep it all contained) I waited by the door to be transferred to the Land Cruiser. I was ready to leave. Of course, I hadn't divested myself of *all* my possessions. My beloved, carefully boxed oven was never out of my sight. Soon, several SUVs appeared on the narrow street with some of the school officials arriving to see us off. Ray and Myra stood amongst them, along with Mr. Zhang and Mr. Liu, small-talking, glad-handing, or whatever one does in these situations. I couldn't imagine there was any sincerity coming from the officials.

It was all too much to handle. My stubbornness and my emotions would not allow it. I walked to the lead SUV where I could be alone, where the on-coming torrent of tears would not be on display. Mr. Liu noticed and walked over to be with me. I don't recall what he said, except that it was something designed to make me feel better, which, of course, only led to more tears. Who could have predicted that Mr. "Motor Mouth" could have spoken such sentiments? Perhaps it should not have been such a surprise. If I'd learned nothing, I'd learned that Mr. Liu, my dance teacher, was a man of good character. Once, he had told me about loaning his brother a considerable amount of money. His brother was a pig farmer and had hit hard times. "What if he can't pay you back?" I'd asked. "He's my brother," Mr. Liu replied. "Being paid back is not important."

More unexpected emotions would come. Walking down the street were children on their way to school. Most of them walked on by, but some of them came near to where I was standing. Through my tears, I recognized a few, possibly part of "the posse." One was Dawa. With the passing of all the years, I try to recall everything about him at that moment. He stood at a respectful distance, shy, with downcast eyes wearing his backpack. Many of my tears, I'm certain, were for the children I'd never see again. They brought their special unconditional love to my life. In my understanding of love, it was pure, maybe spiritual. I was aware that Dawa would be late for school and possibly scolded by his teacher. To bring the moment to a close, I walked over to him, hugged him, and then said goodbye, trying my best for a smile. *Ke li choo*, my little friend.

Somehow, we all packed ourselves and our belongings in the Land Cruiser, making use of all available space in a way that would impress any engineer. We drove out the front gate, over the bridge, and shortly out of town—the beginning of our nine-hour drive over many mountains to reach Lhasa. Bayi and the College of Agriculture and Animal Husbandry were quickly becoming memories.

There was no welcoming committee in Lhasa, no *hada*, and nobody aware, or interested, that three foreigners had arrived. Ray and Myra were taken to their small hotel where they would stay until they departed for an ongoing trip to Nepal a day later. We said our goodbyes, bidding each other well for our ongoing plans.

My first stop was to the classroom building at Tibet University where the foreign language department was located, hoping to find an English speaker there. As before, English was still the *only* foreign language. I found someone who warmly welcomed me back as ESL teacher, and then the driver took me to the three-story foreign residence building which would be my home for the next year.

With my luggage placed outside the SUV and my oven in a safe place, I went in to find someone to show me to my apartment. What I really needed was to get myself quickly organized with the most important things in place. But shortly, I was to have my limits tested. The young woman showing me to my apartment, a Tibetan language student, informed me I'd be living in one of the *third*-floor apartments. Apparently, all the empty lower floor apartments had been delegated to others. I'd learned from three previous introductions to my assigned apartments in China to maintain a non-judgmental attitude, no matter how difficult. But no running water? This was a stretch.

After struggling with my heavy luggage, a few boxes of kitchen/baking supplies, and my beloved oven, I was ready to triage the most important tasks at hand. A thermos of boiled water was a must, meaning that learning how to operate the cooking apparatus to boil the water was right up there at the top. I also needed to become acquainted with the waterless WC, which was... interesting. Locating a bucket for transporting water was a necessity as was micro-inspecting the narrow bed for cleanliness, remembering what I'd found on my bed in Chengdu.

The young woman, definitely not part of my organization, seemed not to care in the least about showing me the ropes, although she did mention that I could get water from a second-floor apartment. This turned out to be a monumental hassle for me as well as the apartment occupiers. How was I to tolerate a year of this?

It wouldn't be long before I would take my bucket and dirty clothes to an outside water spigot where I would squat as I washed my clothes. There was a low iron fence where I would drape the clothes to dry, wiping the fence down first, of course.

Attempting to light the bottled-gas cooking "thing" was frightening in the beginning, as I imagined it exploding upon my lighting of the match. In fact, it made an alarming *whooshing* noise as it flamed to life, and it seemed to me as if it were an evil spirit or maybe some sort of kitchen witch. How I longed for my electric-coil, tripod cooking apparatus of the recent past.

There were two couples from my organization living in my building who were enrolled at Tibet University to study Tibetan. For reasons unknown to me, the younger of the two couples was appointed as team leaders. I'd met them briefly before, but we really didn't know one another. Something happened. I cannot recall specifics, but what I vaguely remember is that one day in their living room, the young woman accused me of being too open to certain Tibetans about Christianity. At least, that's what I remember. But whatever the complaint, what set me off was the manner of it: lecturing me as if I were a child. I knew she'd been in Tibet for a year. I'd been there for three and was older than she was. I took offense. How dare her, team leader or not. The explosion began, a mix of resentment and anger bursting from the pressures I'd been feeling. I could not stop the tears. The brave demeanor of the past months, even the year before, had kept hidden what I dared not expose. But now there was no hiding. The woman didn't care. In fact, another woman happened to knock on the door just then and she invited her in. The two talked in another part of the room, as if I, with my crying, were not even there.

What happened in the following days is not clear to me, except that I know I was still in a precarious state. The new ESL teachers arrived and had begun to settle in. Then, before the English department met with us and assigned classes, someone heard through the pipeline, which originated from the education commission office in Lhasa, that we American teachers would not be allowed to work in Tibet. *What?!* The foreign language department had not even known. An absolute bombshell. It had to have been something political. Tit-for-tat. As far as we could determine from the grapevine, we three teachers would be the only ones affected by this local decree. I was beginning to understand how it worked, the barometer that gauged Chinese-American squabbles.

After my Chengdu supervisor became aware of the situation, he told me to stay put until he could find a school in Chengdu where I could work. The timing could not have been worse; most positions were already filled. Another stressful situation to deal with.

Here in Lhasa, at least, I wasn't far from a trusted safety net. All I was required to do was to wait patiently. My ultimate safety net was my Heavenly Father, in whom I hadn't shown complete faith. I had allowed myself to become mired in circumstances, some of which would eventually come to naught.

Preparing to leave was not as emotional, nor as time-consuming, as departures that had come before. None of that Bayi furniture to dispose of. (Now I could see that God had taken care of that as He knew I'd not need it.) No bicycle purchased. I hadn't even unpacked one of my suitcases.

Lhasa had changed. I had changed. There were a few former students who still lived and worked in Lhasa to whom I would bid farewell. I'd also leave behind the box of my treasured baking items. And my oven. In the whole scheme of a life's path to adventure, what did it matter? There would be other baking supplies and other ovens in my future. Of this, I was sure. What adventures lay ahead only God knew. I was learning to let go, though sometimes with much difficulty.

The day of departure had come. Mr. Li, the department head, accompanied me to the airport. Heading west out of town on Beijing Road, I attempted to take in as much of Lhasa as I could—The Yak Hotel, tea houses, Potala Palace, the familiar jagged mountain peaks. There was a heaviness to it all. I was sadly leaving, maybe forever, three years of my life. And yet I took comfort in Joshua 1:9:

"He will be with you wherever you go."

'93 class students

Graduation party at Holiday Inn

Pastry chef at work in Holiday Inn, 1992

Students visiting Hard Yak Café, Holiday Inn

Friday night entertainment, Holiday Inn

Pedi-cab ride

Epilogue

Twenty-four years had passed since I'd been with my Tibet University students. Here I was in Texas, in 2016, planning my return visit, knowing for certain it would be my last. My plan had been to first spend two weeks in Chengdu, then, with my Chinese friend, Tina, travel to eastern Tibet and onward to Lhasa where I would be reunited with both my 1992 and 1993 classes. But there were snags. Two weeks out, I hadn't heard from a former student whom I was counting on to alert her 1992 classmates that I'd soon be in Lhasa. Moreover, the one person from Bayi I'd contacted told me he couldn't be there when I was scheduled to land at the local airport, and then informed me that other friends and colleagues at the college had already left for their summer break to parts unknown. What a letdown. It appeared it would be nothing more than a sightseeing trip in and around Bayi, and more so for Tina than for me.

Then my miracle happened one week before I was to leave. I received an email from my former student, Christina, who had been in the hospital and had just read my email to her of my plans. She would contact all classmates to tell them of my impending visit. I sat at my desk, thanked God, then wept a little. What a wonderful feeling of hope restored.

A week later, there I was in Chengdu again, the days filled with visiting old friends. After leaving Tibet in 1995, I'd lived in Chengdu for thirteen years. This trip was like coming home again—one of several places, like Lhasa, that had helped shape my life. In those years, teaching ESL, I had developed life-long friends who became my family. Ten of those years were devoted to helping Chinese friends open their own Western-styled restaurants. From those coveted small ovens I'd used in Lhasa and Bayi to the commercial ovens of the restaurants in Chengdu and beyond, there was a golden thread of connection, and that golden thread was of God. I had proof.

After my time in Chengdu, it was off to Bayi. Before leaving the US for China, I'd read about the airport in Bayi. Apparently, it had been built before anybody knew a commercial plane could even land there. Mountains and a narrow valley provided more thrills than I had bargained for. During our landing, I'd never been more aware of a plane's flight path. I was quite literally on the edge of my seat feeling the movements of the plane for at least the final fifty miles as it serpentined around the sides of mountains. Inside the plane, there was an eerie silence, and it felt as if we were floating soundlessly through the valley. How that notion changed when the wheels touched down on the runway with the deafening roar of the engines in full reverse thrust to keep us from rolling off the far end of the short runway.

Tina and I retrieved our luggage and walked out of the terminal into the blinding sunshine, thinking we'd spot our driver and tour guide with ease. In fact, they were at the back of the throng of greeters. Not much of a welcome. We followed them to the parking area while rolling our own luggage. Minor incidents that nevertheless served as a prelude to what would follow. When we saw our ride, we were crestfallen—an older four-door sedan instead of the Land Cruiser we'd ordered. We had no choice but to accept the vehicle, for the driver and guide had driven all the way from Lhasa—nine hours.

Our first stop was at the Public Security Bureau (PSB) in Bayi for me to register as a foreigner. I'd known the man in the visa section when I'd lived in Bayi years before, and he was still there. I was disappointed to learn that I'd not be able to visit the college campus because there was no one there whom I'd known to invite me in. Another example of how things now were. But the man kindly volunteered to accompany us to places I wanted to revisit.

The first place was to the back of the school where I'd go for walks on the path up into the trees and alongside the noisy power station stream that cascaded down the hill, the place where I'd taken my treasured rounded rock. The man warned me that it had all changed and he was right. I didn't recognize it at all. Built up and junky, it made me wish I hadn't gone there. The only bright spot in the area was a yellow raspberry bush that the man instructed the driver to stop at. Never had I seen a bush like it, and I was eager to pluck its fruit and eat all I wanted.

The streets of Bayi were all paved now. No longer were they muddy quagmires. Now there were many, many streets with numerous restaurants, and no "Ptomaine Tavern" in sight. We chose a noodle restaurant for lunch which seemed like a safe choice. Afterward, my friend from the PSB took us to a waterfall that I hadn't known existed and was by then a tourist attraction. Yes, tourists. There were many hotels now, though none rated over three stars. Then we went to the "five-and-dime" where I used to try on the latest hats. I had a picture with me of the proprietor from way back when. The person in the shop told me she was now working at the college, and I gave him the picture to pass along to her.

When my friend decided it was time to get back to work, he asked the driver to let him out at least a block from the PSB. Before exiting the car, he told us that I was not to contact him directly, but only through Tina. I understood his meaning. He had superiors who might not trust him hobnobbing with a foreigner. No communication was safe.

The following day was a tad stormy; Tina and the guide were at each other's throats all day about our travel plans. We'd been told by the tour company in Chengdu that we could travel to areas outside of Bayi, but this was apparently not the guide's understanding. I'd had enough and finally stepped in with some strong words for the guide that even surprised myself. He kept quiet afterward, but silently steamed.

We survived that day to make it back to the hotel and some peace, where a surprise phone call came through from my favorite '93 class student. It hadn't taken long for word to spread that I was back in Tibet. Sadly, he had called to inform me that he couldn't be in Lhasa for our class reunion due to family obligations.

The next morning, we departed for Lhasa, a trip I imagined would be more comfortable than the trips I'd endured years before. Too much to hope for.

We drove for miles without any mishaps. When it was time for a WC stop, our driver pulled off and headed for what looked like a small, modern village. I assumed it was a "show" village for the benefit of tourists because we saw only one person, perhaps the caretaker. But it was sufficient for our needs. Back on the road, it wasn't long before we encountered highway construction and a muddy passageway for miles. At times, I was sure we'd become stuck as the car slip-slided along. Eventually, we crested the Mila Pass without much fanfare and then descended toward Lhasa. My excitement built as we turned onto the main road, approaching those craggy mountains I'd always looked for when returning to Lhasa after an absence, then seeing in the distance the top of the Potala Palace.

I was home again.

The Beijing Road I remembered was now crowded with cars and the walkways were crowded with people. The driver found a place to pull over near the alleyway, adjoining the Barkhor, where our small Tibetan boutique hotel was located. This was where I'd opted to stay. The House of Shambhala Hotel. It was perfect.

Meanwhile, Tina contacted my '92 class student, Zara, to tell her we'd arrived. Zara was the female student I was closest to. We waited downstairs for her to arrive, and when she did, we embraced for a long time, each of us shedding tears. She referred to me as her American mother. A few years before, her own mother had died. She told me about our class reunion the next day. Someone would come for me around noon, she said. I was excited, telling her that I knew more tears would come when I would see all of my students again.

In the meantime, Tina fired our guide. Our fill-in was the owner of Tibetan Kitchen, a popular restaurant. He'd also been a tour guide, and we got along swimmingly. He took Tina on a Potala Palace tour, as I'd wanted to tour the Barkhor alone.

It depressed me to see how its character had changed. It was more appealing from an aesthetic viewpoint. I noticed this with much of Lhasa. It was cleaner than I remembered. There were flowers planted everywhere. But I knew the reason was to help make the city more of a tourist destination, to turn the whole place into some Disney-like attraction. Much of the authenticity was gone, it seemed to me. As for the Barkhor, now everyone had to pass through a checkpoint where backpacks and packages were inspected. I was angry to think it had come to that. More and more controls by the Chinese government. And yet it hadn't stopped Tibetans from prostrating in front of the Jokhang temple and walking the religious path, spinning their prayer wheels and fingering their beads.

Later we walked over to the "island" where Tibetans liked to set up their large tents for a few days and where Mina and I set up our small tent for one night. There was once a swimming hole where young boys liked to swim *au naturale.* Then in the ensuing years, the government opened up many nightspots, discos, and all manner of activities that Chinese would visit. There was a large army presence. The island we once crossed over to on a narrow prayer flag-festooned footbridge was no more.

The day arrived for the Class of 1992 reunion. It had been twenty-four years. I walked out to Beijing Road where Tina and I would meet our ride, and on the way out from the alley, there they were—two students I recognized right away: Paul and Greg. After gusto hugs and smiles all around, we headed to the second-floor banquet room of an unfinished building.

My gentlemen escorts led me through a pair of open French doors where everyone was seated at a U-shaped table awaiting my arrival. My heart leapt at the beautiful sight of my students, a transcendent moment of love and respect that we all felt as our eyes connected. Then came the unabashed tears of us all. All the young women were dressed in chupas adorned with the traditional striped aprons, signifying their marital status. The three young men wore jackets over their regular clothes.

Out of a class of twenty-eight students, almost all had made it. Two young men had died. One of them was Renchen, the class monitor, one of my very favorite students. I had learned of Renchen's death before this trip, and it had filled me with sadness. Renchen had suffered from clinical depression in a time and place where clinical depression was little understood. His pain had become so severe that he had killed himself. If there was any consolation, I had also learned that Renchen had become a believer in Christianity. Perhaps my influence had had some effect on him. And perhaps in his worst moments, he had been comforted at least a little by the good news of the scripture.

Renchen's good friend Spencer was there, now a debonair entrepreneur. In fact, he had arranged almost everything, including a Power Point presentation highlighting the students' school years. Spencer might have been the only one who had owned a camera back then. With the Power Point presentation finished, I was given the opportunity to speak. I talked about how I'd carried them all in my heart for these many years. They could not have known what they had meant to me, the depth of love and concern I'd had all this time for each of them. I presumed my words got through, because it seems everyone benefited from the boxes of tissues that lined the tables.

Next, we all stood and I watched as they lined up. Then, one by one, they draped their *katas*—their long scarves—around my bowed head. As each embraced me, I called them by name, their English name, as I could never remember their Tibetan names. Zara later told me what an impression it made on one student that I'd remembered her name after all the years. I didn't see any reason to let on that I had studied my class list before I'd left home.

Then, the class led me to another large room, this one with an enormous banquet table crowded first with cold dishes, as was the custom, then with a seemingly endless parade of hot dishes. For me, this was a five-star banquet, and it got better still: as an honor to me, someone had remembered that my favorite food was potato, and there it was in abundance. The wine flowed and I watched as the classmates visited with each other, many of them having not seen each other for a very long time. Multiple toasts were made to every conceivable connection: those from the same hometown, best friends, work colleagues. All of it captured by a professional photographer. The final thing to do was to cut a large multilayer cake that was adorned with a large "24" on top. This particular celebration was now coming to a happy, yet sad, ending. But there was soon to be more celebrating.

Some of the girls took me in their car to visit the campus, my home for two years. Unfortunately, our classroom was being repaired and the door locked, so we could only see it through a hallway window. Other parts of the campus had changed. There was more of it. Regretfully, my former upstairs neighbors were not at home. They had been like family to me, but now the children were grown and were away. It was summertime, and people seemed to move around much more than they did back when I lived there. One person we found at home was the wife of the former president. We met again, happy to reconnect.

We left campus and they drove me back to my hotel for a rest. A rather short rest it was, for they had planned something else for the evening. Someone came to take me to another banquet location. This banquet wasn't as elaborate as the earlier one, but it was comfortable and more intimate. I knew a lot of money had been spent on both food and venue, and it didn't escape me that these dear people were making a real sacrifice.

Before the food was served, gifts appeared. Some of the ladies gave me a beautiful, light, dressy jacket, which, to their disappointment, would have fit the Tibetan me years before but not the American me that sat before them now. I assured them I could have it altered, even though I knew I probably couldn't. Spencer also presented a gift—a box of two small, beautiful, mostly golden, chalices. He showed me the price in case I had to declare them when leaving China and I was flabbergasted. They are now proudly displayed in my china cabinet back home.

But the gift I appreciated the most was the one that came at the end of the evening. The photographer's assistant brought all the photos that had been taken earlier that day. Spencer opened the box and handed me a gorgeous, leather-bound album filled with two dozen photos, and a long tube with a rolled-up picture of the class. Each classmate received their own. What a wonderful way to remember each other and this wonderful day.

The following day, we took time off from banqueting—at least for a few hours. Our guide accompanied us to Sera Monastery, the area where I had seen the place for sky burials years before. Then we headed to the Dalai Lama's Summer Palace, passing along the way the scene of so many interesting experiences for me: The Holiday Inn. But she appeared sad to me, an ignored old lady bereft of both the summer-season tourists, and the gaiety of the imaginative slow-season antics of employees and bored ex-pats. The Summer Palace, on the other hand, seemed even more beautiful than before, with flowers tucked in every conceivable space. I couldn't tell if picnicking on the grounds was still permitted as it had been years ago with my students.

Finally, we caught a small bus to upper Beijing Road to take us back to our hotel for a little rest, then a former student came to drive me to an outlying five-star hotel where the class of '93 gathered to eat and get reacquainted. A hotel like this one would have been unthinkable when I'd lived here. Most hotels then were geared mainly to the backpacking sort who seemed to pride themselves on the horrible conditions they had to tolerate. The dirtier the better to impress anyone who would listen to their tales and marvel at their stamina and sense of adventure.

But this hotel...well, when we pulled up, I momentarily forgot where I was. I could have been in Las Vegas. The Intercontinental Lhasa Paradise Hotel rose up in a huge pyramid shape with accompanying triangle-shaped wings, presumably representing the mountains of Tibet. It was a veritable work of art. Inside was even more impressive. The lobby was expansive, and the pyramid-shaped ceiling towered high above us—all glass, allowing sunlight to stream downward. Dining areas here and there were populated with tables that made use of large umbrellas to provide shade. Restaurants, bars, and gift shops were done in a Tibetan motif. There was a tea lounge, a cigar bar, and a billiard room, in addition to the usual ballrooms and conference areas. This was not the Holiday Inn. Nor did it have the Holiday Inn's rustic charm. What it had instead was luxury, luxury Tibetan lodging had certainly never seen before. Everything was clean and polished and first-class.

I took everything in as we crossed the lobby and made our way to the restaurant where I'd finally see my former students. Since the area was immense, I didn't spot them initially, but then, there they were, a beautiful sight to behold. Michael and Eddie saw me first. Our greetings were more restrained than they were with the other class. There was no hugging. After all, we'd been together for just the one year. Many of the students, especially the girls, were still shy and had lost most of their English-speaking ability, which I could tell embarrassed them. But there were smiles all around, and someone volunteered to translate for the ones who had difficulty speaking to me.

After visiting for a while, we went back and forth to the various food stations. The fare was tasty and someone was always giving a toast, causing us all to raise our glasses of Jianlibao, the ever-present honey soda pop that I remembered so well. These people were some of the sweetest I'd ever known. Joel, named after my youngest son, was a little late in arriving, having driven from Shigatse, three hours away. He was working with the city police now. Patricia, named after one of my good college friends, was happy to tell me that she had a short-wave radio program, and had played a song dedicated to me a few days before I arrived. Mary, named after two of my good friends from Longview, Texas, filled me in on her work with a government aid program that was helping deliver Chinese donations to Nepal after the horrific earthquake the year before.

Michael, who had been class monitor, was a teacher, along with Eddie, at an institution in Lhasa, which my conscience will not allow me to divulge. We'd separated ourselves from the group to speak frankly to one another. They wanted to talk and I wanted to listen. Eddie, of course, was the student who'd been in the hospital sharing a room with the Drapchi prisoner. It was Eddie who'd jotted down the notes about the tortures that I had passed along to the Canadian consul. Eddie despised the Chinese even before those discoveries because they had once killed his pet dog in front of him. Both Michael and Eddie said I was lucky to be able to travel internationally. They weren't allowed; they could only travel to inland China.

After our gathering had come to an end, with e-mail addresses exchanged and many pictures taken, I was driven back to the House of Shambhala. It was quite late when my borrowed cell phone rang.

It was my '93 class student, Jack. I didn't know where he was calling from, but he said he wanted to catch the train sometime during the night and come to Lhasa to see me. Apparently, he had just learned that I was there. I told him I'd be leaving for the airport early the following morning and knew I'd have only about thirty minutes to visit with him. Jack was not to be denied. So I said goodnight to him and looked forward to seeing him the next morning. But it was not to be. He called early the next day and said that he could not get a ticket. Such a disappointment. Before we said goodbye, however, he said something that lifted my disappointment, something I knew I would never forget: "I love you, Teacher."

With that, I prepared for yet another departure from Tibet. *Ka li shu,* my top-of-the-world magical home.

Postscript: Today, back home, I grieve for Tibet. The governmental controls I experienced when I lived there, the controls that I saw expanded during my reunion tour with routine searches of backpacks and packages, are only getting worse. Michael and Eddie's remarks stay with me as I read about the increased spying that the government undertakes on Tibetan citizens. Recently, Tibet Watch, a charity organization dedicated to documenting and exposing human rights abuses in Tibet, released, along with the research organization Turquoise Roof, a report that paints a bleak and frightening picture of life as a Tibetan citizen under Chinese rule. Surveillance has come a long way since the days of simple street cameras and plainclothes policemen along the Barkhor. The report— *Weaponizing Big Data: Decoding China's Digital Surveillance in Tibet*—details how China uses a wealth of digital technology, including a mandatory smartphone app (euphemistically called the "National Fraud Center" app), to pry into every citizen's personal life, detailing everyone's movements. And that's not all. According to the report, "The integration of a panoply of advanced technologies in Tibet—AI-driven systems fusing facial recognition with internet browsing and app-based monitoring, to DNA and genomic surveillance, and GIS tracking data—underlines the emergence of a terrifying approach to governance in the 21st century. It uses machine learning to power systems that prioritize state control and suppression over individual liberties and self-determination."

It doesn't help my ire to learn that all of this is helped by a US company. Oracle Corporation out of Austin, Texas, developed a sophisticated database for the Chinese as part of a "big data policing platform." According to the report, the database "is instrumental in a campaign that criminalizes even moderate cultural, religious expressions, language rights advocacy, and social work in Tibet." Shame on Oracle.

The cultural and language controls are especially insidious. What some are calling "linguicide" is the Chinese attempt to erase the Tibetan tongue, the government instead pushing for Mandarin, even insisting that "Tibet" be called "Xizang," the Chinese name for Tibet. In school, Tibetan children are taught Mandarin now as their first language. Language is inseparable from culture. When the language goes, so will much of the Tibetan culture.

For more information on the travails of my top-of-the-world home, please visit https://freetibet.org/.

Class of 1992 reunion, Lhasa, 2016

Class of 1993 reunion, Lhasa, 2016

Acknowledgements

This book could never have been written without English Language Institute/China providing the road in 1990 to my adventure, and for allowing me to spend three wonderful years in Tibet. The individuals who were instrumental for my placement were, among others, Kenneth Wendling, Gary Lausch, Brian Nelson, and Kim Morris Mahr, my wonderful Member Care person, who traveled to Tibet twice a year to check on my group of teachers.

Many thanks to my financial and prayer backers, many of whom were friends from Michigan and Longview, Texas. From Longview, special gratitude to Mary Harrison, Jack Wisdom, Joyce LeTourneau, Debbie Rowe Deason, and many in my Singles group who either faithfully sent letters, and/or contributed to a few Care packages (sadly only one of which made it through the Tibetan postal system). A multitude of thanks to Eddie Knapp who took it upon himself to see that my final financial obligation to the organization was met. No small potatoes, that.

My loving recognition of a dear friend who passed from this life only two months before the release of this book: Marion Smith, ninety-five years old. I'll always remember the trips to my mailbox at Tibet University to find your newsy letters there each month. What a difference letters from home meant to me. I'll always carry with me a sadness that you won't be able to finally read the completed book after inquiring about its progress in our phone conversations. That's on me.

For unwavering support and encouragement from a friend of sixty-plus years, Patricia Austin Johnson, who kept me moving along, even when she was ill. As a retired English teacher, she was happy to hear me read my latest chapter over the phone. And she was not hesitant to question me on points of grammar or sentence structure. Oh my, I read to her as if I were her student. I suppose I was. She died less than a year from seeing the book published. I miss her.

A huge shout-out to Don Walker for getting my slides and photos ready for inclusion in this book while battling major health issues.

To my children, I'm forever grateful that you didn't oppose my leaving for a year at a time. You didn't disown me. My hope is that you are proud of me. You had Iraq and graduate school to occupy your time, while I was fulfilling a quest of my own.

Last, but certainly not least, how could I have been so fortunate to have Jerry Payne as my editor. His website was one of many on my screen. They all seemed the same to me. Finally, my intuitive self made my pick. It's turned out to be a most important choice. His practiced expertise made my stories come alive. After all, he'd written and or edited over thirty-five memoirs. He encouraged me to write even though I had misgivings with my skills. No problem, as he'd do the rewriting and editing as needed. For three years and counting, he's always been the encourager, never seeming to get impatient with my periods of procrastination. In addition to being the kind, thoughtful gentleman he is, he's become my friend. Thank you, Jerry Payne, from the bottom of my heart.

Follow Meredith McLeod Dunton on Facebook

(Meredith Dunton, Author)

CH
Clarion House Publishing

www.ingramcontent.com/pod-product-compliance
Lightning Source LLC
Chambersburg PA
CBHW030357130626
46549CB00004B/1529